A HISTORY OF THE SCOTS BIBLE

AUP Titles of Related Interest

THE PSALMS IN SCOTS
Reprint of P Hately Waddell's
The Psalms: Frae Hebrew Intil Scottis
Introduced by Graham Tulloch

SCOTTISH HANDWRITING 1150–1650
An Introduction to the Reading of Documents
Grant G Simpson

WALTER BOWER'S SCOTICHRONICON
in nine volumes
original Latin with English translation
Volume 8   *edited and translated by D E R Watt*
Volume 2   *edited and translated by John and Winifred MacQueen*

BRYGHT LANTERNIS
Papers on the Language and Literature of Medieval and Renaissance Scotland
edited by J Derrick McClure and Michael R G Spiller

CONCISE SCOTS DICTIONARY
editor-in-chief Mairi Robinson

SCOTTISH NATIONAL DICTIONARY
(18th century to the present day)
editors William Grant and David Murison

DICTIONARY OF THE OLDER SCOTTISH TONGUE
(12th to 17th centuries)
editors Sir William Craigie, A J Aitken, James A C Stevenson et al.

A
HISTORY OF
THE SCOTS
BIBLE

With Selected Texts

GRAHAM TULLOCH

ABERDEEN UNIVERSITY PRESS

First published 1989
Aberdeen University Press
A member of the Pergamon Group

© Graham Tulloch 1989

British Library Cataloguing in Publication Data
Tulloch, Graham
    A history of the Scots Bible.
    1. Bible. Scottish versions.
    Translation, history
    I. Title
    220.5′9163′09

ISBN 0 08 037722 X (hard)
ISBN 0 08 037721 1 (flexi)

PRINTED IN GREAT BRITAIN
THE UNIVERSITY PRESS
ABERDEEN

This Book is Dedicated to the Memory
of my Mother and Father
Betty and John Tulloch

I wish that these were translated into all languages of all people so that they could be read and understood, not only by the Scots and the Irish, but also by the Turks and the Saracens. . . . I wish that the farmer might sing some portion of them at the plough, and the weaver hum some parts at his loom, and the traveller lighten the tedium of his journey with stories of this kind.

Erasmus, on the Gospels and Pauline Epistles, in his Paraclesis

CONTENTS

PREFACE

In 1986, when I was working on a comparison of W W Smith and W L Lorimer as translators of the New Testament into Scots, I became aware of just how much Scots translation there had been over the centuries from the Bible. Much of this has since sat in libraries unread or read only by a few lexicographers and students of Scots. Given the special importance of the Bible to Scotland it seemed worthwhile to try to make this body of work better known. The quality varies from timid adherence to English translations to the brilliant and innovative work of Lorimer and Waddell. But, whether it is good or bad, all the effort that has gone into bringing the Bible alive in the language of the people deserves celebration. The aim of this book is to fulfill the dual function of describing the history of translation into Scots from the Bible and to present a selection of texts chosen both for their inherent importance as translations from the Scriptures and for their linguistic interest. In this study I have confined myself to prose translations. I have also generally limited my discussion to translations of complete books of the Bible. Parts of the Bible, especially the Psalms, have been from time to time translated into Scots verse but these belong to a separate tradition and need to be separately discussed.

I would like to acknowledge the help of Professor David Daiches, Mr Robin Lorimer and Mr Paul Scott in the early stages of my work on this topic. I am also grateful to Mr Colin MacLean of Aberdeen University Press for his continuing interest in and encouragement of this project. I thank Flinders University for allowing me study leave and the Royal Society of Edinburgh for giving me a grant to work with Professor Daiches. Above all I want to thank my wife for tolerating my immersion in waddling through Waddell, riddling through Riddell and forging through Smith for the last two and a half years and for her help in the final preparation of this manuscript. Without her encouragement and help I would not have completed this book.

12 December 1988
The Flinders University of South Australia

ACKNOWLEDGEMENTS

A work of this nature has necessitated the use of material from a vast body of relevant texts, a selection of which appear at the end of the History. The majority of these are out of copyright. For works in copyright permission to reprint passages in this volume has been granted by the following:

R L C Lorimer and the Trustees of the W L Lorimer Memorial Trust, for passages from *The New Testament in Scots*, trans W L Lorimer

Lorna Borrowman, for passages from *The Buik o Ruth and Ither Wark in Lallans*, Alex S Borrowman

Jamie Stuart, for passages from *A Scots Gospel*, Jamie Stuart

The History

THE EARLY PERIOD

Only a few events in the history of Scots language, literature and culture have been as much discussed as a non-event—the failure of the Reformation to produce a Bible in Scots. A translation of the Bible into any language often plays a crucial role in giving that language prestige and in developing it as a standard language. Of this Luther's Bible is a well-known example. Lacking a Scots Bible the Reformers turned to Bibles in English, notably the Geneva Bible. The constant use of English Bibles over the centuries has been more than once credited with much of the blame for the increasing anglicisation of Scots culture. In fact, the absence of a Scots Bible was not the only cause of anglicisation, nor was anglicisation a completely new phenomenon. Nevertheless, the failure to produce a Scots Bible certainly had then and has now great symbolic significance and all the emphasis on this significant symbolic failure has obscured the actual successes.

There has, in fact, been a considerable body of translation of parts of the Bible into Scots even if there has been no translation of the complete text. Few modern readers will be unaware of W L Lorimer's brilliant Scots New Testament published in 1983 but many will not know of the two earlier versions, one by Murdoch Nisbet, made in the earlier sixteenth century but not published until 1901 and a modern one by W W Smith, also published in 1901. Even fewer are likely to know all of the five translations of the Song of Solomon, the two translations of the Ruth, the Psalms and the Gospel of Matthew, and the individual translations of Genesis, Isaiah and Proverbs and of selections from the gospels. This book sets out to remedy that situation. It describes the history of translations from the Bible into Scots and provides an anthology of representative passages.

The history of Scots translations of the Bible falls into two distinct periods. In the sixteenth century only Murdoch Nisbet translated more than just a few verses at a time. Generally in this book I will only be dealing with translations of complete books of the Bible but I have briefly discussed other fragmentary translations of the sixteenth century so as to provide something to set beside Nisbet. After Nisbet there is a gap of some two hundred and fifty years but from 1856 onwards a steady stream of translations of parts of the Bible has been appearing so that there is no shortage of material for comparison in the modern period. Nisbet was clearly a sympathiser with the Reformation ideal of providing vernacular versions of the Bible and his motivation was religious. In the modern period this religious motivation has often been supplemented, or even supplanted by a desire to preserve the Scots language.

Except for Waddell who worked from the Hebrew text and Lorimer who translated from the Greek, all the translators based their translations on English versions. This means that almost all have no independent authority as translations of the original text. As a consequence, the biggest interest lies in what they show us about how the translators see the Scots language, its form, its status and its relationship to its cousin English. The Bible is the one text from which frequent translation has been made into Scots and it offers us a unique opportunity to compare the translators' differing perceptions of what the Scots language means to them. At the same time, we cannot take their translations as straightforward examples of the Scots of their time. All the translators knew English versions before they made a Scots version. Those English versions had presumably been of tremendous importance in their personal religious lives and many of them found it hard to escape from the overwhelming influence of the English version best known to them. One of the major interests of the story lies in tracing the ways the various translators have tried to break free of the English versions in order to achieve a genuinely Scots translation.

If we stretch a point we could claim that the earliest Scots translation from the Bible is the version of the gospels in the Old Northumbrian dialect of Old English since Scots is historically a descendant of this dialect. But this dialect had no distinctively Scottish form and it makes better sense to see Scots as beginning at the point where it starts to diverge from the dialect of the north of England. The first important literary monument of Scots in this normal sense of the word is Barbour's *Brus*, written in 1374 and 1375. More or less contemporary with this is a Scots metrical *Legends of the Saints* at one stage wrongly attributed to Barbour. As it happens, it offers us a translation of a few verses here and there from the Bible. For instance, there is a rather free rendering of the description of John the Baptist's clothing:

> for in-to arsk hare he wes clede
> with a belte of reucht skine made,
> & wyld hony wes his lyflede
> & a thinge callit locusta
> ('Iohannes Baptista', ll.278–81; Matt. 3:4).[1]

Then there are the words from Heaven at Christ's baptism:

> this is my luffit sone and dere
> In quhame it wele compless me
> (ibid., ll.322–3; Matt. 3:17),

the words of Jesus to Satan:

> for wrytine is 'nocht al anerly
> man liffis of bred, bot sykyrly
> In al gud word that procedis
> Of godis mowth'
> ('Egipciane', ll.1023–6; Matt. 4:4),

and his explanation of his purpose:

> I am nocht cumyne rychtwis to cal
> to pennance, bot synfall al
> ('Magdalena', ll.12–13; Matt. 9:13).

Finally, there are his words to Peter, also rather freely translated:

> thu art petir, at is, our stane,
> to byg myn wark one haff I tane; . . .
> to the I gyff the keys of hewyne
> ('Petrus', ll.13–14, 16; Matt. 16:18, 19)

Short passages like these, along with longer passages of paraphrase like that describing the conversion of Paul taken from Acts ('Paulus', ll.533ff.) give us some idea of what a Scots Bible might have looked like at this early stage. However, the time was not ripe. The religious climate was unfavourable, the church remained committed to sole use of the Latin Bible and it was to be another one hundred and fifty years before any substantial section of the Bible was translated into Scots.

NISBET'S NEW TESTAMENT (*c.*1520?)

The first translation of a substantial part of the Bible into Scots was made by Murdoch Nisbet and was nothing less than a version of the whole New Testament and some passages of the Old. No later translator was to equal this in quantity although in the course of time two further versions of the New Testament were to appear, one, Smith's, a much more thorough rewriting of its source than Nisbet's and the other, Lorimer's, the altogether more ambitious task of an entirely new and independent translation.

What little we know about the life of Nisbet can be found in an account of the family written by Nisbet's great-great-grandson, James, who died in 1728. He tells us that

> In the reign of King James the IV., some time before the year 1500, it pleased the eternal Jehovah . . . to cause his marvellous light take influence on Mordoch Nisbet in Hardhill, in the parish of Loudon and shire of Ayr. . . . His eyes were opened to see the vanity and evil of Popery, . . . so he deliberately resolved against it, turned from it, and joined himself with these called Lollards, the first name given to British Protestants, whom Papists call Hereticks. But in the reign of King James the V., the Papists, perceiving the Lollards began to grow numerous, and they not willing any should disturb their kingdom of darkness, raised persecution against them. Then Mordoch fled over seas, and took a copy of the New Testament in writ. What else he did we cannot say; but after some stay abroad he came home to see his native country, with others who had been elsewhere upon the same occasion, two of whom were taken and burnt at Glasgow, viz., Mr Russell and Mr Kennedy, as is to be seen in the first book of Knox's History. Mordoch being in the same danger, digged and built a vault at

the bottom of his own house, to which he retired himself, serving God and reading his new book. Thus he continued, instructing some few that had access to him, until the death of King James the V. But when the Queen Dowager held the regency, the true religion began to be more openly professed, the monuments and ornaments of Satan's kingdom of darkness pulled down. Mordoch, though then an old man crept out of his vault, and joining himself with others of the Lord's people, lent his helping hand to this work....But having served his generation he died, and left his son Alexander Nisbet heir to his New Testament zeal (pp. x–xi).

It appears therefore that Nisbet was born in the late fifteenth century and survived until after 1554 when Marie of Guise became regent. It seems, too, that it was while he was 'over seas', possibly simply in England, he 'took a copy of the New Testament in writ', that is 'transcribed the New Testament'. Nisbet's source was John Purvey's revision of the version ascribed to Wyclif. We do not know when Nisbet returned to Scotland but it was no later than 1539 when his two friends, Russell and Kennedy, were executed. Nisbet's version, if his biographer is correct in suggesting the translation took place outside Scotland, was therefore made between 1513 and 1539. T G Law, editing Nisbet for the Scottish Text Society, concluded that it would have been in the first half of this period on the grounds that Nisbet would not have used Purvey's Vulgate-based version after Tyndale's version, translated from the original Greek and printed in 1525 or 1526, became available. However, it is uncertain how quickly Tyndale's version would have reached Nisbet's hands. Eventually, but we do not know when, except that it was after he had finished his own version, a copy of Tyndale did come into Nisbet's possession and from it he took a long prologue to the Epistle to the Romans and added it at the end of his volume. When Nisbet came to provide a prologue for his completed New Testament he made a translation of Luther's preface which had been first printed in 1522. However, Luther revised his preface in 1534, omitting the first few sentences, and Nisbet follows him in this which suggests this preface was translated after 1534. Nisbet apparently translated from the German which could possibly indicate that he had spent part of his exile in Germany. Interestingly Tyndale had translated the same preface in his fragmentary New Testament of 1525. Either Nisbet did not know this, in which case he would not have seen Tyndale until after 1534, or he was satisfied with his own command of German and preferred his own version.

Whatever date the translation was made, it clearly predates the establishment of the Reformed Church in Scotland. However, once the Reformation had come and the official climate was favourable to vernacular translations, Nisbet's version was still not printed. Several factors may account for this. We should, after all, remember that there was only one edition of the Bible of any version whatsoever printed in Scotland before 1610. This was the Bassendyne Bible of 1579 which was merely a reprint of the second edition of the Geneva Bible which had been first published, in English, in 1560. Bibles in English, whether printed in England or abroad, seem to have presented no insuperable linguistic difficulties for Scottish people and could easily be imported. Moreover, no version based on the Latin text was likely to be printed now that versions based on the Greek were available. It is true that a later hand has occasionally corrected Nisbet's text to make it conform to Tyndale's (e.g. 1 Tim. 6:6) but this sporadic effort could not bring the text into a state acceptable to those requiring a New Testament based on the Greek. Nisbet's version remained therefore unknown to any one except his descendants. The passing on of this precious volume from generation to generation is recorded on one of its blank pages in the successive hands of Nisbet's descendants. After James Nisbet, the family biographer, died in 1728, his widow left the book in trust with Sir Alexander Boswell to be passed on to James's nephew. On receiving it the nephew promptly sold this extraordinary family heirloom whereupon Boswell bought it back from the bookseller and it remained, forgotten, in the library at Auchinleck. As a result James Murray in his *Dialect of the Southern Counties of Scotland* of 1875 confidently claimed that 'there was no translation of the Scriptures into the Northern [i.e. Scots] dialect' (p 65). However, in 1893 the manuscript was offered for sale, its existence became generally known and finally, between 1901 and 1905 it appeared in print for the first time and under the auspices of the Scottish Text Society.

Nisbet's version was, as I remarked earlier, based on Purvey's revision of the version ascribed to Wyclif. Since Nisbet followed Purvey closely it may be helpful to first describe Purvey's work. The history of the Wycliffite Bible is enfolded in controversy and obscurity. Forshall and Madden in their monumental edition of 1850 printed two parallel texts. The first they believed to be by Nicholas of Hereford as far as Baruch 3:20 and thereafter by Wyclif. The second, a revision of the first, they ascribed to Purvey. Sven Fristedt, having re-examined the evidence, concludes in his study *The Wycliffe Bible* that the position was more complex. He believes that there were a series of revisions. First there was a crude translation made by Nicholas of Hereford and his associates, perhaps with some help from Wyclif and Purvey. Then came a first revision made by Purvey and his associates under the auspices of Wyclif. Finally Purvey and others undertook a more thoroughgoing revision. In this Purvey broke with the strict literalism of the earlier version (or versions) explaining in a long prologue his intention to translate sense for sense rather than word for word. It is this final revision which forms the basis for Nisbet's version.

Purvey, as he tells us in his preface, had made great efforts to produce an accurate Latin text. In the hundreds of years since Saint Jerome produced the Vulgate text copies had become contaminated with many false readings. Purvey's efforts to produce an accurate text were not in vain: the footnotes to Law's edition of Nisbet record relatively few departures by Purvey from the best texts and even fewer having no authority at all. One of the few major faults is the omission of the first four verses of Luke. Elsewhere an occasional phrase is omitted (e.g. John 2:25) or an interpolated phrase, found in some manuscripts but not in the best Vulgate manuscripts or the Greek, finds its way into the text (John 7:28) but, in general, Purvey's text is a good one and this, combined with his straightforward and generally intelligible style means that there is much to be said for his translation. Nisbet was fortunate to have access to a text of this quality.

At the same time Purvey's version has certain flaws which are carried over into Nisbet. In particular, although Purvey's version is much less literal than the earlier Wycliffite version, some awkward literalisms are retained. For instance, Latin plurals are retained where English and Scots idiom requires a singular: *nuptiae ... paratae sunt* is rendered as *the weddingis are reddy* (Matt. 22:8) and *tenebris* as *mirknessis* (John 1:5) although here Nisbet has replaced Purvey's *derknessis* with a Scots term. Sometimes a literal translation produces gibberish as with the rendition of *genti facienti fructus eius* as to *a folk doande fruitis of it* (Matt. 21:43); something freer, like Ronald Knox's *to a people which yields the revenues that belong to it*, is required here. Two particularly awkward literalisms are the rendering of *gratias agere* as *do thankingis* (e.g. Mark 14:23) and the use of *will nocht* in translating *noli(te)*. In neither case does this produce Scots idiom as is clear when we compare Nisbet with other sixteenth century writers. John Hamilton in his *Facile Traictise* of 1600 renders *gratias agens* (Mark 14:23) as *giuand thankis* (p 381) and, where Nisbet has given us the clumsy *Will thou nocht litil charge* (1 Tim. 4:14) as a rendering of *noli nelgigere*, Archbishop Hamilton's catechism of 1552 reads *Negleck nocht* (p 232).[2] Fortunately these literal renderings are not too widespread in Purvey.

The relationship of Nisbet to Purvey and, indirectly, to the first Wycliffite version and the Vulgate is best demonstrated by a passage:

PURVEY

And he gaderide to gidre alle the prynces of prestis, and scribis of the puple, and enqueride of hem, where Crist shulde be borun. And thei seiden to hym, In Bethleem of Juda.... Thanne Eroude clepide pryueli the astromyens, and lernyde bisili of hem the tyme of the sterre that apperide to hem. And he sente hem in to Bethleem, and seide, Go ȝe, and axe ȝe bisili of the child, and whanne ȝee han foundun, telle ȝe it to me, that Y also come, and worschipe hym. And whanne thei hadden herd the kyng, thei wenten forth. And lo! the sterre, that thei siȝen in the eest, wente bifore hem, til it cam, and stood aboue, where the child was. And thei siȝen the sterre, and ioyeden with a ful greet ioye. And thei entriden in to the hous, and founden the child with Marie, his modir; and thei felden doun, and worschipiden him. And whanne thei hadden openyd her tresouris, thei offryden to him ȝiftis, gold, encense, and myrre. And whanne thei hadden take an aunswere in sleep, that thei schulden not turne aȝen to Eroude, thei turneden aȝen bi anothir weie in to her cuntrey.

NISBET

And he gaderit togiddir al the princis of prestis and scribis of the pepile, and inquirit of thame quhar Crist suld be born. And thai said to him, In Bethlem of Juda.... Than Erode callit priuelie the astronomyers, and leirit besilie of thame the tyme of the stern that apperit to thame. And he send thame into Bethelem, and said, Ga ye and ask ye besilie of the child; and quhen ye haue fundin, tel ye to me, that alsa I cum and wirschip him. And quhen thai had herde the king, thai went furth; and, lo, the stern, that thai saw in the eest, went before them,

til it come and stude abone quhare the child was. And thai saw the stern and
ioyit with a ful gret ioy. And thai entrit into that hous, and fand the child with
Marie his moder, and thai fel doun and wirschipit him: and quhen thai had
opnyt thar tresouris, thai offrit to him giftis; gold, encens, and myrr. And quhen
thai had tane ane ansuer in slepe that thai suld nocht turn agane to Erode, thai
turnit agane be an vthir way in to thar cuntre (Matt. 2:4–5, 7–12).

Before passing to Nisbet's treatment of Purvey we should note that, in using
Purvey rather than the earlier version, Nisbet has avoided the latter's clumsy
handling of the ablative absolute *et responso accepto* as *and answer taken*.
Purvey also preferred to translate dependent participial constructions as separate main clauses, hence Nisbet follows Purvey with *thai saw the stern* for
videntes stellam and *thai entrit* for *intrantes* where the earlier version had
seeynge the sterre and *entrynge*. While the Latin construction (which parallels
the Greek) is acceptable in English and Scots there is no doubt that a greater
directness and a more typically English and Scots style is achieved by Purvey's
practice. But with these exceptions Purvey follows the Latin closely, even to
the extent of using the unintelligible *answer* to translate the Latin *responso*. A
less literal-minded approach would recognise that *responsum* is here used in
the technical sense of an oracular utterance.[3] Equally literal is *princis of
prestis* for the Latin *principes sacerdotum*. The term *prince* had taken on a
specific meaning in the context of the English and Scottish mediaeval social
structure and the Latin terms *princeps* was used to translate this meaning but
what is needed here is a return to the original Latin meaning of 'chief' or
'leader'. Quintin Kennedy accordingly translated this more accurately, if
somewhat pedantically, as *principalis of the preistis* (p 135).

Nisbet's handling of Purvey's text in this passage is typical of his work in
general. The spelling has been carefully scoticised and so has the grammar:
hem and *her* are replaced by their Scots equivalents *thame* and *thar* and the
en plural ending of verbs is removed giving way to the inflections of Scots
usage. Thus the second and third person singular pronouns are both followed
by an *is* inflection, as in *quhen thou dois almes, know nocht thi left hand quhat
thi richt hande dois* (Matt. 6:3) and this same inflection is extended to the first
person singular and to the plural either when the pronoun is separated from
the verb, as in *I am a man ordanit vndir power, and has knychtis vndir me* (Matt.
8:9) and *thai saw nocht, nouthir scheris, nouthir gaderis* (Matt. 6:26), or when
the subject is a plural noun, as in *men kendlis nocht a lantern, and puttis it vndir
a buschel* (Matt. 5:15). Nisbet also carefully makes a distinction between
participles ending in *and* and verbal nouns and adjectives ending in *ing*:
Blessit be tha seruandis, that quhen the Lord sal cum he sal find walkand [Latin
vigilantes]... *And gif he cum, in the secund walking* [Latin *vigilia*], *and gif
he cum in the thrid walking, and find sa, tha seruandis are blessit* (Luke 12:37–
8). This distinction goes back to Old English; it was already lost in Purvey's
Middle English but survived until much later in Scotland; Murray records the
persistence of a distinction in Southern Scots in the later nineteenth century
and exhibits it in his version of the Book of Ruth. These regular and systematic
changes have an immediate scoticising effect, an effect not available to Scots

translators of the modern period who had lost many distinctive Scots spellings like *sch* and *quh* for English *sh* and *wh* and are often unwilling to use *s* endings with plural subjects for fear of their language being labelled illiterate and ungrammatical.

With vocabulary Nisbet is more circumspect. Certain words are regularly replaced. *Clepide* in this passage is one of them; it was rarely used in Scots, and then mainly in verse and under English influence. Other changes regularly carried out by Nisbet are from *bild* to *bigg* (Matt. 21:33), *gospel* to *euangele* (1 Cor. 9:23) and *sue* to *follow* (John 1:20). Likewise *walk* is replaced by *gang* (John 1:36) with the spelling *walk* being employed as the Scots equivalent of English *wake* as in the verses quoted in the previous paragraph. Returning to the passage, *lernyde* yields to *leirit*, by now a distinctively Scots usage and *above*, *aȝen*, and *sterre* change to their slightly different Scots equivalents *abone*, *agane* and *stern*. All this involves quite a bit of change but nevertheless represents the minimum change necessary. Nisbet feels no need to change *ask* and *inquirit* to the Scots *spere* and *sperit* or *apperit* to *kythit* which was by his time largely confined to Scots. Nor is there any reason why he should— all, though shared with English, were still current Scots terms. If a term is found in Scots Nisbet retains it, even if it is shared with English and even if a purely Scots equivalent exists. In similar fashion, he merely plays with the form of *astromyens*, using forms shared with English and eschewing the purely Scots *spaemen*.

The contrast between Nisbet and modern translators in their handling of vocabulary is highly instructive. The two nineteenth-century translators Riddell and Henderson are also working from a translation, the Authorised Version, which uses *enquired* and *appeared* (both in verse 7). It is true that Riddell, rather hesitant, as always, to change the Authorised Version, uses *inquairet* but Henderson, in revising him, turns to *spier't* and both Riddell and Henderson use *kythet* rather than *appeared*. For Nisbet the minimum change was sufficient to turn English into Scots, just as nowadays minimal change might in many cases change Dutch into German, but modern translators, much more concerned about maintaining the separate identity of Scots, will use distinctively Scots terms whenever they are available. Specifically this often means the replacement of formal terms shared with English, like *appear* and *enquire*, by exclusively Scots informal terms. By comparison with modern texts, and starting with modern preconceptions about Scots, Nisbet's Scots may seem to share too much with English. Many words that we have come to expect in modern Scots texts do not appear: Nisbet, for instance, regularly uses *ask*, *child* and *knaw* rather than *speir*, *bairn* and *ken* as a modern writer would do. These latter three words were already in use in Scots but Nisbet evidently had no feeling that Scots writers should prefer them to the terms shared with English. All in all, then, the distinctively Scots element in Nisbet's vocabulary is relatively small. Nevertheless in the quite different linguistic circumstances of early sixteenth century Scotland the distinctive spelling and grammar are sufficient to make this a quite clearly Scots text.

All these changes towards scoticising the text seem to be Nisbet's own work. He could conceivably have been working from a text which had already been rendered into Scots but no other Scots version of Purvey has been found and, as his editor points out, some of the words that have been corrected or erased by the scribe in the course of producing the manuscript before us show that he was working from an English original (I xvi). There is no reason to doubt that we have here Nisbet's holograph since his descendants's account makes it clear that Nisbet himself made the copy and it was this copy that was passed down through the generations.

Other differences from Purvey's text, where for instance Nisbet's version is based on a manuscript different from Purvey's, may well be from the specific manuscript Nisbet was working from rather than his own work. The scribes producing copies of Purvey's text occasionally attempted to improve it either by turning to Latin manuscripts rejected by or unknown to Purvey or by adopting readings from the earlier Wycliffite version. The latter practice may explain those occasions where Nisbet's text agrees with the earlier rather than the later version, as when Nisbet reads *glorie* (Matt. 4:8), Purvey *ioye* and the earlier version *glorie* (although Forshall and Madden found no manuscript of Purvey's version in which this mistake was corrected) or when Nisbet reads *corrumps* (1 Cor 5:6), Purvey *apeyrith* and the earlier version *corrumpith*. However both of these changes could also have been brought about by Nisbet or his source referring back to the Latin text which here reads *gloriam* and *corrumpit*. Consultation with the Vulgate would certainly seem to have produced the reading *tribunale* (Rom. 14:10) where Purvey and Wyclif both have *trone* and the more literal translation of the Vulgate's *inebriari* as *be dronkinn* (Luke 12:45) where the English versions have be *fulfillid* [or *fillid*] *ouer mesure*. In further instances where the Latin has been consulted the text used differs from that adopted in the Wycliffite versions and produces variations like *behaldand* (Luke 23:35) based on a text reading *spectans* where both the Wycliffite versions have *abidynge* based on the alternative textual reading *expectans*.

All this, then, suggests that either Nisbet or the scribe of an earlier English manuscript of Purvey had been making separate use of a Latin Bible. Nevertheless the variations produced are neither numerous nor particularly important: the basic accuracy of Purvey's text is not seriously undermined. It is all the more a pity therefore that Nisbet's New Testament was not printed in his own time. The production of a Scots Bible at this stage could well have had an important effect in maintaining a separate written identity for the Scots tongue just as the production of Luther's Bible helped stabilise and standardise German. For us, accustomed in the modern period to forms of written Scots which are heavily Scots in vocabulary but often quite English in spelling and grammar, Nisbet's Scots, where the converse is true, may well seem too English. But, in the long run, what was needed to maintain a standard of written Scots distinct from that of English was a separate spelling and grammar. As we shall see, later writers like Allan Ramsay gave Scots a certain literary status but simultaneously undermined it by using an anglified spelling and grammar. If, on the other hand, they had retained, where appropriate the elements of Scots spelling and grammar found in Nisbet they would have bequeathed to subsequent writers a recognisable identity for Scots which would allow them to use as much or as little purely Scots diction as they wished without calling the Scots identity of their language into question.

SIXTEENTH CENTURY PROSE FRAGMENTS

After Nisbet, no one else made a translation of a whole book of the Bible into Scots until the mid nineteenth century. The Reformation brought with it English Bibles and slowly but surely English became the language of Scottish religion with the Geneva Bible dominating the Scottish scene until well into the seventeenth century. Nevertheless in the course of the sixteenth century a great deal of religious material in Scots was produced and in it are embodied many quotations from the Bible. Rarely do these amount to more than one or two verses at a time but they still give us some hints as to what sorts of language might have been used if other, longer translations had been undertaken. Since they are not translations of complete books, they do not strictly belong to the subject matter of this study yet it may be interesting to briefly survey them.

One of the earliest is also one of the most interesting, at least as an example of Scots language. John Gau (or Gow) was a native of Perth and a graduate of St Andrews having matriculated in 1509. His name appears on the rolls of the university for a few years and then he disappears from sight until his *Richt Vay to the Kingdom of Heuine* is printed in Malmö (then part of Denmark but now in Sweden) in 1533. Later we find him acting as a chaplain in Copenhagen. He died, apparently, in 1553. Gau had been long enough in Denmark before 1533 to learn the language since his *Richt Vay* is largely a translation of *Den rette vey till Hiemmerigis Rige* written in Danish by Christiern Pedersen and published by him in exile in Antwerp in 1531. Most of Pedersen's work was itself a translation of a work in German by Urbanus Rhegius so that behind Pedersen's Danish lies German influence. Various short passages from the Bible are scattered throughout Gau's work and some are unusual in being translated neither from an English nor from a Latin Bible. In his editor's opinion, Gau sometimes cited from the Vulgate in the Old Testament passages but 'Those from the New Testament are generally taken from the Danish or Tyndale's or Luther's version' (p xl) and he cites the case of the Matthew 17:5 which is once quoted in exactly the words of Tyndale (p 29) and another time in quite different words (p 109). In fact, most of the quotations are very short and many of them are more in the nature of paraphrases so that it would be a hard job to determine what was Gau's source in each case. What we can say is that the influence of the Danish is discernible in Gau's language. His spelling, or that of his printer, shows possible Danish influence in the use of *v* in the place of *w* and possible German influence in the use of *sz* as an alternative to *s*. Gau's vocabulary also occasionally shows this influence though not particularly in the passages from the Bible. When he uses the very rare word *leirfaders* to mean 'masters in learning' (p 15) he is modelling himself on the Danish *lerefedre* and he stands alone amongst Scots and English writers in using *marklie* from the Danish *merkilig* to mean 'clearly' (p 69). Finally Gau's very unusual *wordine* as a past participle of the verb *worth* meaning 'become' may derive from the German *worden*.

Gau's characteristics may be seen in a comparison of one of his few longer passages with Nisbet's treatment of the same passage.

NISBET

Quham sais men to be mannis son? And thai said, Sum, Johnne Baptist; vther, Helie; and vther, Jeremie, or ane of the prophetis. Jesus said to thame, Bot quhat say ye me to be? Symon Petir ansuerd and saide, Thou art Christ, the sonn of God levand. Jesus ansuerede and said to him, Thou art blessit, Simon Bariona; for flesche and blude schewit nocht to thee, bot my fader that is in heuenis. And I say to thee, that thou art Petir, and on this staan I sal big my kirk; and the yettis of hell sal nocht haue mycht aganis it (Matt. 16:13–18).

GAU

quhom sais men yat I ye sone of man am? thay said, part sais that thow art Ihone the Baptist / part sais thow art Helias / part sais thow art Iheremias / or ane of ye prophetis / he said to thayme quhom say ze that i am? symon Petrus ansuert and said thow art Christ the sone of the liffand god Iesus ansuert and said to hime happy art thow Simon the sone of Ihone for flesch and blwid hesz noth rewelit this to ye bot my fader quhilk is in ye heuine / and I say alsua to ye that thow art Peter and apone this steyne I sal big my kirk ... and ye portis of hel sal noth preuail aganis it (p 61).

As examples of Scots of this period these are much of a muchness: Nisbet has been led by Purvey to use *that* where we would expect *quhilk* and Gau has used the English form *quhom* and his usual idiosyncratic spellings like *blwid* and *hesz* but otherwise both are writing good Scots. All the same Gau's translation flows more freely because it avoids the literalisms carried over by Nisbet from Purvey. For instance, he uses normal Scots word order in *liffand God* where Nisbet keeps the order of the Latin *Deu uiui* and adds an article where Nisbet had the unidiomatic *in heuenis* based on the Latin *in caelis*. Gau clearly demonstrates what Nisbet had shown at greater length, that Scots was fully equipped at this stage as a vehicle for Bible translation and, in doing this, it would naturally retain the formal diction like *reveal* and *prevail* which it shared with English.

This point was to be strikingly illustrated not long after in *The Complaynt of Scotland* written in 1549 and 1550, probably by Robert Wedderburn (*c*.1510–*c*.1552), Vicar of Dundee and one of three brothers who made a contribution to the literature of the period. It is easy to make fun of an author who writes 'i thocht it nocht necessair, til hef fardit ande lardit this tracteit vitht exquisite termis, quhilkis ar nocht daly vsit, bot rather i hef vsit domestic scottis langage, maist intelligibil for the vlgare pepil' (p 13) where the language used seems to contradict what he is saying but there are several things to bear in mind here. Firstly this is part of an appeal to 'al philosophouris historigraphours & oratours of our scottis natione to support & til excuse my

barbir agrest termis': at this particular point the author is addressing the
learned. Secondly, the author simply does not share our notions that Scots is
largely a spoken and colloquial language. For him Scots can also be a written,
formal language and, when it is such, it will include formal Latinate diction.
Thirdly, the author employs a variety of styles of Scots in his work: it is
therefore unfair of Murray to cite the dedication to the queen, a set piece of
aureate diction, with the implication that it is typical of the work in general
(*DSCS*, pp 64–5). In translating or paraphrasing the Bible the author employs
a full range of Scots diction including both the formal and the informal. Take
this translation of parts of Leviticus 26:

> Gyf 3e keip my ordinance, i sal send 3ou rane on 3our grond in conuenient
> tyme, 3our feildis sal bryng furtht cornis, 3our treis sal bayr frute, 3e sal eyt
> 3our breyde in suficiens, 3e sal sleipt at 3our eyse, i sal sende pace amang 3ou,
> the sourde of vengeance sal nocht pas throucht 3our cuntre, 3e sal follou 3our
> enemeis, and 3our sourdis sal gar them fal befor 3ou, fiue of 3ou sal follou &
> chaisse an hundretht, & ane hundretht of 3ou sal chaisse ten thousand, ande
> 3our enemeis sal fal to the grond venquest in 3our presens, sa that 3e vil obeye
> to my command (pp 20–21).

A comparison with the Vulgate will moreover reveal that it is not in deference
to the Latin text that the Latinate terms have been introduced: none of the
Latinate words correspond with the same words in the Vulgate. What we
have here then is a translator who feels free to use Latinate diction in exactly
the way the translators of the Authorised Version did, although they did it to
a lesser extent. This and other passages in *The Complaynt* give us some idea
of what a Scots translation might have been like if it had been intended for a
moderately educated audience and made without a close adherence to either
the English or the Latin.

As moves towards the Reformation gathered pace the Scottish Church tried
to undertake some reform from inside, especially at the council of 1552
under Archbishop Hamilton. From this council issued, under the Archbishop's
name, a Catechism written in Scots, possibly by John Wynram, sub-prior of
St Andrews. This contains some quotations of Scripture including quite a
long passage from the Sermon on the Mount. At some points, at least, the
catechist has apparently made use of Tyndale's translation as can be seen in
the following passage:

TYNDALE

> Agayne ye haue hearde how it was said to them of olde tyme / thou shalt
> not forswere thy self / but shalt performe thyne othe to God. But I saye vnto
> you / swere not at all: nether by heuen / for it ys Goddes seate: nor yet by the
> erth, for it is his fote stole: nether by Ierusalem, for it ys the cyte of that greate
> kynge: nether shalt thou sweare by thy heed / because thou canst not make one
> white heer / or blacke: But your communicacion shalbe / ye / ye: nay / nay. For
> what soeuer is more then that / commeth of yvell (Matt. 5:33–37)

Ye haif hard quhow it was said to thame of old tyme, thow sall nocht forsweir thi self, bot sall performe thi eith to God: bot I say to yow, sweir nocht alutterly ...nother be hevin, for it is Goddis seit, nor yit be the erd, for it is his futstule, nother be Jerusalem, for it is the citie of the greit king, nother sall thow sweir be thi heid, because thow can nocht mak ane hair qhuyt or black. Bot your talking sal be, ye, ye, na, na, for quhatsaevir is mair thane this, that cummis of evil (p 62)

For one short passage we are able to compare the catechism not only with Nisbet and the Vulgate but also with Gau:

constituens [illum] ad dexteram suam in caelestibus: supra omnem principatum, et potestatem, et uirtutem, et dominationem, et omne nomen quod nominatur non solum in hoc saeculo, sed et in futuro.... et ipsum dedit caput supra omnia ecclesiae [or, omnem ecclesiam]: quae est corpus ipsius (Eph. 1:20–22).

hes set Jesus...at his rycht hand in hevinly thingis, abone all the principattis, potestatis, vertewis and dominationis,...and also abone all uther creatouris that may be namit, nocht only in this warld, bot also in the warld to cum (p 163) [and] hais ordanit Christ to be heid ouir all the kirk, quhilk is his body (p 171)

and setting him on his richthalf in heuenlie thingis. Abone ilk principate, and potestate, and virtue, and dominatioun, and abone ilk name that is namet, nocht aanly in this warld bot alsa in the warld to cummand;...and gaue to him to be hede ouir al the kirk, That is the body of him

and hes set hime at his richt hand in the heuine ower al kingdome and power and hes giffine hime pouer and lordschip ower al thing quhilk is or cane be namit notht alanerlie in this vardil / bot alsua in the vardil to cum ... and hes made hime heid ower al thing to the halie kirk quhilk is his body (p 49).

Here it is noticeable that Nisbet and the catechism are sticking close to the Latin especially in rendering *principatem, et potestatem, et uirtutem, et dominationem* while Gau adopts a much freer rendering. Tyndale's version here is rather different.

For the rest of the century it is the Catholics, mostly after they had ceased to be the established party, who kept alive the use of Scots in religious contexts. It is well known that Knox adopted a rather anglified style of language and Ninian Winȝet, one of the Catholic controversialists, drew attention to this in an equally well known jibe at Knox: 'Gif ze, throw curiositie of nouationis, hes forzet our auld plane Scottis quhilk zour mother lerit zou[,] in tymes cuming, I sall wryte to zou my mynd in Latin, for I am nocht acquyntit with zour Southeroun' (i 138). In general, then, the controversialists write in Scots and in their works offer a wide range of Biblical quotations. Later in the century there is some indication of the being influenced by the New Testament published by the English Catholic exiles in Rheims in 1582. For instance, when John Hamilton published his *Facile Traictise* in Louvain in 1600, he rendered two verses of Luke's Gospel as

> And it come to pas that sa sune as Elizabeth hard the salutation of Maria, the barne reiosit in his mother's wombe; and Elizabeth was replenisit with the halie Spirit, and scho cryit with a loud voce and sayd, Blissit art thow amangis al wemen, and blissit is the fruit of thy wombe; and how is this commit to me, that the Mother of my lord suld come to visie me (p 152; Luke 1:41–3).

This shows some divergence from the Rheims version but it shares with it the unusual *replenished* where most English versions have *filled*.

As for the Reformers, many of their central documents were originally written in English and only lightly scoticised in spelling when printed in Scotland. The liturgy of the Reformed church, later known as *The Book of Common Order*, was originally compiled in English in Geneva and proclaimed its origins in the title of its first printing in Edinburgh in 1562: *The forme of prayers and Ministration of the Sacrament, etc ... used in the English Church at Geneva*. Even the Scots Confession of Faith of 1560, a home-grown product of Scotland, is heavily influenced in its language by English Bibles and was printed in editions showing various degrees of anglicisation, although Mairi Robinson, having studied its various manuscripts and editions in detail concludes that there was no deliberate policy of anglicisation.[4] When parliament enacted a law requiring all well-off people to have a copy of the Bible in the 'vulgar tongue' it seems that the possession of a Bible in English was considered as fulfilling this requirement. Indeed, this act was the sequel to a national effort in which all parishes were required to contribute to the printing for the first time in Scotland of a vernacular Bible, but, as we have already noted, the so-called Bassendyne Bible which resulted was merely a reprint of the Geneva Bible without any attempt at scoticising even the spelling. One of the few exceptions to the Reformers' preference for English texts, whether lightly scoticised or not, were the metrical versions of the psalms in the *Gude and Godlie Ballatis* which are not part of the subject of this book. This volume also contained a few Biblical quotations at the beginning most of which are somewhat dependent on Tyndale or some other English version as can be seen from the following example:

TYNDALE

That which I delyvered vnto you / I receaved of the lorde. For the lorde Iesus the same nyght in which he was betrayed / toke breed: and thanked and brake / and sayde. Take ye / and eate ye: this is my body which is broken for you. This do ye in the remembraunce of me (1 Cor. 11:23–24.

GUDE AND GODLIE BALLATIS

That quhilk I have deliuerit vnto zow, I resauit of the Lord, for ye Lord Jesus the same nycht, in the quhilk he was betrayit, tuke the breid, brak it, & gaif thankis and said. Take ze, eit ze, this is my body quhilk is brokin for zow, do ze this in remembrance of me (pp 5–6).

This mild scoticisation represents the furthest that the Reformers were willing to go in the provision of a Scots text of the Bible. By the end of the sixteenth century the idea that a Scots Bible was an English Bible had fully triumphed.

The problem was that Lowland Scots did, indeed, encounter few problems in reading English Bibles. No such idea could prevail in relation to Gaelic. In striking contrast to the absence of a Scots Bible for Scots-speakers, Gaelic-speakers had a printed Gaelic New Testament by 1767 and an Old Testament by 1801. Gaelic was greatly advantaged by this as it provided a universally known standard for Gaelic prose. The absence of any such standard for Scots was one of the many reasons for the declining role and status of Scots in subsequent centuries.

THE MODERN PERIOD

Apart from Nisbet, none of the sixteenth century writers translated more than a few verses at a time. It was to be more than three hundred years after Nisbet's work before another translation of a whole book of the Bible into Scots was to appear. In that intervening period the fortunes of the Scots language had changed enormously. The history of Scots in that period is well known but it is appropriate to summarise it here as it has an important influence on the sort of Scots used by modern translators.

After the period of the Reformation the use of Scots began to decline in various ways. The removal of the court to London following the union of the crowns deprived Scots of its most prestigious speakers and began that process by which the upper classes and, later on, the middle classes abandoned Scots in their speech in favour of English. For a long time it was only the aristocracy that were affected by this change but in the latter half of the eighteenth century the professional classes also began to adopt English as their speech on formal occasions. At first, no doubt, they could also speak Scots on informal occasions but by the mid nineteenth century many middle and upper class Scots were growing up as speakers of English alone. By the time that the first modern translation of part of the Bible into Scots appeared in 1856 Scots had come to be seen as basically a tongue of the rural and urban working classes, although there were exceptions to this at all levels of society. This had a fundamental effect on the status of the language. It was no longer the normal speech of educated people and this inevitably led, for some people at least, to the idea that it was inferior, limited and vulgar. Sir Walter Scott described this relegation of spoken Scots to the status of vulgarity as taking place in his own lifetime. In 1822 he wrote to Constable:

> Scotch was a language which we have heard spoken by the learnd and the wise & witty & the accomplishd and which had not a trace of vulgarity in it but on the contrary sounded rather graceful and genteel. You remember how well Mrs Murray Keith—the late Lady Dumfries—my poor mother & other ladies of that day spoke their native language—it was different from the English as the Venetian is from the Tuscan dialect of Italy but it never occurd to anyone that the Scottish any more than the Venetian was more vulgar than those who spoke the purer and more classical—But that is all gone and the remembrance will be drownd with us the elders of this existing generation.[5]

But this is not the whole of the story: the history of Scots in writing is somewhat different. The use of Scots in printed texts declined dramatically in the seventeenth century as Scottish writers and publishers both copied the language of English printed books and tried to gain access to the larger English market. While Scots held its own in handwritten material, like letters and diaries and burgh and church records, these too became much more English from the beginning of the eighteenth century. By the latter half of that century the authors of the Scottish Enlightenment were writing consistently in English. English had taken over as the first choice for the written medium and was the normal functional language of writing, a situation which continues today. Yet at the same time certain kinds of writing in Scots had undergone a dramatic revival. Allan Ramsay, and after him Fergusson and Burns, gave Scots a secure place in poetry, but it was at a cost. Ramsay was a writer of both Scots and English verse. His Scots verse tends to informal, comic and often satiric while his English verse tends to be formal and serious. Fergusson and Burns by and large continued and thus reinforced this distinction. Meanwhile the use of Scots in printed prose virtually disappeared until Scott made such important use of it in his novels. Scott influenced many other novelists to use Scots in their work but it was almost always under the same limitations as Scott set himself. Even with novels like *The Fortunes of Nigel* which were set well back in the past, Scott's use of Scots conforms to the sociolinguistic pattern of Scottish speech in his own time which means that the use of Scots is determined by social class. With the one glorious exception of Nigel's King James, all Scott's upper class characters speak English while his middle class characters are divided between English and Scots speech so that his working class characters provide the only consistently Scots-speaking group. Scots in nineteenth century novels is largely the language of either working class characters or of slightly unusual and often comic characters of a higher class. Consequently the kind of Scots used is almost always, as in the poetry, informal. Furthermore, the subjects dealt with are generally not serious ones.

Much had been saved in this revival of Scots as a written language but what was largely lost was the notion of a formal Scots register for prose and verse. Ramsay's one long formal and serious poem in Scots, *The Vision*, had, for instance to be disguised as a newly discovered Middle Scots work. Originally Scots and English had shared a large amount of formal diction much of it borrowed from Latin. Now this diction was much more likely to appear in purely English contexts and tended therefore to be regarded as English. Scots was redefined as existing mainly, or even wholly, in its colloquial register. Some recognised this trend and deplored it. Writing in 1792, Alexander Geddes protested that 'every exotic term which the English have borrowed from other languages, the Scots had an equal right to appropriate'. But the tide was against him and his protests went unregarded, partly, perhaps, because he combined them with some unfair criticism of recent writers of Scots, including presumably Burns, for taking the attitude that 'to write Scottish poetry . . . nothing more was deemed necessary than to interlard the composition with a number of low words and trite proverbial phrases, in common use among the illiterate'.[6] In part, too, the exclusion of shared Scots-English formal diction arose from the shaky identity of Scots. If writers wished to emphasise the separate identity of Scots they could do so by using lots of exclusively Scots words which were mostly informal in style as is the case with those many European languages which share a common stock of Latinate formal diction but are less likely to share a stock of informal diction. A few Scots formal terms, like *ordinar* and *exeme*, had different terminations but most were identical with English, at least in spelling. Using terms identical to English ones did not help writers establish a separate Scots identity for their language. For this reason they might avoid using them.

The result of all this is that Scots had by the middle of the nineteenth century a somewhat equivocal status. On the one hand it was seen as the language of the uneducated or the eccentric, with no formal register and in imminent danger of dying out with the spread of education. On the other hand it was seen as the language of a poet who was a national hero and of a novelist who was an international hero and it was thus a source of justifiable pride. If it was largely the language of the uneducated it would not generally be seen as suitable for writing; yet if Scott, one of the giants of the literary scene used it, it must be suitable for writing. In these circumstances it will not be surprising if we find equivocal and confused attitudes to Scots on the part of our translators.[7]

On top of this we must look specifically at the language of religion in Scotland. As we know, Nisbet's New Testament was not printed for about four centuries and only English versions of the Bible were available to Scottish people. For a while the Geneva Bible, written in the Standard English of England, was the most popular version in Scotland but it was overtaken by the Authorised Version around the middle of the seventeenth century. Even the Scottish Metrical Psalter of 1650, destined to become so dear to Scottish hearts, was in English. The language of religion in its basic texts was thus overwhelmingly English. This carried through to the speech of ordinary Scots people, as we can see in many nineteenth century novels where speakers of Scots, like Davie Deans in Scott's *Heart of Mid-Lothian*, will often, when discussing religious matters, switch into English—not contemporary English, however, but the English of 1611—or they will intermingle this English with their Scots. In this respect the Scots were like the English: for both peoples the language of religion was archaic and distinct from everyday contemporary usage both in speech and writing. Scottish writers thus faced a double feeling of strangeness in using Scots as a language for a religious text. It was strange because it was not English, the normal Scottish language of religion, and, in the absence of any recognised model for the writing of archaic Scots, it was also strange because it was necessarily a contemporary Scots that must be used and not an archaic style of Scots. In addition to this, Scots had, as we have already seen, been re-defined as an informal language. Although the language of the Authorised Version originally included some less formal elements it also included a lot of formal diction and as it became older the sense of its formality probably increased. So the translator of the Bible into Scots, accustomed to reading it in English of an archaic and rather formal nature, was now called upon to render it not only into Scots but also into a form of Scots which could only be informal and could not be archaic.

PRINCE LOUIS LUCIEN BONAPARTE

At this stage an unlikely figure enters the story of the Scots Bible in the form of a prince of the house of Bonaparte. Prince Louis Lucien Bonaparte (1813–1891) was the son of Napoleon's brother Lucien. He was born in England and spent most of his life there. His passion was the study of the languages and dialects of Europe, particularly the Basque and Celtic languages. To further this study he commissioned a large number of new translations of various books of the Bible into the dialects of English, Basque, Italian, German and other languages and reprinted a number of existing translations. These were all privately printed, and, according to Victor Collins, who later produced a catalogue of them, he 'was very chary in parting with copies of his works, and thus it happened that after his death whole editions were found just as they had come from the printers forty years before'. The prince had merely taken out a few copies 'for presentation to Mr Gladstone, Sir James Lacaita, Dr Max Müller, Mr Halbertsma and a few other friends'.[8] The prince's design of providing a written record of so many dialects was a grand one. Unfortunately, at least with the Scots texts, there were some real problems.

Amongst the various attitudes to Scots that could be adopted at that time the one exhibited by Prince Louis appears to have been what we might expect from a dialectologist and philologist. According to Collins:

> In conversation the Prince would often say that he worked rather for posterity than for his own generation. He sought to record for future ages the dying dialects of to-day. Steam and electricity were rapidly killing space, and, in their destructive career, were obliterating the distinctive characteristics of outlandish speech. He would, in so far as in him lay, hand down to coming centuries the manner of speech of the British yokel, of the French peasant, of the Basque mountaineer, of the Italian workman, of the Corsican and Sardinian islander, and many more, just as it was in vogue during the golden era of Victoria (pp vii–viii).

In his mind Scots was clearly included amongst these dying tongues and was to be recorded in its contemporary form before it died out. It further seems that he wanted to record speech, not literary dialect. He saw literary dialect as a corruption and wrote to James Murray, in a letter quoted by Murray in his *Dialect of the Southern Counties of Scotland* that

> The only corrupters of dialects, that I know of, are the *literary men* who 'improve nature,' by writing them, not as they *are*, but according to their notions of what they *ought to be*—i.e., in accordance with 'rules of grammar' derived from other languages with which they may be acquainted. As though grammar were anything but a systematic statement of usage! What would be thought of the botanist who should mutilate his specimens of flowers and plants to improve their symmetry, or make them fit into pre-arranged artificial systems, instead of following nature and drawing his laws and systems from her! (*DSCS*, p 75n).

Such was his view of 'literary men' yet, in choosing his translators into Scots, the prince at least twice turned to writers of literary Scots. As he had himself suggested, such writers were unlikely to view Scots in quite the same way as he did. On top of this, all the translations into English and Scots dialects were from the Authorised Version. This was no doubt intended to provide a measure of comparability for later philologists but it had unfortunate side-effects. The Authorised Version was a revered text and the translators were reluctant, in varying degrees, to change it. As a result none of the seven translations into Scots commissioned by Bonaparte is entirely satisfactory as a record of mid nineteenth century Scots. All contain at least some non-Scots features carried over from the Authorised Version. Moreover there is no attempt to differentiate between the different dialects of Scots. This conflicts with the prince's desire to record the actual spoken dialects. Instead we are presented with a somewhat ideal notion of Standard Scots derived from literary texts. Nevertheless these works provide a fascinating insight into what four translators of the 1850s and 1860s thought was an appropriate Scots language for Biblical translation. We can watch them feeling their way and not always finding it. Some are better than others and the later ones learn from the earlier ones. Several are more interesting for what they attempt than for what they achieve.

RIDDELL'S ST MATTHEW (1856)

The first translator employed by Prince Louis was Henry Scott Riddell (1798–1870), the son of a shepherd and himself a shepherd before seeking a university education. He trained as a minister but was prevented from taking up a position in the church by a period of insanity. He spent almost all his life in the Borders, latterly at Teviothead in a cottage provided by the Duke of Buccleuch. In his lifetime he was well known as a writer of songs about Scotland ('The Land of Gallant Hearts'), love ('The Wild Glen Sae Green') and the Forty-Five ('The Yellow Locks of Charlie'). He also wrote lengthier poems and prose works and, during his period of madness, he translated the Psalms into verse.[9] Riddell's social background and his lack of early education make it certain that he would have grown up as a Scots-speaker. He was also friendly in early life with James Hogg and John Wilson, both prominent users of Scots in prose. How he came to be chosen by Prince Louis I do not know, although his Scots songs were well known by this time, but it is obvious that he was well qualified through his knowledge of both spoken and written Scots and as a writer of a solid body of Scots verse. Riddell's metrical translation of the Psalms does not seem to have been printed but a prose version was one of the three books of the Bible he translated for Prince Louis. He began, however, in 1856 with a translation of St Matthew. Whatever the defects of this work—and, especially when it is considered as a translation into Scots, they are considerable—it deserves close attention as the first Scots Bible translation of the modern period. Riddell's work directly and indirectly influenced others and was the first stage in the evolution of a modern Scots prose for Bible translation which can be seen as having culminated in the work of W L Lorimer in this century.

This, the first of the Bonaparte translations, is a handsomely produced work but there is unfortunately no preface other than a note by the printers certifying that no more than eighteen copies were printed, listing all the recipients and noting that it had been done 'solely for linguistic purposes' (p v). This one short phrase of explanation, presumably printed under the prince's direction, conforms with what we have already said about his aims. Riddell's aims, on the other hand, can only be deduced from the work itself, if they can be deduced at all. As it happens, examination of the text leaves us still not entirely sure of Riddell's precise aims or rather leaves us with the impression that his aims were rather mixed.

Unlike with the other Bonaparte translations, we are not informed on the title page that the translation is 'from the Authorised English Version' but it is immediately obvious when one examines Riddell's Matthew that this is the case. A few verses from the story of the arrival of the Wise Men which we examined in considering Nisbet will illustrate how closely he sticks to it.

AUTHORISED VERSION

Then Herod, when he had privily called the wise men, enquired of them diligently what time the star appeared. And he sent them to Bethlehem, and said, Go and search diligently for the young child; and when ye have found him, bring me word again, that I may come and worship him also. When they had heard the king, they departed; and, lo, the star, which they saw in the east, went before them, till it came and stood over where the young child was. When they saw the star, they rejoiced with exceeding great joy.

RIDDELL

Than Herod, whan he had hiddlinslie ca't the wyse men, inquairet o' them eidentlie what time the stern had kythet. An' he sendet them til Bethlehem, an' said, Gang an' seek eidentlie for the young childe; an' whan ye hae fund him, bring me back word, that I may come an' wurship him alsua. An' whan they had heard the king, they set out; an', lo, the stern whilk they saw in the east gaed afore them, till it cam' an' stude ower whare the young childe was. An' whan they saw the stern they rejoicet wi' verra grit joy (2:7–10)

In general terms, we can see that quite a large number of changes have been made but they are all either matters of spelling or simple substitutions of one word for another. Very rarely in his translations does Riddell recast the structure of the sentence. In more specific terms, and dealing first with the vocabulary, it is obvious, even in this short passage, that there are several different kinds of changes. Firstly, and most straightforwardly, Scots terms replace English ones. In this passage *afore* and *gang* replace *before* and *go* and elsewhere in Riddell's Matthew we find the similar replacement of *concerning, from, knew,* and *weeping* with *anent* (4:6), *frae* (1:21), *kennet* (1:25) and *greetin'* (2:18). These changes could hardly be avoided. In other cases the Authorised Version's word could have been retained but the substituted term is possibly more common in Scots, as when Riddell replaces *buy* and *stretch* with *coffe*

(14:15) and *rax* (14:31). On the whole, however, Riddell's approach is a minimalist one. Where words are used at all in Scots they are retained even where a more common Scots word exists: he retains *child* (2:8) with its old-fashioned plural *childer* (2:16) even though Murray, writing about the dialect of the area that Riddell came from less than twenty years later, says that 'the synonym *bairn, bairns*, being generally used in the south of Scotland *cheyld, cheyder*, have become nearly obsolete' (*DSCS*, p 159).

Secondly, because he is working from a translation which was by his time archaic, Riddell is also at pains to remove obsolete words and meanings of words. Indeed this accounts for almost as much change as the simple replacement of English by Scots. In the passage quoted the archaic *privily* gives way to *hiddinslie* and on other occasions *charger, divers* and *wroth* are replaced by *aschet* (14:8), *sindrie* (4:24) and *angrie* (2:16). His handling of the archaic intensive *exceeding* is variable, perhaps suggesting dissatisfaction with both his *verra*, used in this passage, and his *excessiv* (2:16; 4:8). Certainly the first is rather pale and the second a somewhat odd revival of seventeenth and eighteenth century literary English usage; it remained for Henderson, who was to become in effect his reviser, to find much better translations in *unco* (2:10, 4:8) and *sair* (2:16). From changes such as these it is obvious that Riddell's version is as much a modernisation as a scoticisation. Nevertheless there are some inconsistencies. While removing some archaisms, he keeps others: here he retains *lo* and elsewhere *despitefully* (5:44) and *verily* (10:23).

Thirdly, the most interesting aspect of all in his changes of vocabulary is his persistent practice of replacing formal with less formal terms. Once again, this is not fully carried through and a number of formal words survive from the Authorised Version like *adversary* (5:25), *descend* (3:16), *fragment* (14:20) and, in this passage, *enquired*. All the same, many formal terms are removed: for instance, in this passage *departed* yields to *set out* and in other places *exceed* and be *reconciled* give way to *gae ayont* (5:20) and *mak' friens* (5:24). These moves towards a more informal style of Scots are at first puzzling, given Riddell's reverence for the Authorised Version, as evidenced by his retention of other terms and his minimalist approach to lexical change. In the Authorised Version formal and less formal terms happily co-exist in what becomes a unified style. Why cannot Riddell retain a similar mixed style? The answer seems to be that this removal of formal terms reflects the fundamental change I have already outlined in the way that Scots had come to be seen since the great days of the Middle Scots makars. In those days Nisbet had also closely followed an English version, one, it is true, without too many Latinate formal words, but where they did occur he was quite content to retain words like *perturbatioun* (1 Pet. 3:6), *purgatioun* (Luke 2:22), *propositioun* (Luke 6:4), *reconceilit* (Mat. 5:24), *stabliset* (Luke 16:26) and *subiectioun* (Gal. 2:5). But, as we have seen, since Nisbet's time Scots had been redefined as existing mainly, or even wholly, in a colloquial register. Its formal register had yielded its place to English.

Riddell's removal of formal diction can be seen as part of this overall trend. Formal terms which in the sixteenth century had been seen as part of the joint diction of English and Scots were now seen as purely English: to be considered truly Scots a piece of prose must stick to informal terms, or, at the very least, it must avoid highly formal and literary terms also found in English and where it used the shared diction of Scots and English it should only be the informal or stylistically neutral elements. To use formal terms was to write English. Now Riddell was translating the Bible and not writing a comic, informal poem. We would expect him to prefer a somewhat formal style. In these circumstances his reluctance to accommodate formal, literary terms is striking testimony to the way in which Scots had come to be seen as not including a formal register.

Curiously, when we turn to Riddell's grammar we find quite different principles at work. Scoticisation, it is true, is evident but modernisation is not. On the contrary, he seems in his grammar to actually want to increase the archaic elements rather than remove them. This is most noticeable in his use throughout of the Middle Scots article *ane* for the Authorised Version's *a*, even to the extent of rendering *ahungered* as *ane hungert* (4:2), an idiom not actually found in Middle Scots. *Ane* as an article was thoroughly obsolete by Riddell's time so that he is here introducing archaism where there is none in the Authorised Version. On top of this Riddell makes what can only be described as a very odd decision with regard to verbal inflections. Even in the earliest Scots texts the *eth* ending has yielded to *s* or *is* but Riddell chooses to retain the Authorised Version's *eth* in his Scots version and merely changes the spelling to *ith*. This inflection, and this spelling of it, are only found in those earlier Scots texts where there is evidence of considerable anglicisation. It is not a native Scots form. It looks particularly odd where it is combined with Riddell's change of the Authorised Version's *not* to enclitic *na* as in *bringithna* (3:10). The rare exceptions to this use of *ith* are special cases. With *tarrows* (13:21) he is also changing the whole word since the Authorised Version has *dureth*: this exceptional case suggests that Riddell's natural impulse to write *s* as in Modern Scots was only controlled by his strict allegiance to the Authorised Version. He also fails to record the Scots use of an *s* ending after *thou* rather than the *st* and associated forms of English. Hence we find *thou art* (16:16) and *thou hest* (17:27) rather than *thou is* and *thou hes*. The retention of *thou* is itself an archaism since *thou* had gone out of use in most parts of Scotland by this time. The further retention of the Authorised Version's *you* (spelt as *yow* to reflect Riddell's Border pronunciation) can be defended on the grounds that it was in use at the time in the Borders but Murray claims that *ye* was the normal object in Southern Scots and *yow* was only used in special cases particularly when emphasis fell on the pronoun (*DSCS*, p 190). One suspects that it would have been generally rendered as *ye* if Riddell had not been following the Authorised Version so closely.

By contrast, other aspects of grammar are scoticised. I have already mentioned the use of *na* and to this we may add the regular use of Scots forms of past tenses and participles. Here, indeed, Riddell is a more thorough scoticiser than is strictly necessary, giving an ending in *et* (this is his usual spelling) to verbs like *kythe* (1:20) and *thole* (3:15) which would normally in Scots have an *ed* ending, as in English. The contradiction of aims in the handling of verbal inflections is striking: the non-Scots *eth* retained on the one hand and the excessive use of Scots *et* on the other. But given the climate of the time these contradictory practices are not surprising. To present the Bible in Scots was to face the danger of its being seen as written in an inappropriately informal medium. To retain the *eth* inflection, by now firmly associated both with biblical English and with high-flown poetic diction, was to offer a counterbalance to this danger. Riddell's language can best be understood as an outcome of two contradictory impulses, one to present the Bible in Scots, a medium with strong associations of informality and colloquialism, the other to retain the general stylistic nature of the Authorised Version which had been characterised by the mixture of formal and more stylistically neutral vocabulary. The tension between these two aims of true Scots and a suitably 'biblical' style was to continue as a fundamental problem for translators after Riddell and has only been to any real degree resolved in this century in the work of Lorimer.

It is fascinating to see Riddell grappling with the problems of using an informal, contemporary Scots for the Bible long before informal, contemporary English had gained the widespread acceptance as a medium for translations which it now enjoys. He was forced into this style of language because he had no models of either formal Scots or an agreed kind of archaic Scots which he could follow. It is true that Andrew Norton in his Gospels (1855) and Leicester Ambrose Sawyer in his New Testament (1858) were, in the same decade as Riddell, experimenting with the use of contemporary English but it was a matter of choice and an archaic, more formal style was still available in English. The most important English translation of the century was, in fact, the Revised Version completed in 1885 and this was, as we shall see, an attempt to preserve as far as possible the language of the Authorised Version. As such it was far from being either contemporary or informal in its language. It would be interesting to know how Riddell felt about the challenge facing him: his practice in his translation suggests he approached it with mixed feelings.

Riddell's spelling is notable both in its carefulness and general consistency and in its originality. Consistency and carefulness in spelling Scots are certainly not features which mark the major authors that Riddell could have modelled himself on. Scott, for instance, both uses different Scots spellings of the same word at different times and intermingles English and Scots spellings even in passages of broad Scots. But Riddell does follow Scott and his predecessors in defining many Scots pronunciations by reference to English spelling. Apostrophes, indicating the absence of a letter found in English spelling, abound. A few formal words are however spelt without apostrophes: *corrup, excep, exak*. The trouble with using the apostrophe, as later writers have realised, is that it tends to suggest that English is the norm from which Scots is a deviation, that Scots is in some sense a corrupt form of English. Few things reveal more than spelling does about how a language is seen by its users and the implication is very strong in Riddell's spelling that he sees Scots as a non-standard dialect rather than a language in its own right.

Where Riddell most radically departs from his contemporaries is in the use of æ, which fills a number of roles in his spelling scheme. Its function is often somewhat analogous to that of the apostrophe: it allows for differentiation of pronunciation but enables the reader to recognise the related English word which will use an a or e in that position. Unfortunately its phonetic significance is rather less clear; it seems to represent a range of sounds in words like *ganæration, hæle, hæven, leæven, næther* and *ræise*. All in all, the use of æ was an interesting experiment but it seems that Riddell made it bear too varied a weight of meaning for it to be really useful as a phonetic guide.

A few of Riddell's spellings like *fisch* and *schip* are taken from earlier Scots. Riddell's use of earlier Scots spellings like these, of the Middle Scots inflection *ith*, of the article *ane*, and of *thou* might indicate some impulse to match the archaic qualities of the Authorised Version's language by translating it into archaic Scots. If this is so, and such an impulse would not be surprising, Riddell is not consistent. In vocabulary and spelling he departs considerably from Middle Scots. Despite these few archaic features, his is basically nineteenth century Scots.

One's first impression on reading Riddell is that his translation into Scots is a rather half-hearted affair. In particular, the retention of the English *eth* inflection, evident on every page, gives one the impression that Riddell can scarcely bear to change the Authorised Version at all. This impression is increased by his use of the anglicised *et* spelling for past tenses and participles rather than the traditional Scots *it*. This first impression is somewhat unfair. Closer inspection shows that there is considerable change in both spelling and vocabulary, albeit not in grammar. The spelling changes are necessarily pervasive and the vocabulary changes affect roughly half the verses. Its biggest failure is in grammar but this is a more thoroughly Scots version than one at first realises.

Nevertheless there was a fundamental problem in Riddell's approach. The identity of Scots was by now thoroughly under threat from English. One way of reasserting its identity was to emphasise as much as possible the ways in which it could differ from English. The minimalist approach adopted by Riddell, whereby all words shared with English are retained, leads to a language with the smallest possible amount of differentiation from English. Its perceived identity as Scots is thus very weak. Add to this the use of English grammar and archaic English vocabulary and you have a kind of language which few readers are going to accept as possessing a strong Scots identity.

The effect of Riddell's methods of translation is variable: his reluctance to do more than substitute one word for another at times works quite effectively as in the description of the arrival of the Wise Men quoted above; at other times it produces a stilted and discordant effect as in Christ's words to the disciples in the Garden of Gethsemane: *My saul is excessiv sorrafu', een untill deæth: taigle ye here, an' watch wi' me* (26:38) where the formal and archaic *excessiv* is ill at ease in the company of the colloquial and contemporary *taigle*. Above all, in judging his work we should not forget that he was the first person to put any book of the Bible into Scots for about three hundred years. The Bible and seventeenth century English had been for so long united in the minds of all people in Scotland that it was very hard to think in terms of any other language for biblical translation and especially difficult to translate it, not into an utterly distinct language, but one which still shared a great deal with the English of 1611. Additionally Riddell was used to reading the Bible in an archaic, rather formal language and must now turn it into an informal, contemporary language. He was bound to encounter problems.

Riddell went on to translate the Song of Solomon and the Psalms for Prince Louis but before we consider those texts it will be best to view the other version of St Matthew commissioned by the prince.

HENDERSON'S ST MATTHEW (1862)

In 1862 Prince Louis again paid for the printing of a version of St Matthew. The translator was one George Henderson but I have not been able to identify him. Perhaps he is the same as the George Henderson who in 1859 wrote a prefatory Notice to the *Discourses* of his father, another George Henderson (d.1784), and who gave his place of residence in 1860 in the National Library of Scotland copy of those *Discourses* as Glendarroch. There was also a George Henderson, minister of Cullen, who died in 1885 aged 86 and two matriculants of Glasgow University whose ages make them possible candidates. There is thus no shortage of possibilities but at this stage I have no evidence for positive identification.

Henderson's *The Gospel of St Matthew translated into Lowland Scotch* has more than just a name in common with the earlier version of Riddell. It is, in fact, a revision of Riddell although it contains no acknowledgement of this debt. There is, however, a useful preface by Henderson and notes on pronunciation by Prince Louis. This time two hundred and fifty were printed rather than a mere eighteen; perhaps the prince felt an obligation to make the work more widely available. Presumably he commissioned this second version for the sake of comparison. No other reason can be gleaned from his notes unless there is a hint to be found in his comment that it 'is much to be regretted, in the interests of comparative philology, that the Scotch, as well as the English, the French, the Gaelic, and all their dialects, does not follow in its ordinary spelling a more phonetic principle, such as to be found in every other European language' (p 8). In fact, Riddell is considerably 'more phonetic' than Henderson, but this comment may be read as a realistic acceptance that no phonetic spelling of Scots stood any real chance of being adopted. This might explain his willingness to finance Henderson's more conventionally spelt version.

Henderson's preface expresses a clear aim: 'to show that the language of the Lowland Scotch is not merely a corrupt form of that spoken in England, but that it possesses claims to be considered a branch of the Anglo-Saxon family' (p 5). As part of this endeavour he wishes to give a '"local habitation"' to various words that 'though retained among the peasantry—in all countries the faithful depositaries of ancient languages—are fast fading away before the schoolmaster and the march of modern civilisation, and are too frequently affectedly considered as mere vulgar "barbarisms"'. But while he thus wishes to make clear the ancient origins of Scots he also wishes to produce a version in contemporary language: he anticipates that 'objections may be raised to the use of certain words, as *kythe* for "appear," *eydently* for "diligently," *hiddinslie* for "privately," &c. as too archaic for a version of the Lowland Scotch of the present day' but argues that such words are still current and may legitimately be used. It is a defence that writers of Scots, amongst them MacDiarmid, have used again and again. Henderson's expressed aim is therefore clear: a version in modern Scots which will nevertheless make clear the language's ancient origins. How far he fulfilled this complex aim can be best considered in the context of a discussion of his revisions to Riddell, beginning with his vocabulary. Firstly, however, as an illustration of Henderson's work as a reviser of Riddell, I repeat Riddell's account of the arrival of the Wise Men along with Henderson's rendering:

RIDDELL

Than Herod, whan he had hiddlinslie ca't the wyse men, inquairet o' them eidentlie what time the stern had kythet. An' he sendet them til Bethlehem, an' said, Gang an' seek eidentlie for the young childe; an' whan he hae fund him, bring me back word, that I may come an' wurship him alsua. An' whan they had heard the king, they set out; an', lo, the stern whilk they saw in the east gaed afore them, till it cam' an stude ower whare the young childe was. An' whan they saw the stern they rejoicet wi' verra grit joy.

HENDERSON

Syne Herod, whan he had hiddlinsly ca'd the wise men, spier't at them eydently what time the star kythet. An' he sendet them til Bethlehem; an' said, Gang an' seek eydently for the young bairn; an' whan ye hae fund him, bring me back word, that I may come an' worship him alsua. Whan they had hear't the king, they set out; an', lo, the star, whilk they saw in the east, gaed afore them till it cam' an' stood owre whare the young bairn was. Whan they saw the star, they rejoicet wi' unco meikle joy (2:7–10).

In the gospel as a whole about three quarters of the Scots terms introduced by Riddell are carried over unchanged into Henderson but, in rejecting some of Riddell's terms and in introducing a number of his own, Henderson exercises considerable independent judgement. All the same it is noticeable that most of Henderson's further departures from the Authorised Version conform to the trends already evident in Riddell. Riddell had replaced most of the words that Scots does not share with English but Henderson could extend the list of shared English-Scots words that are replaced by entirely Scots terms. Where Riddell was willing to retain the Authorised Version's *child, evening* and *great* which belong to the common stock of English and Scots, Henderson replaces them with the purely Scots alternatives *bairn* (1:18), *gloamin'* (14:15) and *meikle* (2:10) although he sometimes keeps Riddell's plural *childer* (5:9). Henderson also extends the replacement of archaisms: *slew* gives way to *killet* (2:16) and *troubled* meaning 'terrified' to *fleyed* (14:26). He further changes the archaic asseveration *of a truth* to *verament* (14:33) but the latter is itself an archaism found in Middle English. Finally, he extends the application of Riddell's policy of removing formal terms: *descending, fragments* and *inquire* are replaced by *comin' doun* (3:16), *orra bits* (14:20) and *speir* (2:7).

The same principles continue to apply when Henderson rejects Riddell's changes, either retaining the Authorised Version reading or introducing his own new term. Riddell's change of *cast* to *thraw* (5:29) is not accepted, presumably because *cast* is the more common term in Scots except in Lothian and the Borders. Riddell, a Borderer, opted for *thraw* but until Henderson is identified it is impossible to say whether *cast* or *thraw* was the more common in his dialect. Perhaps we have here some shaky evidence that Henderson was not from the Borders or Lothians. The changes of *moved* and *treasures* to the Middle Scots terms *amovet* (14:14) and *thesaures* (2:11) and of *dwelt* to the highly archaic *wonet* (2:2) or *won* (4:13) are likewise rejected in line with Henderson's policy of using only vocabulary in contemporary use.

Henderson explicitly states his rejection of certain Scots terms which he regards as too informal: 'Various vernacular words, as *lug* for "ear," *crack* for "talk," *cuddy* for "ass," &c. have been discarded as unsuitable in a translation of a portion of the Holy Scriptures' (p 5). Like Riddell before him and others after him Henderson was encountering the problem that the most familiar Scots diction was colloquial diction and colloquial diction did not fit with their notions of appropriate biblical style. Several times, indeed, it seems that Henderson felt that Riddell himself had been too informal. Riddell's change of *least* to *weest* (2:6) does not appear in Henderson and, where Riddell replaces *multitudes* with *ferkishins*, Henderson prefers *thrang* (5:1). Other departures from Riddell are harder to explain: did he think Riddell had been too free in applying the vivid word *eerie* to the disciples when Christ walks on the water and they fear he is a 'ghaist'? In any case he opted for the much tamer *fleyed* (14:26). And why did he reject Riddell's thoroughly Scots *boundes* and the Authorised Version's *region* in favour of the rather colourless *kintra* (3:5) but later retain the Authorised Version's *region* when rejecting Riddell's rather free *damain* (4:16)? Finally we see him correcting clear mistakes on Riddell's part and restoring omitted words and phrases. In short, it might be said that Henderson has carried through Riddell's aims more thoroughly than Riddell himself, indeed has out-Riddelled Riddell.

Something similar happens with the grammar. It is true that Henderson, like Riddell, retains the entirely non-Scots *eth* inflection (spelling it, however, in the normal English fashion) but he does remove Riddell's archaic use of *ane* as an article and of the relative pronoun *whilk* in relation to persons. He is freer, too, in introducing auxiliaries and this gives his grammar a more modern flavour: Riddell retains the Authorised Version's *knew her not* and *bringeth not* as *kennet her na* and *bringithna* but Henderson reads *didna ken* (1:25) and *dothna bring* (3:10). So, while the use of the *eth* inflection remains an irritant, Henderson reads much more like a piece of modern Scots prose.

This impression is increased by the spelling. Henderson tells us in his preface that the 'orthography adopted is that of Burns, Sir Walter Scott, and other recent writers, their inconsistencies being avoided in order to ensure uniformity' (p 5). This proves to be an only partially accurate description. It is true that he has dropped some of Riddell's conventions, which brings him closer to Burns and Scott, but other features remain which are not found in those authors. One major difference from Riddell is the dropping of æ, but he retains Riddell's apostrophes and adds others in formal words like *corrup'* and *excep'* so that he ends up using rather more apostrophes than either Scott or Burns. Nevertheless the spelling of Henderson's work makes it look much more like other Scots writing of the previous one hundred years or so. It is consequently easier to read than Riddell but less distinct from English. Moreover, by retaining and even extending Riddell's widespread use of the apostrophe, Henderson maintains the impression of Scots as a corruption of English.

How well then has he fulfilled his expressed aims? As regards vocabulary, he has certainly given many Scots words a 'local habitation' and thus demonstrated the considerable resources of Scots diction not shared with English. On the other hand, he has fulfilled his aim of showing Scots as a separate 'branch of the Anglo-Saxon family' rather less satisfactorily with regard to spelling. By opting for a spelling much closer to the practice of modern Scots writers he has achieved one positive result. He has reminded us that Scots does have a separate modern set of spelling conventions, albeit a somewhat confused one, whereas Riddell had given the impression that a separate spelling of Scots could only be achieved by a rather quaint phonetic spelling. A tongue without its own established spelling which can only be rendered phonetically is liable to be seen as purely a spoken dialect without any real literary register. Henderson avoids this at least. But his widespread use of apostrophes has a contrary effect: it sets up English as the norm from which Scots is seen to be a mere spoken deviation.

It would be unfair to judge Henderson purely in terms of the high aims he set himself. It is better to see him in terms of his place in the history of Scots translation of the Bible. While his sadly unacknowledged debt to Riddell is considerable this should not blind us to the fact that his translation is a considerable improvement on his predecessor's. His work is more thoroughly Scots, more consistently modern, more idiomatic, more accurate and more sensibly spelt. He faces the same difficulties as Riddell in using informal and contemporary Scots for a Bible translation and his comments show that he was aware of these difficulties but he seems more at ease in dealing with them. Riddell had blazed the trail; Henderson followed and laid down a rough track for others to tread on.

RIDDELL'S PSALMS (1857)

In 1857 Riddell was again employed by Bonaparte, this time to translate the Psalms. Riddell's method here is very much as in his Matthew with one significant variation: he abandons the *ith* inflections with the third person singular and uses the historic and contemporary Scots *s* inflection. This goes some way towards making the translation more genuinely Scots and modern but he still retains his *ist* inflection after *thou* and, since this latter inflection is very frequent in the Psalms, it gives an archaic and unScots tone to the whole translation.

The same kinds of choice about vocabulary are made here as in his Matthew. For example, the formal *calamity*, the English *knoweth* and the archaic *stablished* are replaced by *sair wanluck* (18:18), *kens* (1:6) and *sete siccer* (93:1). At the same time many formal terms are not removed: while *transgression* is at least once changed to *wranggangin'* (89:32), it is elsewhere retained (19:13). Riddell surely has every justification in keeping both *covenant* and *testimonies* (25:10)—these words had been enshrined in Scots speech by the Covenanters—but, as we shall see, a later, more thorough Scoticiser, Waddell, replaced them. Also, as in his Matthew, certain archaisms of the Authorised Version are left untouched like *innocency* (26:6) and *holpen* (83:8) as a past participle of *help*. To this Riddell has added some further Scots archaisms which I suspect are taken from Jamieson. The Authorised Version's *mercy* is displaced by *misrecorde* (37:26), *promotion* becomes *promovall* (75:6) and *nobles* gives way to *riolyse* which Jamieson cites only from *Colagros and Gawane* and glosses as 'princely person, nobles'. Jamieson's influence is also to be traced in the use of *frennet* 'raged' (46:6) otherwise found only in Jamieson and the translation of the Authorised Version's *suddenly* as *in ane wanwuth* (64:4): this derives from a phrase only recorded in his dictionary, *to be ta'en at a wanwuth* meaning 'to be taken by surprise'. Riddell also has a few innovations of his own like the new compound *maigmayden* (86:16). According to the *Scottish National Dictionary*, *maig* is normally used with 'contemptuous force' which makes it rather a strange rendering of the Authorised Version's *handmaid*. The mixture, then, of colloquial modern Scots vocabulary with archaic English and Scots terms and modern Scots grammar with archaic English grammar is much the same as in Riddell's Matthew.

This is the only prose version of the Psalms in Scots except that of P H Waddell. Waddell fashioned something quite distinctive, a passionate and intimate overflow of powerful feelings. Riddell remained too close to the 1611 text to produce a really new version, but changed it enough to give his version a quaintness the Authorised Version never had.

RIDDELL'S SONG OF SOLOMON (1858)

The following year Riddell made yet another translation for Prince Louis, this time of one of the prince's favourite sample texts, the Song of Solomon. This was to be the first of four Scots versions of this text commissioned by Bonaparte. Once again the familiar features of Riddell's technique occur. On the one hand he retains the Authorised Version's formal *countenance* (2:14) and *terrible* (6:4) and the archaic *espousals* (2:11) and on the other he removes the formal *abundantly*, changing it to *routhlie* (5:1) and the archaic *substance*, replacing it with *guids an' geer* (8:7). At the same time he introduces the Scots archaism *amene* (1:16) for *pleasant* and the English archaism *arrayemints* (4:11) for *garment*. Typically, too, he includes a few of his own creations like *wate-men* (3:3) for the Authorised Version's *watchmen* and *wassail-ha'* (2:4), a translation of *banqueting-house* which was perhaps influenced by the Authorised Version's marginal note *house of wine*. In short, this is a typical Riddell translation and, as with his Matthew, provided the basis for subsequent translations for Prince Louis, all of which draw heavily on him.

ROBSON'S SONG OF SOLOMON (1860)

In 1860 Prince Louis published two more translations of the Song of Solomon. One was anonymous, the other by Joseph Philip Robson. Despite the description of him on the title page as 'Author of "Scotch Songs"', Robson was not a Scot. He spent his life in Newcastle where he was born in 1808 and died in 1870. He was a schoolmaster there and wrote both a column for a local newspaper under the name of 'A Retiort Keelman' and a number of books of poems. On the face of it someone who called himself the Minstrel of Tyne and Wear seems a strange choice for making a translation into Scots and, indeed, in this same year of 1860 Robson also produced for Prince Louis translations of the Song of Solomon into the Northumberland and Newcastle dialects: on their title pages he is described as the author of *Tyneside Songs* and *Bards of the Tyne*! Nevertheless he acquitted himself creditably in Scots.

Like Riddell's translations, and indeed all the translations into English dialects for Prince Louis, Robson's is based on the Authorised Version but he draws heavily on Riddell even if he shows a good deal more willingness to depart from the Authorised Version. Riddell's influence is evident throughout the translation, Robson's frequent concurrence with him being too great to be merely accidental. Robson agrees with Riddell, for example, in rendering *tents* as *shielins* (1:5), *comely* as *winsome* (1:10), *pleasant* as *leesome* (4:17) and *choice one* as *dawtie-bairn* (6:9) and he makes use of two of Riddell's coinages, *waitmen* (5:7) for watchmen and the somewhat archaic *wassail-ha'* (2:4). (Indeed, all the Bonaparte translators use *wassail-ha'*). On the other occasions, however, while he follows Riddell in replacing particular English words with Scots and in removing certain archaisms and formal terms of the Authorised Version, he does not always make the same choice of replacement as Riddell. Riddell replaces *abundantly, virgins* and the archaism *fitly* with *routhlie, mays* and *deftlie*; Robson uses *fouthlie* (5:1), *lasses* (1:3) and *bonnilie* (5:12). Riddell had found *pleasant* insufficiently Scots and had used the archaic *amene*, a word favoured by Scottish writers though not unknown in English; Robson rejects the archaism and uses a word shared with English but made Scots by its intensive, *unco' beautifu'* (1:16). On top of this Robson changes many words left unchanged by Riddell. Formal or archaic terms like *countenance, espousals, excellent, terrible* and *valiant* which Riddell had not changed give way to *face, weddin', gran', dreedfu'* and *braw*. Nor are his changes limited to removing archaisms and formal diction. He has an eye for the vivid word and rather than keep the colourless *haudet, luiks* and *tuuk* (which Riddell rightly identified as perfectly acceptable Scots equivalents of the English *held, looketh* and *took*) he goes for the much more effective *grippet* (3:4), *keeks* (2:9) and *clicket* (5:7). As these changes indicate, Robson's language, as well as being more vivid, is altogether more colloquial and everyday than Riddell's. This is especially evident in his handling of the Authorised Version's exclamatory *behold* which Riddell had left untouched. Compare the Authorised Version's

> Behold, thou art fair, my beloved, yea, pleasant: also our bed is green

and

> The voice of my beloved! behold, he cometh leaping upon the mountains, skipping upon the hills

with Robson's

> Guid sooth, but thou art bonnie, my lo'ed ane, aye, unco' beautifu'; an' alang wi' a', oor couch is green (1:16)

and

> The voice o' my ain love! wow, he comes loupin' upo' the moontans, skippin' upo' the hills (2:8)

and the colloquial and familiar tone of Robson is at once obvious. The tones of everyday colloquial speech also come through strongly in

> An' what is thy lo'ed ane mair nor anither's lo'ed ane, that thou keeps churmin' sae til us? (5:9)

where the Authorised Version, followed by Riddell, has the archaic and formal

> what is thy beloved more than another beloved, that thou dost so charge us?

Robson's rather free translation of the Authorised Version here maintains a colloquial tone established by small details elsewhere, for instance by rendering *every man* as *ilka chiel'*, *while* as *the hale time* and *withdrawn himself* as *ta'en hissel aff*. There are some exceptions, as when he simply changes Riddell's clumsy *arrayemints* to *raiment* (4:11) rather than moving, as the anonymous translator did, to the obvious colloquial *claes*, but normally Robson opts for colloquial vocabulary and idioms and achieves a stylistically consistent translation, intimate and familiar in tone, modern and up-to-date in idiom and arguably more suitable for such a passionate work as the Song of Solomon than Riddell's more archaic and formal style. Whether or not it is appropriate to the work, such a style entirely fits the then current view of Scots as primarily a colloquial tongue, a language of speech rather than of formal literary modes. By choosing such a style, well developed in Scots writing over the last one hundred and fifty years, Robson abandons any attempt to produce a special elevated style for Biblical translation. He also foreshadows modern translators who have believed that their aim should be to render the Bible into everyday colloquial English.

Robson's desire for modern and colloquial language prevails at times at the expense of distinctively Scots diction. Riddell had translated the Authorised Version's *a cunning workman* as *ane warkman o' artish ingyne* using his own formation *artish* and the Scots *ingine*. Robson does not continue with this rather artificial circumlocution but his simple *guid warkman* (7:1) has nothing distinctively Scots about it beyond the spelling. What he loses in Scots flavour he gains in colloquial strength and clarity of meaning.

The choices made by Robson in his grammar are consistent with the principles at work in the vocabulary. The English *eth* and *est* forms are abandoned in favour of the Scots *s*—*the king hes, thou has*—but one case of Riddell's *ist* has been retained, perhaps accidentally, in *wonist* (8:13), and *art* is preferred to *is* after *thou*. Of course, Robson is following Riddell in not giving up the Authorised Version's use of *thou* despite its general disappearance in Scots by this time but the presence of the associated Scots *s* inflections gives *thou* a more colloquial tone than it has in Riddell. Robson also abandons Riddell's elaborate phonetic spelling for a conventional Scots spelling with all its drawbacks and inconsistencies but Prince Louis has supplied notes on pronunciation. There are a few idiosyncracies that might be traced to the fact that Robson was not a Scot: it seems likely that the spelling *dreed hour* (3:8) indicates that Robson failed to recognise the Scots *dreaddour* meaning 'fear' in Riddell's *dreædour in the nicht* and interpreted it as 'dread hour' and it is certain that *thaw* (4:5), used once as a spelling for *thy*, has been accidentally carried over from Robson's Newcastle and Northumberland versions where it is the normal form.

A comparison of these versions with the Scots version points up several interesting differences. In his Notes to the Newcastle and Northumberland versions Robson enters into some detail about variations in pronunciation within the one area. Of this word *thaw*, for instance, he writes in the Newcastle version that '*Thy* is generally pronounced *thaw*. Occasionally you hear "*thy*" pronounced like *thēy-ĕ*, but the broad *thaw* is almost universal in the colliery districts of the Tyne' (p 3). This is, one supposes, exactly the sort of information the Bonaparte texts were intended to provide. In the Scots version there is no such detail; we are presented with a text in generalised Standard Scots. No doubt the fact that Robson was not a Scot has something to do with this but it also testifies to the unique status of Scots amongst dialects in Britain. For the dialects of England the only authority is the usage of speakers. For Scots there is also another authority, the texts of the modern Scots literary tradition. These are mostly in a standard literary Scots and it is this kind of Scots that we find in Robson and the other Bonaparte translators except, to some degree, Riddell. The special position of Scots as possessing the only fully established modern dialectal literature in Britain interfered with the achievement of Prince Louis's aims. The authority of the literary tradition overwhelmed the authority of the contemporary speakers. This was a loss for the study of spoken dialect but it did mean that the Scots translations are much more likely to appeal to us as satisfying literary texts and not just linguistic documents.

All in all, we can say that Robson, compared to both Riddell and Henderson, has much more thoroughly accepted the idea that to use Scots is to use a necessarily informal and contemporary register. Nevertheless his retention of *thou*, even with the more colloquial Scots *s* inflection, suggests a desire to retain something of the archaic and formal qualities of the Authorised Version since *thou* was both largely obsolete in Scots and strongly associated with a rather formal English poetic style.

ANONYMOUS SONG OF SOLOMON (1860)

Like Robson's, the other translation of 1860, published anonymously, owes a considerable debt to Riddell. Indeed, it is rather closer to Riddell than Robson is, the translator being less willing to vary Riddell's language. For instance he keeps Riddell's very unusual word *raftries* (1:17) where Henderson and Robson, the two other Bonaparte translators, return to the Authorised Version's *rafters* and he uses Riddell's translation of *pillars of smoke* as *towiricks o' reek* (3:6), merely changing the spelling to *tooricks*, where the others have *lunts*, a much more ordinary word to use in Scots in connection with smoke. We also find some of Riddell's grammar, especially the *ist* forms after *thoo* and the occasional use of *th* forms as in *heth* (1:4). On the other hand, his archaic use of *ane* as an indefinite article has given way to the use of *ae*, but, while Riddell's usage can be defended as an archaism, the use of *ae* as an article is not a normal feature of Scots of any period unless it can be considered as an unusual spelling of *a*.

Despite its closeness to Riddell, the translation does have certain independent features, the spelling being one. For Riddell's idiosyncratic phonetic spelling the translator substitutes a more conventional Scots spelling system, although he does make use of diacritics as in *ĭntments* 'ointments', *prïën* 'tasting' and find *'fĭnd'*, and, foreshadowing Lorimer, in the personal name *Sōlomon*. Like Robson, but more cautiously, he extends Riddell's practice of removing archaisms and formal terms and of replacing English terms or shared English-Scots terms with distinctively Scots ones so that *whaur* replaces *whither* (6:1), *awsome* replaces *terrible* (6:4) and *stowps* replaces *flagons* (2:5). He also disagrees with some of Riddell's changes to the Authorised Version, either reverting to the Authorised Version's words or providing his own new term. Like Robson and Henderson he rejects Riddell's *hippertiein'* which seems to be a purely Southern Scots word and reverts to the Authorised Version with *skippin'* (2:8) and replaces Riddell's euphemistic *middel* for the Authorised Version's *belly* with the genuinely Scots *wame* (7:2). On the other hand he stands alone in rejecting Riddell's *smitch* and retaining the Authorised Version's *spot* (4:7) and in translating *the chiefest* as *the maist kenspeckle* (5:10). By and large, then, because it sticks closer to Riddell and the Authorised Version, this is not as thoroughly colloquial a translation as Robson's but, compared to Riddell, it does represent a further move towards presenting Scots as a primarily colloquial tongue.

As we have noted this work was published anonymously. Being a translation it presents few clues to the translator's identity. A possible clue is the use of the form *shaddie* (2:3) to translate the Authorised Version's *shadow*.

This is a Lothian and Berwickshire form and suggests that the translator came from that area. It is also noticeable that the notes on pronunciation, which occur in the Robson and Henderson versions over Prince Louis's initials, are here unsigned. A somewhat unlikely surmise might be that Prince Louis himself was the translator and that he omitted his initials to remove all trace of his role.

HENDERSON'S SONG OF SOLOMON (1862)

For his final commissioning of a version of the Song of Solomon Prince Louis again turned to George Henderson. Henderson's Song of Solomon bears much the same relation to Riddell's Song as his Matthew does to Riddell's Matthew: he both keeps and changes a great deal from Riddell and he is more thorough than Riddell in removing archaisms, anglicisms and formal terms. In this case, however, Henderson had two other intervening translators to draw on and he makes good use of their work, borrowing about equally from Robson and the anonymous translator. From the former he takes *grippet* (3:4) *keeks* (2:9) and *lunts* (2:6) for the Authorised Version's, *held, looks* and *pillars*, and from the latter he takes *awsome* (6:4), *douchty* (4:4), and *hingin's* (1:5) for the Authorised Version's *terrible, valiant* and *curtains*. At the same time he introduces a number of new translations of his own. Whereas the others follow Riddell in rendering *barren* as *kebbet*, *lodge* as *won* and *substance* as *gudes an' geer* Henderson uses *yeld* (4:2), *dwall* (7:11) and *haudins* (8:7).

Stylistically Henderson is closest to Robson. He shows a distinct preference for more colloquial idioms even where they are less distinctively Scots: *a good smell* becomes *a nice smell* (2:13), *ravished* is changed to *stown awa* (4:9) and *utterly ... contemned* appears as *a'thegither scornet* (8:7). Robson had replaced the archaic and formal *behold* with the very informal *wow!*. Henderson doesn't go as far as this but he does change it once to *leuk!* (2:8) and he breaks down a rather formal phrase like *in the day of the gladness of his heart* into something much more informal: *in the day whan his hairt was fu' o' glee* (3:11).

One aspect of his grammar, found also in his Matthew, is more informal even than Robson: he uses auxiliaries with negative verbs so that he writes *dinna glower* (1:6) where all the others have *glowerna* but his grammar is in general more formal than Robson because he adheres more to Riddell's use of the *st* inflections after *thou* rather than the Scots *s* and he is more likely than Riddell to replace the Authorised Version's *that* with *wha* (3:4) or *whilk* (4:1) which are only found in very formal, literary Scots.

A prefatory note by Prince Louis presents this translation as different in its spelling from the anonymous translation and Robson:

> The following translation of the Song of Solomon into Lowland Scotch has been executed on a plan entirely different from that of the two versions which have preceded it. They were intended to represent, so far as possible, the Scotch pronunciation in an *English* form; this is designed to be a monument of genuine Scotch orthography of the present day (p 3).

The comment is a little puzzling since the spelling differences between the three are not great and neither of the first two seem to me to depart greatly from current practices in spelling Scots in, for instance, Scottish novels. Possibly Prince Louis was thinking of the three translators' use of either *oo* or *ou* to render the Scots [u] sound. *Ou* was the historic spelling and was preferred by Scott and Galt earlier in the century but increasingly through the nineteenth century *oo* became more common, providing as it did for English readers a clear indication of the Scottish pronunciation. Perhaps Prince Louis or Henderson still saw *ou* as 'genuine Scotch orthography of the present day' and still saw *oo* as an English form though it was increasingly popular with Scottish writers. Certainly Henderson prefers *ou*, Robson uses both *ou* and *oo* and the anonymous translator opts for *oo*. Otherwise it is hard to see much justification for Prince Louis' comment.

Altogether then, Henderson's Song of Solomon is stylistically similar to his Matthew. It is more informal, more modern and more distinctively Scots than Riddell but still adheres to certain non-Scots characteristics of the Authorised Version.

'Anonymous' Song Of Solomon (Undated)

The Bonaparte translations seem to have had little effect on later translations, owing no doubt to their very limited distribution. However, there is an intriguing tailpiece to this story. Later in the century there appeared anonymously in Glasgow *The Song of Solomon Printed in ye olde Scottish Dialect*. This short pamphlet, selling for two pence, is undated but on the front page it carries a quotation from Waddell's Isaiah which dates it later than 1879. It is also identified as part of 'The Kailyard Series' which strongly suggests a date after 1895 when J H Millar gave the term *kailyard* notoriety as a name for a school of writing.

Despite the absence of a translator's name it is clearly an adaptation of George Henderson's version. The printing is slaphappy in the extreme and obvious errors abound: individual words and groups of words are omitted, *O* (the vocative) appears as *o'*, *waled* changes into *warld*, meaningless in the particular context, and *gar't* becomes *gait*. With a text in this condition it is difficult to be sure what changes are intentional but there are some consistent elements. The spelling, for instance, is much more thoroughly differentiated from English spelling than Henderson's: his *after, gladsome, head, house, my* and *our* are regularly changed to *aifter, glaidsome, heid, hoose, ma* and *oor*. As regards vocabulary, *wee*, perhaps felt to be too colloquial, usually but not always yields to *sma'* or *young*, and *piece*, retained by Henderson from the Authorised Version, gives way to *bit*. One curious feature is the replacement of *gie* 'give', *gied* 'gave' and *gae* 'go' by the attested but highly unusual alternatives *gae, gaed* and *gie*. Where Henderson changes the Authorised Version's *clusters* to *bunches*, the pamphlet makes a further change to *bundles*. This last appears rather odd in its context and looks very much like a mis-

reading of manuscript *bunches*. This, along with other readings like *gait* for
gar't, suggest the pamphlet was set up from manuscript, most probably a
transcript prepared to avoid the obvious plagiarism of setting up directly from
Henderson's printed text. Alternatively, it is not impossible that Henderson's
original manuscript or one of its drafts was the copy text.

Henderson had not been willing to make very drastic changes to the
Authorised Version. Whoever it was who prepared this text for publication
was no more adventurous than Henderson with regard to vocabulary but did
have a clear notion that a Scots text should be spelt in a more thoroughly
Scots fashion than Henderson had used. Careless work that it is, at least in
its printing, it represents a further small step towards a genuinely Scots
translation. What it does not do, despite its title page, is give us a translation
in Early or Middle Scots.

The Bonaparte translations make an interesting group. Apart from Riddell
who was the first to translate each of the three texts, these translators are in
effect working both from an English translation, the Authorised Version, and
one or more Scots translations. We can see that they all learnt something
from Riddell's mistakes although they also all owe a lot to him. Being the first
modern translator, Riddell is, as we might expect, rather cautious. He feels
reluctant to depart from the Authorised Version but even he shows himself
more adventurous in his later translations, especially in dropping the use of
the *ith* inflection. The others move a step beyond him in eliminating
archaisms, formal terms and anglicisms but only Robson achieves a satisfactorily consistent style. Since Henderson comes after Robson but does not
achieve the same consistency of style it does not seem to be simply a matter
of each translator learning from his predecessors. Perhaps Robson was more
willing to adopt a more colloquial style because he also had experience of
translating the Song of Solomon into two other dialects which were primarily
spoken varieties of language and lacked the strong literary traditions of Scots.
Perhaps he simply was more willing to change the hallowed Authorised
Version. It was no easy matter for the translators to come to terms with the
idea of translating the Bible into language very different to the English of
1611. Though each translator helped his successors, ultimately the break
from the overriding influence of the English version had to come from a
personal determination on the part of the individual translator. Such a determination is clearly evinced in our next translator.

WADDELL'S PSALMS (1871) AND ISAIAH (1879)

With P Hately Waddell (1817?–1891) we move into a class quite different
from that of the Bonaparte translators. Waddell tried singlehandedly to remedy the deficiencies of Scots as a vehicle for Bible translation and produced a
kind of language which strongly influenced subsequent translators. He was
a man of great energy and widely varied interests. After being called to the
Free Church in Girvan in 1844 he shortly afterwards left his charge to found

an independent congregation. He moved to Glasgow in 1862 where he was an independent minister preaching in various locations, including the Trades Hall, until he rejoined the Church of Scotland in 1888. He gave a series of lectures on Renan's *Life of Jesus* and wrote various books including a drama on the life of Jesus called *Behold the Man: A Tragedy for the Closet* (1872) and a short novel or tract called *Life at the Loom, or The Weaver's Daughter: Being an Illustration of the Miseries and Misfortunes of a Poor Weaving Population* (1848). In his *Ossian and the Clyde, Fingal in Ireland, Oscar in Iceland; or Ossian Historical and Authentic* of 1875 he attempted to prove that the poems of Ossian were indeed genuine and not by Macpherson. In a demonstration of his long-standing interest in geography he argued that the poems contained geographical references that would not have been known to Macpherson. His income was meagre and he supplemented it for several years by undertaking tours throughout Scotland, and sometimes in England and Ireland, lecturing on various subjects but especially on Burns whose works he also edited. Nor was his work limited to lecturing and writing. When the weaving industry was depressed he organised work for the unemployed, only one example of the active side of his ministry.

Altogether, Waddell brought strong qualifications to his work in translating the Psalms and Isaiah. The circumstances of his life would have given him a good knowledge of spoken Scots and he edited not only Burns but also the Waverley Novels. As their titles proclaim *The Psalms frae Hebrew intil Scottis* and *Isaiah frae Hebrew intil Scottis* were translated directly from the original Hebrew. Waddell was thus the first translator of the Bible into Scots to work from the original text. He approached the task with scholarly thoroughness. He tells us in a 'Notice to the General Reader' appended to the Psalms and, with alterations, to Isaiah, that, as well as using the Hebrew text, he consulted the Authorised Version, the Geneva Bible 'in which our own most distinguished Reformers had a share', and 'the Septuagint, and the Vulgate old and new; the individual versions of Pagninus, Praten, Tremellius, Junius, and Cocceius, in Latin; of Diodati in Italian, of Luther and Ulenberg in German, with the French and Belgian Versions old and new' (p2).[10] The year before Waddell published his Psalms approval had been given for work on the new Revised Version of the Bible. This grew out of a recognition of how far Biblical scholarship had progressed since 1611. The Revised Version of the Old Testament appeared in 1885, too late for Waddell to use it in his own translations, but he attempted in Scots to provide the same greater accuracy of translation as the Revised Version aimed at in English, asserting that

> the Translator ought also now to state, that where any difference as between the present and the authorised English Version may occur, he is not responsible. His own work is done directly from the Original, which he has attended to with the utmost care—Scotch for Hebrew, with all possible fidelity; and he has not much doubt that any impartial scholar, who is sufficiently acquainted with the spirit and the idioms of both languages, will admit that the present Scotch translation in general is much closer to the Original in many ways than our well-known English Version is, and that no variation anywhere occurs in it greater than what occurs everywhere and constantly in the English (p 2).

The Authorised Version is 'often utterly inadequate, and sometimes even erroneous, as a measure of the Hebrew Sense'. Nevertheless, he is 'far from depreciating in any way the acknowledged merits of so grand a work' (p 2).

Waddell has thus set himself a dual task; to produce translations which are both more accurate than the Authorised Version and are in Scots. The question of accuracy has not arisen up to this point since the translations so far considered have been based on English translations: their accuracy or inaccuracy is dependent on the accuracy or inaccuracy of the English version they are using. Our central concern so far has therefore been the kind of Scots used by the translators. Waddell is different because he translated direct from Hebrew but in the context of the wider history we are following here I will be concentrating with Waddell, too, on the nature of his Scots. I cannot myself make a claim to be 'sufficiently acquainted with the spirit and idioms of both languages' but those who can make such a claim may well find Waddell's accuracy as an interpreter of the Hebrew text is a subject worthy of attention. By the way of brief comment it is interesting to note that on the ten occasions when Waddell in his marginal notes on the Psalms specifically draws our attention to the fact that he is departing from the Authorised Version he sometimes has the agreement of the foremost Biblical scholars of the day as expressed in the Revised Version, either in its main text or in its notes (7:13, 15:4, 16:2, 42:10), and sometimes does not (29:9, 48:14, 50:23, 51:16, 54:7, 68:13). More recently, however, in two of these latter cases, the New English Bible has adopted a reading similar to Waddell's (50:23, 51:16).

The difference between a translator working from the original and one who is working from another translation written in a language closely related to the translator's is immediately obvious when we read Waddell. Even when taking the same text as the Authorised Version and rendering it with the same meaning Waddell regularly casts his translation in a quite different mould. Compare the Authorised Version's *O thou enemy, destructions are come to a perpetual end: and thou hast destroyed cities; their memorial is perished with them* with his *O ill-will'd man, surely swurd-wark's by for evir: hail towns ye hae rutet frae the yird; themsels an' a' min' o' them's dwafflet* (Ps. 9:6). The variation is especially marked in Isaiah where Waddell has often arranged his translation so as to provide the verses with rhyme and assonance. The Authorised Version's

> And he fenced it, and gathered out the stones thereof, and planted it with the choicest vine, and built a tower in the midst of it, and also made a winepress therein: and he looked that it should bring forth grapes, and it brought forth wild grapes

can be compared with Waddell's

> An' he dykit it roun', and flang stanes out enew; an' he set it with stoks of the wale'dest; an' he bigget a towir i' the mids o' the yaird, an' he howket a troch whar the wine maun be shair'd; an' he ettled it syne till gie grapes in rewaird, bot it gie'd-na a grape but the wildest (Is. 5:2).

Where the translation is not so radically different from the Authorised Version as this we still find that the word-order is frequently changed. Where the Authorised Version has *The foolish shall stand not in thy sight: thou hatest all workers of iniquity* Waddell gives us *Wha roose themsels, sal ne'er stan' frontin thee; a' do'ers o' wrang, ye mislo'e them utterlie* (Ps. 5:5) and, even where the word order is the same as the Authorised Version's, he is much more likely to use distinctively Scots terms than, for instance, Riddell. Take the Authorised Version's *Let us break their bands asunder, and cast away their cords from us* and Riddell's *Let us brik thair ban's asinder, an' thraw thair coords awa frae us* beside Waddell's *Lat's rive their thirlbans syndry, an' fling atowre their tows frae us* (Ps. 2:3). One suspects, indeed, that Waddell is sometimes deliberately avoiding the Authorised Version's language and that, in this sense, the Authorised Version had a powerful negative effect on his diction. In this verse, for instance, he has created his own new compound *thirlbans* where the Authorised Version's *bands* could have been much more easily and naturally rendered as *bans* (as Riddell does).

Yet if he has avoided the diction of the Authorised Version, he has managed to imitate its cadences, particularly in the Psalms where he has not introduced rhyme to the same degree as in his Isaiah. In his own time Waddell was renowned as an orator and he produced translations which can be read aloud with great effect. Perhaps it is in this that the influence of the Authorised Version shows itself.

Waddell's independence from the Authorised Version shows itself in another important respect: his language is thoroughly Scots, not a mixed Scots-English. Waddell himself describes his language in his 'Notice to the General Reader'. The terms of his description reveal a lot about how he saw the contemporary status of Scots: like so many Scots writers of the modern period he looks to the Scots of his childhood for his inspiration:

> The bulk of the language, both in terms and phraseology, is such as was in daily use by all well-educated peasants and country gentlemen of the last generation, and such as they had received by tradition from their own fore-fathers—men who represented the true vernacular of their country, from the days of the Reformation and of the Covenant. With such language the Trans-lator was familiar in his youth, as many of his readers must also have been (p 1).

Clearly, in Waddell's perception, the best Scots models belong to the past although he avoided using early Scots and claimed that 'there are not, on an average, more than five words in a thousand exclusively very old Scotch, such as is to be found in the earliest Scottish authors. Whoever may imagine otherwise is mistaken'. But, as Waddell recognised, using writers even of the recent past, and especially Burns, as a source presented problems: 'A very large number of terms employed by Burns are also employed here, as may easily be ascertained by consulting the Glossary for his Poems. But the expressions or phraseology most frequently employed by Burns could not, for very obvious reasons, be admitted in a translation of the Bible' (p 1). The problem was one that we have already identified: Burns, like most writers of

Scots in the modern period, tended to use an informal and colloquial style of Scots. To some extent this informal Scots suited the highly personal tone of the Psalms but a more formal style was also needed. As we have seen, by this time English had been adopted by the Scottish writers as their language for formal prose and a register of formal Scots had ceased to exist. Yet while Waddell saw Burns' language as presenting some problems for Biblical translators he also believed that it was Burns who had made Scots the preeminent language for lyric poetry and thus, presumably, a highly suitable medium for translating the Psalms. According to his lecture *Genius and Morality of Burns*, Burns was 'the very foremost lyric man since the days of DAVID' (p 4). He saw many similarities between Burns and David and called Burns 'this singer and psalmist of the people' (p 15). Through his poetry he had given Scots a safe and secure position as 'the language of passion and of sympathy'—so much so that Waddell was happy to accept the use of English for more mundane purposes in Scotland, believing that Scots 'may be disused if necessary in commerce, in politics, or in philosophy, without reproach' (p 10).

One solution to the absence of formal Scots diction would have been to reclaim for Scots the many formal words which it originally shared with English but, if we examine Waddell's Scots, we see that he adopted a narrow definition of Scots which denied him that resource. He saw Scots as mainly those elements not shared with English; as far as possible he avoids using the common stock of English and Scots vocabulary. Although he proclaimed in *Genius and Morality of Burns* that Scots was 'not a mere dialect...but a *tongue* cognate with the English' (p 4), he evidently felt the need to demonstrate the separateness of Scots by emphasising, indeed overemphasising, its distinctive diction. His solution to the problem of formal language is not, then, to reclaim the Latinate terms known in formal English but to look within the resources of Scots and to use what he calls 'one or two compound terms, made up of well-known simple terms, in the very spirit and according to the recognised idioms of the Scottish language, to express words or ideas in the Hebrew language which no Scotch or English or Latin terms *alone* ever will or can express' ('Notice', p 1). There is some understatement here; there are more than one or two and they are not all made up of well-known elements. Where a formal term, especially a Latinate one, is to be found in the Authorised Version Waddell will generally use one of his compounds. His *gaen-free* (Ps. 32:7), *heal-haddin* (Is. 25:9), *heigh-ha'din* (Ps. 59:17), *kith-gettin* (Ps. 12:7), *thought-takins* (Ps. 5:10) and *truthtryst* (Ps. 19:7) correspond to the Authorised Version's *deliverance, salvation, defence, generation, counsels* and *testimony*. But there is more to this than just the rejection of formal terms shared with English. This becomes obvious when we find Waddell replacing *decree* with *redden-right* (Ps. 2:7) and *glory* with *nameliheid* (Ps. 8:1) even though the completely Scots forms *decreet* and *glore* exist and also when a word of no great formality like *judge* is replaced, as a noun, by *rechter* (7:11) or *righter* (Ps. 2:10) and, as a verb, by *right-recht* (Ps. 9:4) or simply *right* (Ps. 7:8). *Decreet, glore* and *judge*, long established in Scots usage, are apparently not acceptable to Waddell. Why? The answer, as I have suggested elsewhere, can be found in comments made by Waddell in *Genius and Morality of Burns*.

While many Scots have liked to lay emphasis on the special contribution of French to Scots and while Waddell himself recognised this element as important, he attached much more significance to its Germanic roots. For Waddell Scots remains an essentially Germanic tongue:

> notwithstanding all the changes to which the vernacular of Scotland has been subjected by the commerce and world-wide relations of her sons, it adheres more perfectly in its root to the old Teutonic than the English does; and an uneducated Scotchman would be better able to make himself understood in Germany, than any other man that was not a German. He instinctively passes by the English door that is only across the border, and goes right to the old Teutonic homestead that is across the sea (p 7).

The Germanic element in Burns' language gives it its special quality: the words

> thrill through you, and revive and quicken you, as sweet and as congenial as your mother's milk. You feel than the man who speaks thus is your own mother's son—bone of your bone and flesh of your flesh: a son o' the faitherland—a Teuton and a Scotchman (p 7).

To be truly Scots is to be truly Germanic. No wonder then that Waddell weeds out the Romance vocabulary and replaces it with words of Germanic origin. Sometimes he can do this using normal Scots diction as when he changes *thou beholdest mischief and spite, to requite it with thy hand; the poor committeth himself unto thee* into *yersel can see baith cark an' care, till take a' i' yer han'. Till yersel the puir man leuks an' lippens* (Ps. 10:14). But if the resources of Scots fail him he creates new compounds or derivatives from Germanic elements. Indeed, the very use of compounds, Waddell's favourite method of producing new words, was, as he must have known, typically Germanic. The Romance languages prefer to create new words with affixes, to derive rather than combine. In pointing out Germanic elements in 'Auld Lang Syne' Waddell noted their equivalents in German and it is clearly German of all the Germanic languages that has particularly influenced him. The words for *judge* mentioned before show clear German influence: *righter* is from the German noun *Richter* and *right* from the German verb *richten*. Waddell's *to-flight* meaning 'refuge' (Ps. 62:8) is a calque of German *Zuflucht* and it seems possible that the word *torne* may be taken from German *Zorn* 'anger' with the initial letter changed to allow for the same phonetic difference as between *to* and *zu*.[11] It is used in the phrase *in your bleezan torne* (Ps. 6:1) where the Authorised Version has *in thy hot displeasure*. It could alternatively be explained, as I have elsewhere,[12] as the use of the word *torne* in the sense recorded by Jamieson 'a turn, an action done to one, whether favourable or injurious' but the meaning 'anger' fits the context more easily. Waddell also used another word to mean 'anger'; this is *wuth* (Ps. 2:5). It had not been used before in Scots but was taken up by the later Bible translator Cameron (Gen. 27:45). It seems to be based on the German *Wut* which has the same meaning, although it may also be influenced by the rare Scots adjective *wuth* meaning 'deranged'.

Returning to the words meaning 'judge', the compound verb *right-recht* shows the specific influence of Luther's translation of the Bible: compare, for instance, Waddell's *the warld he sal right-recht* (Ps. 9:8) with Luther's *er wird den Erdboden recht richten*. More difficult to account for is Waddell's use of *rechter* (Ps. 7:11) for the noun 'judge' and *rechtin* (Ps. 50:6) for 'judgement'. Here the German adjective *recht* meaning 'right' is treated as if it were a verb meaning 'judge'. Luther's influence is apparent from the very first verse of the Psalms where his use of *Gottlosen* inspired Waddell to create *godlowse* to mean 'wicked' and he continues to influence Waddell's translation even where he does not inspire the creation of new words: compare Waddell's *stark an' mighty* (Ps. 24:8) and Luther's *stark und mächtig* or Waddell's *furder . . . the right* (Ps. 7:9) and Luther's *fördere die Gerechten* where the Authorised Version has *establish the just*.

Given Waddell's emphasis on the essentially Germanic nature of Scots, it is no surprise to realise that he does not draw heavily on Celtic sources. All the same they did provide him with one useful word. Wanting an alternative to the Latin-derived *altar*, Waddell sometimes opted for his own creation *slachtir-cairn* (Ps. 84:3) and sometimes made use of the Celtic name given to certain prehistoric structures found in various places through the British Isles where a large stone is placed horizontally on three vertical stones. Somewhat inappropriately for a Scottish text, he uses the Welsh form *cromlech* (Is. 36:7) rather than the Gaelic *cromleac*. Cameron in his version of Genesis was later to feel the same need and used both *cromlech* (22:9) and *offran-stane* (12:7).

Creation of new words and borrowing from other languages are only two of the ways Waddell provides himself with extra diction. Another resource is the use of archaisms although Waddell is accurate in his claim that he uses few of these. Amongst the few that he does use are *frett* 'devour' (Ps. 52:4), *furthschaw* 'display' (Ps. 19:1), *gree* 'favour' (Ps. 21:7), *redd* 'deliver' (Is. 36:20) and *thring* 'oppress' (Is. 52:4). Some of these Waddell further uses in his new compounds like *gude-gree* 'mercy' (Ps. 5:7), *redd-but* 'deliver' (Ps.6:4) and *redd single* 'save singlehandedly' (Ps. 33:17). One may well suspect that some at least of the archaisms come from Jamieson. Certainly Jamieson would seem to have been his source for certain rare words like *lucken* 'grow and thrive' (Ps. 1:3) and possibly *glaum* 'a mouthful' (Ps. 63:10) although the latter could be a case of Waddell's using the better-known verb *glaum* 'devour' as a noun.

Amongst Waddell's diction there are a number of words used with unusual senses. It is hard to know whether we should identify these as mistakes or as deliberate extensions of existing words. In the case of compounds Waddell may well have put together the constituent elements independently without reference to the existing word. *Misfaur* (Ps. 109:14) usually denotes a 'misfortune' but Waddell uses it to mean a metaphorical 'going astray', a 'sin'. The very similar *misgate* meaning 'transgression' (Ps. 25:7) is one of Waddell's new creations. Waddell's two nouns *owregaens* 'transgressions' (Ps. 25:7) and *owre-gangers* 'transgressors' (Ps. 37:38) presumably arise from a literal translation of *transgress*, literally 'overgo'. Both *owergae* and *owergang* exist in Scots but do not normally have this meaning. In *The Monastery* Scott had used the rare and archaic word *halidome* to describe the lands attached to St

Mary's. It provides Waddell with a useful and legitimate Germanic alternative to *sanctuary* (Ps. 74:3). Waddell goes on also to use *halirude* (Ps. 78:54) or *haly-rood* (Ps. 150:1) with the same meaning. This is a mistake. The Abbey of Holyrood (Halierude) was indeed a sanctuary but *Halierude* is a proper name applied to the particular abbey and not a generic term for a sanctuary.

Waddell's grammar is fairly thoroughly Scots. He uses the non-Scots *eth* verbal ending only very rarely (e.g. Ps. 1:2; 24:4) and equally uncommon is his use of the English *st* forms after *thou* (e.g. 8:1). We find that he either uses the Scots *s* inflection as in *LORD, thou hauds them heal* (Ps. 36:6) or, on one exceptional occasion, the plural form *are*, as in present-day Orkney usage: *the frien' o' the faitherless yerlane are Thou* (Ps. 10:14). Even in addressing God, Waddell generally uses *ye* (occasionally *yo* for the object) or, very frequently, *yersel* or *yerlane*, although there are just a few appearances of *thou* (as already mentioned) and *thee* (Ps. 2:7; 5:5). This use of *ye* and *yersel* gives a much more personal and familiar tone, to the Psalms in particular. It contrasts markedly with the unwillingness of the English translations to use *you* in addressing God even as late as the Revised Standard Version of 1952 and the New English Bible of 1970. In pronouns, as in other things, Waddell reduces to the minimum any overlap with English, using the spellings *yo* for *you* and *scho* for *she*. The Scots pronunciation of the first person subject pronoun as *ah* is indicated by using the spelling *'am*, meaning 'I am'. However, he does avoid using a feature of Scots grammar that might be condemned by some readers as illiterate rather than truly dialectal: like most modern Scots authors, he avoids the use of *s* inflections after plural subjects despite its clear survival in spoken usage.

For all that he uses many informal elements, Waddell clearly aimed at a language that would have a formal, literary quality suitable for the sacred text. This is partly achieved by the frequently inverted word order which can give a literary quality to sentences formed from very colloquial diction, and partly by the use of *wha, whase* and *whasae* (e.g. in Ps. 15) which are always marks of a literary style in Scots, the normal Scots relative being *that* or *at*.

Waddell's spelling shows no particular innovations. It is pretty consistent and he mostly employs Scot forms where they are available. Nevertheless, he accepts certain established anglicisms of spelling like *gh* and *ow* for the older Scots *ch* and *ou*. He does, however, include a list of such spellings indicating how they should be pronounced and offering a stern warning that to 'pronounce on the English principle any word in which one of these syllables occurs, is to destroy at once both the character and the force of the sound' ('Notice to the General Reader', p 1). Apart from the use of *Scottis* in his titles, the only regular archaic spelling is *sch* for *sh*. In keeping with his time he uses many apostrophe spellings but in a context that is so thoroughly Scots that they have less of their usual impact in suggesting that Scots is corrupted English. It is clear to any reader that we are here dealing with an independent tongue.

Waddell's texts present us with an idealised notion of Scots which nevertheless seems realistic in context. The overlap of Scots and English is greatly underplayed; the country gentlemen and well-educated peasants whom

Waddell saw as his source would have used far more of the shared English-Scots diction than Waddell allows for. Ironically, one of his most distinctive features, the use of new compounds to replace words like *generation, redeemer, salvation* and *testimony*, is the very feature that it is least likely of all that his ideal speakers would have used. Those 'men who represented the true vernacular of their country, from the days of the Reformation and of the Covenant' ('Notice', p 1) were far too well versed in the English Bible not to use words like these: indeed, their speech, as represented more accurately in Scott's novels, is characterised by the presence of such words. Peasants who continued to speak Scots had long been accustomed to using the language of the English Bible in discussing religious matters. As Waddell was aware, it was Scots, not English, that sounded strange in religious contexts. He admits that any 'strangeness' to be found in his Scots, apart from its being strange and unknown to the younger generation, 'must result solely from its grammatical application to so solemn a theme as the Word of God' ('Notice', p 1). This was particularly a problem for a writer like Waddell whose conception of Scots involved the exclusion of Latinate terms. Yet, in spite of this, Waddell did succeed in creating a plausible Scots for his Biblical translations. It may be a partly artificial creation but so, in some way or another, is most literary language. If literary, it has not lost its contacts with speech and it draws strength from those contacts. What he showed was that, extended over a sizeable text, a consistently Scots style, kept free from hankerings after the language of an English version, establishes its own linguistic validity.

I have so far talked as if the Authorised Version would be the main English version in the back of Waddell's mind as he worked. Despite his consultation of the Geneva Bible I believe this is true but we must not forget that, with the Psalms and with parts of Isaiah, another English version was equally well known to a Scot, the Scottish Metrical Psalms and Paraphrases. This is the background to one of the stylistic peculiarities of Waddell's version, the use of rhythm, rhyme and assonance within his prose. The translator himself draws our attention to this feature of this work:

> In the translation of the PSALMS, the reader will find that most of them fall naturally into a sort of rhythmical cadence, and many of them into rhyme itself. It may be proper to state, with respect to this peculiarity, that no device whatever has been employed to produce such effect—the fact being, that in many cases the Psalms which present this rhythmical aspect are more literally translated than they could well have been otherwise; and that there is generally a corresponding rhythm, and sometimes even a corresponding rhyme, in the Hebrew original ('Notice', p 2).

This is somewhat disingenuous. No one reading some of the more complexly rhymed verses can doubt that the rhymes were deliberately contrived. At times, too, a few words have been added to allow a rhyme, as Waddell's italicisation of words not in the original makes clear:

> Up, O LORD, i' yer angir; redd my ill-willers by, i' yer wuth: an' steer for me till the rightin ye ettled, wi' yer ain word *o' mouthe* (Ps. 7:6).

Nevertheless, contrived or not, Waddell often uses rhyme with considerable effect. In this verse from Isaiah the rhyme reinforces the contrast of opposites:

> An' syne it sal be; for scentit stuff, sal be gruesome gluff; an' for ban' sae tight sal be screed out-right; and for weel-set hair, sal be beld an' bare; an' for boddice boun, a bit harn dight roun; an' for beauty a', a bleezan sca'! (Is. 3:24).

and in the following verse the rhyme and assonance build up to the climax of the last few unrhymed words:

> The cotter's een sal be daze'd; an' the height o' the carl sal be baise'd; an' JEHOVAH himlane sal be heize'd, or that day be owre! (Is. 2:11).

Within a single verse there can be a quite complex set of rhymes:

> Bot siclike, he sal swear an' say, i' that dulesome day: I'se be laird till yo nane; for in houss o' my ain 's neither meat nor cleedin; [nae gifts can I gie]; owre the folk gie me nane o' the leadin (Is. 3:7).

These examples are all from Isaiah where rhyme is used much more extensively than in the Psalms. Some readers may find the device irritating at times since it both splits up the verses into small units and leads to very frequent inversion of the normal word order:

> The folk that gaed lang i' the gloam, sic a bleeze o' light they hae seen; and wha won'd in the deid-mirk holm, the light it comes down on their een (Is. 9:2).

The effect is often more exaggerated than in the Metrical Paraphrases. They rhyme only two of each four lines and have fewer inversions of word order than Waddell and they render this same verse as:

> The race that long in darkness pin'd
> have seen a glorious light;
> The people dwell in day, who dwelt
> in death's surrounding night
> (Paraphrase 19, 11.1–4)

The main influence of the metrical psalms and paraphrases seems to have been in encouraging Waddell to introduce rhyme and rhythm. Only occasionally do they influence the actual wording of his translation. One possible case occurs in Psalm 50. Here the metrical Psalter's 'Sion hill' may have been in Waddell's mind when he used 'Zioun-*Hill*' since, as Waddell's italics inform us, the word *hill* has no counterpart here in the Hebrew text.

Having gone to some lengths to cast some of his verses in rhyme, Waddell, not surprisingly, rises to the challenge of Psalm 119 where in the original Hebrew text the verses of each section begin with a particular letter of the alphabet. As far as possible Waddell uses the same sounds to begin the verses of his sections. The device is cleverly carried through with the one exception of the forced use of the archaic spelling *zit* for *yit* (119:55) and the spurious spelling *zat* for *that* (119:56, 140). *Zit* was in fact pronounced as *yit* and *zat* seems to be based on the false assumption that, where early Scots printed texts used *z* as a way of representing the earlier letter ȝ, the contraction *yt* for *that* (where *y* represents the earlier English letter þ) can also be rendered as *zat*.

Waddell's translations are impressive attempts to create a form of Scots suitable for Bible translations. If his language is sometimes rather idio-syncratic it finally wins us over by its vigour and inventiveness and makes itself a fitting medium for the 'radiant, soul-satisfying joy', the 'absorbing pathos' and 'consuming zeal' which, as Waddell asserted in his lecture on Burns, inform 'these sweet and often terrible effusions' (p 23). Yet the trans-lations themselves were only part of his endeavour. Determined to give his readers the equivalent in Scots of the English translations they were accus-tomed to, he provided for his own translations the full apparatus of marginal notes, psalm and chapter headings, page titles and lengthy introductions, all in Scots. The marginal notes are of various kinds. They include comments on the translation like 'Sae Luther reads, an' mae. Our ain Inglis, *wha swears till the wrang, an' bides by't*, canna be thol'd. *His ain wrang* is nane i' the Hebrew' (Ps. 15:4n) and the characteristic 'Sae stan's the Hebrew, an' wi' unco pith it stan's. Our Inglis reads anither gate, wi' but little pith an' less grammar' (Ps. 29:9n). One note comments on his choice of diction: 'Heb. *voice*: nae word but *ca'* in Scots till neibor't. *Voce*, frae the Italian, 's but feckless' (Ps. 68:33n) and others provide explanations of the headings like that on 'Till the sang-maister on Muth-labben' which suggests 'Aiblins on the downfa', or dead, o' some reivan carl' (Ps.9). Yet other notes highlight his favourite psalms, like Psalm 8 next to which a hand points to the note 'Tak tent as ye read: thar'e no mony grander kirk sangs nor this'. The headings are often vivid and concise: Psalm 10 is prefixed with 'The yird-born carl has baith a heigh head an' a heavy han'; kens little, an' cares less: bot the Lord rights a', baith puir and faitherless, wha lippen till himsel' and in some Waddell can indulge his penchant for rhyme: chapter 3 of Isaiah is headed: 'An unco reddin maun be, or Jerusalem's flytin-free, either wi' God or her niebors. Her dochtirs sae braw, they're glaiket an' a; an' her sons they're nae better nor rievers'. Finally the two introductions, as well as including such scholarly material as explanations of the terms used in the original psalms, offer us examples of extended Scots discursive prose of a length which it would be very difficult to find in any printed book of the Modern Scots period. Translations, introductions and notes all add up to a very extensive and impressive piece of Scots writing.

MURRAY'S RUTH (1873)

Riddell lived at Teviothead. Only a short distance away was Hawick where there was an Archaeological Society whose energetic secretary was James A H Murray (1837–1915), then relatively unknown but later to become the editor of the *New English Dictionary* (later renamed the *Oxford English Dictionary*) and one of the greatest of all lexicographers. One evening the President read an extract from Riddell's version of the Sermon on the Mount to the Society. Murray was inspired to obtain a longer extract from a London literary magazine and included criticisms of Riddell's Matthew in a lecture to the Society on 'The Origin and History of the Scottish Language' given in April 1859. As we would expect of someone who was later to write what still remains one of the best histories of Scots, Murray's comments on Riddell are very much to the point.

> It is an attempted *restoration*, and not the Scotch of any particular time or district ... Thus, though interesting, the work has not to posterity the scientific value that would attach to the rendering of any passage into the precise spoken language ... which would then appear before the world, not as an opinion but as a testimony—not a picture from memory or from fancy, but an actual photograph of the very tones in the middle of the nineteenth century.[13]

As we can see, for Murray, Riddell's major failing was that his language belonged to no specific place or time. It was a guess at what Scots might have become if it had followed a different history, rather than an attempt to provide a 'photograph' (to use the word he uses here and in his Preface to *The Dialect of the Southern Counties of Scotland*) of real Scots of a particular time and place. Riddell's peculiar spelling, presented without any key to its phonetic significance, could not find favour with one who later condemned 'the sort of infatuation which possesses writers, that because certain letters seem to them the fittest spelling of a particular sound, the same sound will, without any explanation, be suggested to their readers by those letters' (*DSCS*, p 90).

Dissatisfied with Riddell's version, Murray began to work on his own translations of parts of the Bible into Scots, a natural activity for someone whose preferred way of learning a language was to obtain a grammar and a copy of the Bible in that language. Two important differences in Murray's attempted versions were that he used phonetic symbols and that he tried to translate into a particular local variety of Scots, that spoken in Upper Teviotdale, which he, as a native of Denholm, calls 'my native dialect' (*DSCS*, p 89). He started work on Matthew and Acts but decided neither was appropriate for his endeavours and finally settled on Ruth and Jonah (neither of them texts favoured by Prince Louis) and finished translations of both of these.[14]

When he later moved to London he was introduced to Prince Louis who asked him to translate part of the Gospel into Scots, both in phonetic script and in the sort of spelling in which 'Scotchmen like to see Scotch written',[15] Murray tried but was dissatisfied with the results and wrote to the Prince that:

> I know no rule, no standard whatever for the modern Scottish forms of speech. The spelling of Burns for example is *simply English*, partly disguised by the fact that he uses a considerable percentage of *words not English*: these words unfortunately are such as can scarcely ever be pressed into service in the Gospel

of Matthew, and the result is that when I try to write in Burns's orthography, my version looks scarcely different from the English certainly not worth publishing as Scotch, inasmuch as it conveys almost no idea as to the *actual living thing* a Scotch dialect, and its utter difference from English sounds.[16]

Once again the problem of spelling had proved a major stumbling block for a writer of Scots. When his version of Ruth finally appeared as an appendix to *The Dialect of the Southern Counties of Scotland* in 1873 he used his own special, carefully explained, spelling system. Murray's comment also shows him struggling with the attempt to provide a distinctively Scots vocabulary which is not too informal. It would appear that he found no solution to this and in his Ruth the Scots element lies particularly in spelling and grammar and much less in distinctively Scots lexis.

Because, unlike all the other translations here considered, Murray's Ruth appeared merely as an appendix to a much larger work it comes in a context from which we can deduce a lot of about the translator's intentions. While his Historical Introduction covers all varieties of Scots the actual description of pronunciation and grammar is confined to the dialect of the Borders, which is now, following Murray's lead, called Southern Scots. He was anxious to point out that Scots was not one united entity as the Bonaparte translators had tacitly assumed it to be:

> It is customary to speak of Scotch as one dialect (or language), whereas there are in Scotland several distinct types, and numerous varieties of the northern tongue, differing from each other markedly in pronunciation, and to some extent also in the vocabulary and grammar (*DSCS*, p 77).

In classifying the various geographical varieties of Scots he was 'led to arrange them in three groups—a *North-Eastern*, a *Central*, and a *Southern*—which may be further subdivided into eight minor divisions, or sub-dialects' (*DSCS*, p 78). It had been his intention to provide versions of the first chapter of Ruth in each of his eight 'sub-dialects' in palæotype, the phonetic transcription invented by A J Ellis, 'but doubts as to the accuracy of my palæotypic renderings in some cases, which I have not at present the means of testing, have induced me to give only three of these, viz one from each of the three great dialectic groups' (*DSCS*, p 239). He thus gave palæotype versions of the first chapter of Ruth in Teviotdale, Buchan and Ayrshire Scots and a Teviotdale version of the whole of Ruth in conventional type but with a special spelling.

Southern Scots was of particular interest to him, not only as his native dialect but as 'the least changed representative of the ancient tongue of Cædmon, Cuthbert, and Beda, and the Northern writers of the 13th and 14th centuries' (*DSCS*, p 89). It descended from the earliest English spoken in Scotland, the Old English of Northumbria, and in Murray's opinion was its purest surviving form since south of the Border it had lost its gutturals and in Lothian it had 'received an artificial culture' and 'changed considerably from the original type as found in the Early Scottish writers' (*DSCS*, p 89).

From the outset Murray makes it clear that he is interested not in literary Scots, which he refers to disparagingly as 'artificially trimmed Literary idioms', but in actual contemporary spoken Scots which, if it was not corrupted, could provide valuable 'witnesses of the usages of the past and the natural tendencies of the present' (*DSCS*, p v). The works of recent writers like Burns, Galt and Scott 'are more or less *conventional* representations. To a greater or less extent they are almost all contaminated with the influence of the literary English—the language which their authors have been *educated* to write—whose rules of grammatical inflection and construction they impose upon their Scotch, to the corruption of the vernacular idiom' (*DSCS*, p 74) and in support of his view he quotes the letter from Prince Louis on literary dialects which I have already cited.

Turning to his Ruth, we find that it is the sort of translation these comments would lead us to expect. It is clear that Murray always has the Authorised Version in his mind but he shows no hesitation in departing from it to achieve the style of language he wants. As a representation of spoken Scots unadulterated by literary influences it is necessarily informal and colloquial. The formal terms of the Authorised Version like *continued* (1:2), *perform* (3:13) and *require* (3:11) are replaced by informal words or sometimes periphrases as with *testimony* which is changed to *seyne ăt a bàrgain was meade* (4:7). Because formal terms are often of Latin or French origin this leaves a basically Germanic vocabulary although a few very well established romance terms like *deacent* (3:11) and *faimus* (4:14) are retained. Murray regarded many of the Middle Scots borrowings from French as 'a bizarre and incongrous element in the language' (p 58) and many of the Latin borrowings as 'grotesque' (p 60). He found it surprising 'how few of these foreign accretions remained as permanent elements of the language' but believed that this was because sixteenth century Scots had not been 'perpetuated as a literary medium' and 'the speech of the people has cast out most of these foreign ingredients, and remains almost as purely Teutonic as it was in the 13th and 14th centuries' (*DSCS*, p 61). The notion of Modern Scots as fundamentally a Germanic tongue will be encountered again in the work of P H Waddell. Being a translation into modern Scots, Murray's version completely removes all the Authorised Version's archaisms like *advertise* (4:4) meaning 'inform'. Likewise the Authorised Version's exclamations and asservations give way to genuine Scots alternatives: *behold* becomes *Aweil thăn* (2:4) and *surely, Ah but* (1:10). Nor does Murray confine himself to word for word substitutions; for instance, the Authorised Version's *he shall be unto thee a restorer of thy life, and a nourisher of thine old age* becomes *hey'll meake-ye leive (y)eir leyfe ower agean leyke an' hey'll teake cayr o'ye quhan (y)e're aald* (4:15). Henderson and Robson had moved in this direction but not with Murray's thoroughness.

In grammar especially Murray distances himself from his predecessors' practices. Not for him English *th* inflections or even English-influenced use of *wha* as a relative. A comment of his on a well-loved Burns poem makes clear his attitude on the relative. According to Murray *wha* as a relative is 'unknown to the living dialects of Scotland' (*DSCS*, pp 70–71) and

> 'Scots wha hae' is *fancy* Scotch—that is, it is merely the English 'Scots who have,' spelt as Scotch. Barbour would have written 'Scottis at hes;' Dunbar or

Douglas, 'Scottis quhilkis hes;' and even Henry Charteris in the end of the sixteenth century 'Scottis quha hes'...The vernacular is still 'Scots at hæs,' which Burns apparently considered ungrammatical, and therefore shaped the words after an English model. Much of the contemporary Scotch is of this character; it is Scotch in spelling, English in everything else (*DSCS*, p 71n).

Similarly English *whose* he expresses with *at* and a possessive pronoun: *Boaz..., hym ăt (y)e was aseyde 'ys maydens* (3:2). The comment on Burns recalls another observation of Murray's, that an *s* inflection is used with all persons of the verb in the present tense except when the verb immediately follows its subject pronoun, hence the inflection in *thaim ăt's geane* (1:8). Such inflections, he tells us, 'are not vulgar corruptions, but strictly grammatical' when used in Scots (*DSCS*, p 212). The use of *s* inflections where English has none is still a prominent feature of present-day spoken Scots yet Scots writers from about 1700 have been most reluctant to use it. It generally appears only in texts representing the speech of people of very little education as does the use of *us* as a singular pronoun. According to Murray 'the true Objective Singular mă...is now almost obsolete, except among old people, the plural *us* being regularly used instead' (*DSCS*, p 188) and he uses *us* consistently throughout his Ruth (e.g. 1:2; 2:2). (Interestingly, Robson records a similar use of *us* in his Newcastle and Northumberland versions of the Song of Solomon, which are, like Murray's work, a record of spoken usage, but uses *me* in his Scots version, which is based on literary models). For English *than* after a comparative Murray offers four alternatives in Scots: *nor, than, as* and *be* or *bey* (*DSCS*, p 169). Typically Murray uses *as*, a word which is particularly likely to be seen as 'corrupt English' rather than 'true dialect', and which is avoided by the Bonaparte translators. Murray strongly objected to writers who were, as he said of Scott, 'led astray by unconscious deference to English grammar' (*DSCS*, p 75). Scott he saw as only an occasional offender but

> where Scott and Burns have thus occasionally Anglicised the native idiom, many other writers have done so systematically, apparently looking upon the vernacular usage, where it differs from that of literary English, as 'bad grammar,' or 'ignorant corruption,' and it is hardly too much to adopt the phrase of the author of the Cleveland Glossary, and say that their Scotch is only 'ordinary English in masquerade,' and of about the same value philologically as the snuff-shop Highlander is in ethnology (*DSCS*, p 75).

It is one of the great strengths of Murray's work, and an important advance in the study of dialect, that he recognised that dialects have their own 'good grammar' which may not be the same as that in English. Thus *s* inflections with plural subjects, *us* as a singular and *as* after comparatives are good Scots despite their being bad English. This insight was not shared by a number of other Scots writers, including many of our translators.

Murray informs us that 'As in Dutch and Flemish the second person singular pronoun has quite disappeared from the spoken dialect. Even in prayer I have heard an old shepherd say "Ye war oor faither, aathoa wey hæd forseaken ye," but as a rule *English* is the liturgical language even among the illiterate, and *thou, thy, thee*, of course used' (*DSCS*, pp 188–9). Murray's being a translation into Scots he does not use the liturgical English and consistently uses *ye*, or *yow* in emphatic positions (1:10), where the Authorised Version has *thou* and *thee*. It is interesting, in passing, to see Murray's Scots-speaking shepherd preceding English-speakers of our own day in abandoning *thou* in addressing God.

Finally, Murray records that in Southern Scots there was still a distinction between the present participle and the gerund such as we noticed in Nisbet. As an example he cites *hey beguid a*-greitin, *but feint o' eane kœnnd quhat hey was* greitand *fòr* and tells us with typical humour that 'It is as absurd to a Southern Scot to hear *eating* used for both his *eiting* and *eitand*, as it is for an Englishman to hear *will* used for both his *will* and *shall*. When he is told that "John was eating," he is strongly tempted to ask what kind of eating he proved to be?' (*DSCS*, p 211). Similarly in his Ruth we find *schui... beguid a gœtherin* (2:3) but *Quhayr hœ-ye bein gœtheran' the day* (2:19). Murray is alone in the modern period in making this distinction. This is to be expected as it only survived in Southern Scots: for instance, in Lothian, as Murray tells us, the construction would be *He begood a-greit'n, but quha kènt, quhat he wus greit'n fur?* (*DSCS*, p 211). Smith, who shared Murray's southern dialect, was to use various spellings for the gerund and participle in his 1901 version of the New Testament, but not according to any discernible pattern.

As we have seen, Murray was unhappy with the spelling used in most contemporary Scots texts. In *The Dialect of the Southern Counties of Scotland* he points out that 'the Scotch so written is not a witness to the actual spoken dialects; it does not represent—as it does not pretend to represent—the amount of difference, but rather to show the maximum of likeness, between them and the usual English' (*DSCS*, pp 76–7). For his purpose of representing the 'actual spoken dialects' some other spelling was necessary. Having the aim of 'truth and distinctness' in phonetic representation he developed his own spellings although he confessed some reluctance to 'discard the drapery with which [Scots] was clothed in earlier times, and which in so many cases is our only guide to the living organism which once breathed within'. Nevertheless, 'in dealing with a living dialect of the 19th century, one cannot always do justice to its own form and spirit by confining it to the winding sheet which decently enough envelopes the dead language of the 16th' (*DSCS*, p vi). In Murray's spelling each letter or combination of letters represents a single sound and the phonetic value of each is carefully explained. Where others merely use either the traditional Scots *ch* or English *gh*, Murray has four spellings: '(kh) the simple "guttural"...; (kh) or (kjh) the palatalized guttural...; (kwh) the labialized guttural' (*DSCS*, p 240). Thus even when he uses the conventional alphabet he aims at phonetic exactitude. Moreover, as we have seen, he also made use of palæotype.

Murray tells us that to provide the originally planned eight specimens of Scots of different areas he 'had for this purpose taken down the first chapter of Ruth in the vernacular from the dictation of native speakers' (*DSCS*, p 239). For the Buchan and Ayrshire versions which he finally printed he names his informants and a reviser but he names no informant for the Teviotdale version; we are presumably to take it that the last is entirely Murray's own work. He did, after all, claim to speak of Upper Teviotdale Scots 'with perfect confidence' and to be for it 'a competent witness' (*DSCS*, p 89). Apart from pronunciation differences, there are considerable verbal differences between the three versions. Unless Murray himself provided a text to be read aloud which differed from his own Teviotdale version, an unlikely procedure, it seems that he must have encouraged his informants to translate the Authorised Version into contemporary colloquial Scots of their own locality.

Since there are often several options open in any one dialect for recasting archaic or formal passages in the Authorised Version many of the verbal differences between the three versions may merely arise from different translation choices rather than from actual local differences. For instance, part of the ninth verse is rendered in the Teviotdale version as *thay beguid a-greitein lood an' sayr*, in the Ayrshire version as *they beguid a-greitin an' grat sair sair* and in the Buchan version as *they roar't an' grat*.[17] The differences in these cases do not seem to reflect dialectal variation. The same is mostly true of verse 5 where Teviotdale reads *wui naither bairn nor man belangan' 'er, Ayr wi' naither man nor wean* and Buchan *without aither bairn or man*. The exception is the variation between *bairn* in Teviotdale and Buchan and *wean* in Ayr. This is a genuine dialectal difference which Murray himself comments on, telling how he misunderstood a 'Wast-Cuintre' girl as speaking of a *wain* (waggon) when she was using *wean* 'a word not in ordinary use in our dialect [i.e. Southern Scots], but familiar enough in the writings of Burns' (*DSCS*, p 77n).[18] The Teviotdale version is also the only one to use *us* as a singular pronoun: does this mean that the usage, now common throughout Scotland, was then confined to Southern Scots or is it just that Murray is more wholeheartedly committed than his informants in Ayrshire and Buchan to presenting dialect grammar even if it is liable to be seen as illiterate? Altogether then, the most significant differences between the three versions are those of pronunciation since they are the only differences which consistently reflect actual local variation within Scotland.

Murray also gives us another piece of Bible translation. In a short digression on 'Scotch Pronunciation of English' he points out that, although English is the liturgical language of Scotland, it is spoken in a fashion quite different from that of England. He then provides phonetic transcripts of 'Standard English', 'English of Scotland' and 'Scotch' readings of the metrical version of Psalm 100. Finally, pointing out that a fully Scots version would also have different diction, he translates the metrical psalm into Scots prose, a rare instance of a Scots prose version of a Biblical text begin based on the metrical version. The translation exhibits Murray's familiar characteristics, including an *s* inflection considered illiterate in English: *Aa fuok ăt leeves . . . ònna the yerth*.

Murray's work stands well apart from the Bonaparte translations which preceded it in that Murray has an absolutely clear idea of what he means by Scots and consistently adheres to it regardless of either the proprieties of English grammar or the familiar renderings of the Authorised Version. Murray knows exactly what he is doing. He is reproducing contemporary spoken

Scots, not a literary register of Scots. He accepts that modern Scots has rejected most of the earlier Latinate borrowings and is thus essentially informal. He makes it quite clear, too, that he is using Scots in spite of knowing that the normal religious language of Scotland is English. He thus has no qualms about the correctness of displacing the Authorised Version's *thou* in favour of *ye* even though he acknowledges that *thou* would be a modern Scot's most common chòice in religious contexts. While Murray's translation was not finally published under Prince Louis's auspices, it fulfills the prince's aim of recording actual spoken dialect much more fully than any of the Bonaparte translations themselves do. Because Murray is simply illustrating spoken Scots and not trying to produce a religious text he also completely accepts that his language·will be both informal and contemporary.

SMITH'S NEW TESTAMENT (1901)

Two new features distinguished the work of William Wye Smith. For the first time in the modern period an English translation other than the Authorised Version forms the basis of a Scots translation. The Revised Version of the New Testament had appeared in 1881 with that of the Old Testament coming out in 1885, too late for Waddell to refer to it in his translations, but when Smith published his *New Testament in Braid Scots* in 1901 he mostly based his translation on the Revised Version. Smith's work also represents the first contribution of the Scots diaspora to the history of Scots Bible translation. He was born in Scotland but spent most of his life in North America. It was only to be expected that the fervent nationalism of exiled Scots would lead them to preserve and adorn the tongue of their childhood in this way and we will see the pattern repeated in the work of Henry Paterson Cameron, a Scot living in Australia.

Smith, like Riddell and Murray, was a Borderer. He was born in Jedburgh in 1827 and was taken by his parents to the United States in 1830 and to Canada in 1837. After being a school-teacher, businessman and journalist he became in 1865 a minister of the Congregational Church, retiring from his parochial work in 1907 and dying in 1917. Smith published several books of poetry and contributed various pieces from his New Testament translation to newspapers before bringing out *The Gospel of Matthew in Broad Scotch* in Toronto in 1898. This was intended as a specimen of the whole work and in due course the complete New Testament was published in Paisley in the first year of the new century.[19]

With Smith's work, as with Waddell's, we have the advantage of helpful comments by the translator himself. In an address 'To the Reader' printed on the inside front cover of his separate 1898 publication of Matthew, Smith makes it quite clear that his aims differ from those of both Murray and Waddell. He tells us that

> With respect to the style: whoever now writes in Scotch must necessarily conform to the dialect of Burns. The Translator is a Borderer; but in many

respects he departs from Border usages, in order to conform to Burns—whose influence has made the 'Ayrshire' the classical dialect of the Lowland Scotch: exactly as Petrarch and Dante, 500 years ago, by their writings, made their 'Florentine' the literary dialect of the Italian.

It is thus clear that he differs from Murray in using literary Scots, not spoken Scots, as his base and from Waddell in his willingness to confine himself to the language used by Burns rather than to invent new terms.

Smith's response to the problem of the status of Scots as an almost exclusively informal tongue is particularly interesting. For the first time we encounter a writer who sees a positive virtue in the necessity of using an informal register. In this same address 'To the Reader' he claims:

> over and above its dialectic peculiarities, this version claims to be a colloquial rendering. Many of us have wished—not as a public version, but for private study—for a familiar and colloquial rendering of the New Testament. It is a thing which will never be satisfactorily done in English; and he would be a bold man indeed who would attempt it. But, under cover of the 'Scotch', the present Translator humbly intimates that he has done that very thing!

Clearly, too, Smith was aware that what he was obliged to do in Scots was something for which English translators were not yet fully prepared. It is true that Smith does not see the use of informal Scots as a necessity and claims that it 'could have been rendered in a stately style, equally as native to the soil' but it is difficult indeed to conceive what kind of 'stately' style Smith could have used in the days before MacDiarmid and synthetic Scots. Nevertheless it is refreshing to see a writer who not only has no regrets about using informal Scots for serious subject-matter like biblical translation but also sees himself as belonging to a tradition in doing so:

> To those who may imagine that a solemn and reverent theme must needs suffer in a familiar and 'dialect' rendering, it is only necessary to pass in our reading from Burns and Scott to Samuel Rutherford and John Knox, to see how the pithy terseness of the 'Scotch' equally adapts itself to the most weighty and solemn themes and thoughts.

After all this it comes as something of a disappointment to find that Smith's language is by no means as consistently colloquial as his comments suggest. Or perhaps we should be alerted to this possibility by the reference to Knox who can certainly be colloquial but who, with his heavily anglicised style, is hardly a model for writing Scots. In part Smith's failure to produce the informal style he desired can be attributed to his unwillingness to depart too far from the Revised Version. At first sight one might expect the use of a more modern English translation to produce a more modern style of Scots but the Revised Version was not in contemporary English. It was intended simply as a revision of the Authorised Version and the revisers were strictly enjoined, as they tell us in the separate prefaces to both the Old and New Testaments, firstly to 'introduce as few alterations as possible into the text of the Authorized

Version consistently with faithfulness' and secondly to 'limit, as far as possible, the expression of such alterations to the language of the Authorized and earlier English Versions'. The text from which Smith was working was thus no more modern in its language than the Authorised Version used by previous translators. Any language retained from the Revised Version had a strong chance of being archaic.

Before we consider how much Smith was willing to change the Revised Version, we need to note that he occasionally departs from the Revised Version in favour of the Authorised Version or even from both of them in favour of their marginal notes. The following verse provides a nice example of his eclectic approach:

> And they that heard him slippit cannilie oot, frae the auldest e'en to the last ane; and Jesus was left alane, wi' the wumman staunin i' the mids (John 8:9).

In the first sentence he follows the Revised rather than the Authorised Version in omitting the words *being convicted by their own conscience* but in the second sentence *wi' the wumman staunin i' the mids* is from the Authorised Version and replaces the Revised Version's *the woman, where she was, in the midst* presumably because it gives a smoother style in the Scots. As for following the marginal notes, the reading *for the sma'est tribunal* in 1 Cor. 6:2 comes from the Revised Version margin and not from either its main text or that of the Authorised Version.

I have said that Smith set limits to his willingness to change the Revised Version but I should make it clear that these limits were nowhere near as restrictive as those adopted by Riddell or even Henderson. While naturally he makes a number of word-for-word substitutions he does not confine himself to such minimalist change. In the verse already quoted *slipped cannilie oot* is an effective alternative to the two English versions' *went out one by one*. A typical verse will have some word-for-word changes, some minor recasting of the sentence structure and perhaps some more significant variations. Take, for instance, the verse rendered by both English versions as

> When Jesus therefore saw her weeping, and the Jews also weeping which came with her, he groaned in the spirit and was troubled.

Here Smith reads:

> Whan Jesus saw her sabbin, and the Jews a' greetin that cam wi' her, he was unco touched at the heart, and was wrocht-on (John 11:33).

Apart from replacing weeping with two Scots words and recasting the archaic *groaned in the spirit and was troubled* Smith has slightly changed the second clause to give it a more colloquial style and added the thoroughly Scots touch of the intensive *unco*. Similarly, in the verse *Sae whan they gaed on, ask-askin him, he straughtit his sel, and quo' he to them, "The ane that's wantin sin amang ye, let him cast the first stane at her!"* (John 8:7). Smith has, amongst other things, recast the Revised Version's *He that is without sin among you* in a more colloquial form and employed the device of the repeated verb, which Lorimer was later to find useful, to remove the formality of the Revised Version's *they continued asking him*. Note also that, here as elsewhere, Smith is willing to introduce the typically Scots use of the continuous verbal forms (cf. 1 Cor. 1:4; 14:27, 28). Occasionally, but not consistently, he uses past participles ending in *ate*, originally a feature of both English and Scots but latterly confined to Scots: compare *they soud be consecrate i' the truth* (John 17:19) and *wisdom is vindicatit* (Luke 7:35).

Like Riddell and Henderson, Smith consistently uses the enclitic negative *na*: this seems, indeed, to be one universally agreed *sine qua non* of Scots grammar in Bible translations. Further, being freed from strict adherence to the Authorised/Revised Version, Smith can tackle the problem of *thou*. By Smith's time *thou* was as archaic in Scots as in English. Nevertheless, the Revised Version, true to its linguistic principles, retains the Authorised Version's use of *thou* for singular address. All the same, things were changing in the English Bible with the appearance of various Bibles in modern English. Amongst these Ferrar Fenton's complete Bible and James Moffat's *Historical New Testament* appeared in 1901, the same year as Smith's work. Two years later Weymouth in his *New Testament in Modern Speech* compromised by adopting *you* for all occasions except in address to God whether by Christ (e.g. John 17) or others (e.g. Matt. 25:37–44) but not in address to Christ as a man in this world. With the Authorised Version still setting the style for religious language in Scotland and with *thou* still firmly entrenched in prayer, Smith, too, compromised. His compromise is not as radical: he further retains *thou* for any respectful speech to Jesus. Thus Peter (Matt. 16:16), the leper (Luke 5:12), Martha (John 11:21) and Mary (John 11:32) address Jesus as *thou* while the High Priest addresses him as *ye* (Matt. 26:62, 63). Smith's handling of the verbal inflection after *thou* is variable. Riddell, it will be remembered, used *ist* Henderson merely changed this to English *est*. In John 17, a chapter devoted to Christ's address to the Father, Smith has the Scots *s* in *thou has* (24, 26) and *thou gies* (24) but also English *st* in *thou hast* (2, 7, 23) and *thou gi'est* (9, 11). It would seem that the *st* forms still exerted a powerful hold over Smith's mind in such contexts. Generally, however, he forms past tenses without *st* as in *thou had* (John 11:21) and *thou gied* (John 17:4).

In other respects Smith adheres more closely to the Revised Version, often to the detriment of his colloquial register. Thus, while he is sometimes willing to use *s* after *thou*, I have noted only one use of the *s* inflection in the much more stigmatised situation where it can extend to any person of the verb if the verb does not immediately follow the pronoun: *Hoo's I to ken this? For I'm an auld man?* (Luke 1:18). Moreover, he completely avoids, as far as I have noted, the equally stigmatised use of *us* as a singular pronoun: Murray had, of course, used this and had described it as a universal feature of his and Smith's dialect but Smith could reasonably argue that is was not a feature of the classic tongue of Burns and Scott which he was attempting to imitate. Where the Revised Version uses *who, whom,* and *whose* Smith generally uses *wha, wham,* and *whase.* By contrast, Murray had always replaced these with *at,* the Scots equivalent of *that.* There can be no doubt that Murray's practice reflects actual spoken usage but Smith can be defended in that *wha,* and to a lesser extent *wham* and *whase,* do appear in Scots literary texts even if this is probably under the influence of literary English usage. What is certain is that the use of *wham* and *whase* in particular intrudes an inappropriately formal element into Smith's supposedly colloquial style. Lorimer later this century follows Murray in using only *at* and achieves a genuinely colloquial style: compare Smith's *this is he o' wham it is written* (Matt. 11:10) with Lorimer's *This is him at Scriptur speaks o.* Smith also keeps from the Authorised and Revised Versions the common device of using dependent participial clauses, itself based on the original Greek: *Jesus . . . cry't, 'It is dune!' and loutin doon his heid, gied up his spirit* (John 19:30). This structure, common in English written texts, is not common in either Scots or English colloquial speech. In these cases Lorimer prefers independent clauses even though he is working from the Greek. Here he writes: *he said, 'It is dune.' Syne he boued his heid an gíed up his spírit.* Even where Smith does change the structures it is often not sufficient to produce a fully colloquial style. For instance, where the Revised Version, here following the Authorised Version, reads

> But he answered and said unto them, An evil and adulterous generation seeketh after a sign; and there shall no sign be given to it but the sign of Jonah the prophet

Smith has

> But he answer't to them, 'An ill-doin and adulterous race seek for a token; and nae token sal be gien till't, but the token o' Jonah the prophet' (Matt. 12:39).

Smith has omitted *and said* and recast *there shall no sign be given* but he still has the archaic *answer't to* and the rather formal passive *nae token sal be gien.* Lorimer's greater flexibility avoids both of these:

> Jesus answert, 'An ill-gíen, onfaithfu generâtion wad hae a míracle, na? A-weill, the ne'er a míracle will it get, binna the Míracle o Jonah.'

All the same we should not forget how far Smith has advanced beyond Riddell and even beyond the slightly more colloquial Henderson who in this verse shows scarcely any variation from the Authorised Version at all:

> But he answer't an' said until them, An evil an' adult'rous generation seeketh after a sign: an' ther sall nae sign be gien til it but the sign o' the prophet Jonas.

Similarly, Smith's handling of the passage quoted earlier from Riddell's version of Matthew shows him taking a much freer hand with the Authorised and Revised Versions and producing a much more modern and colloquial translation:

Than, Herod, convenin the Wyss Men privately, faund oot mair strickly o' the comin o' the starn; And bad them gang to Bethlehem; and quo' he, 'Gang, and seek ye oot the wee bairn; and whan ye ken, fesh me word again, that I as weel may come and worship.' Eftir hearin the King, they gaed awa'; and lo! the starn whilk they saw i' the East gaed on afore them, till it stood whaur the wee bairn was. And whan they saw the starn, they were blythe wi' unco blytheness (Matt. 2:7–10)

Smith's most recent predecessor, and the only widely published one, was Waddell but Smith shows only minimal influence from him. Where the Revised Version has *bondservant* he sometimes uses Waddell's *thirlman* (1 Cor. 7:22) but in the same verse he also renders it as *bondman* and only a few verses later he translates the same word as *servant* (7:23), the Authorised Version term which Waddell took such pains to avoid. Aside from this use of *thirlman* the other possible influence is the presence of a limited number of new compounds. The uncharacteristic *fain-waitin* (1 Cor. 1:7) is reminiscent in form of some of Waddell's more outré creations but most of Smith's creations are very obvious combinations like *Risin-frae-the-deid* (1 Cor. 15:22) and *schawin-forth* (1 Cor. 12:7) which replace the Revised Version's *resurrection* and *manifestation*. Waddell had used his creations to avoid using formal Latinate terms but Smith by and large remains content to use such terms except where obvious Scots alternatives exist like *misca'* and *thole* (1 Cor. 4:12) for *revile* and *endure*. Hence we find words like *generation, glorify, magnify, redemption, sanctification* and *testimony*. The disadvantage of these, as we have seen before, is that they were no longer seen as Scots but as English and they thus dilute the Scots identity of his language. This difficulty is partly overcome when alternative Scots spellings are used as in *diveesions* (John 1:10) and *exerceese* (1 Tim. 4:8) but even these can to some readers give the appearance of being merely English terms ignorantly mispronounced since we tend to expect literary tongues to preserve the Latin spellings of the vowels in such words, as happens in English and French. Lorimer's later use of accent marks avoids this problem. The distinctively Scots element can also be enhanced by the use of the few Scots formal terms which are either obsolete in English like *expone* (1 Cor. 14:5) or are rarely used in English like *depone* (John 17:26) or have different forms of long standing like *contrar* (Acts 17:7) and *necessar* (1 Cor. 4:2). Alternatively but very infrequently Smith resorts to archaisms to give him formal Scots terms like *inhabiters* (Luke 2:1) and *inscrivit* (2 Cor. 3:7). Despite the attendant dilution of the Scots identity of his language, Smith's decision to retain the established Latinate diction of the Authorised and Revised Versions seems to me to have been a wise one. Any alternatives are liable to seem artificial. His retention of these terms is one of the reasons why Smith's work presents few difficulties for the reader. Another is the use of a traditional modern Scots style of spelling. Readers of Scott and Burns will have no problems with his vocabulary or with his spelling which shows only a few innovations: he shares with Riddell a fondness for the Middle Scots *sch* as in *schaw* (Luke 5:14) and, rather unusually, by using the spelling *fing'er* (John 8:6), he reminds us that *finger* and *singer* form a perfect rhyme in Scots whereas in English the presence of a [g] after the [ŋ] sound in *finger* makes them an imperfect rhyme. As with most Scots texts of his time, Smith makes considerable use of apostrophes and of English spellings even where accepted Scots ones exist: no more need be added here to what has been said before about the implications of such practices for the identity of Scots.

The anonymous Bonaparte translator of the Song of Solomon had used a length mark in spelling Solomon's name, but Smith is the first modern translator to move tentatively beyond this in employing Scots spellings of proper names. Like Lorimer he uses *Andro* (Mark 1:29) and *Sautan* (Mark 3:23) but is less adventurous with other names. He chooses the forms *Aylsander* (2 Tim. 4:14) and *Dauvid* (Mark 2:25) rather than Lorimer's more distinctively Scots *Saunders* and *Dauvit* and retains *Elizabeth* (Luke 1:5) and *James* (Mark 1:29) where Lorimer has *Elspeth* and *Jeames*.

The main problem with Smith's translation is the unevenness of style, alternating between formal and informal. The mixing of formal and informal diction is less irritating than the intermingling of colloquial sentence structures with formal and archaic ones derived from the Authorised and Revised Versions. The new English translations were beginning to challenge the supremacy of the Authorised/Revised Version style but it was still too close to Smith's heart for him to change that style as much as was really needed. It was hard enough for a translator using English to develop a new style of language for Biblical translation and even more difficult for a translator using Scots, given all the associations of vulgarity popularly attached to Scots. Smith must, at times, have experienced the feeling, expressed by George Douglas Brown whose *The House with the Green Shutters* appeared in the same year as his *New Testament*, that it is 'very difficult . . . to write Scots that is not fatuous and vulgar—I mean, to keep the racy twang of the native dialect, and yet make it fit to appear in a "prent beuk"'.[20] At the same time his is a far more thoroughly Scots version than either Riddell's or Henderson's and, if his style is uneven, Smith did make real efforts to profit from the informal nature of Scots and to produce a 'familiar and colloquial rendering'. Furthermore, compared to Waddell he is easy to read, mainly because he makes no real innovations in language. He himself wrote:

> I have had before me, all throughout, the probability of this translation being counted, in a modest way, as one of the standards of the language in time to come; and have endeavoured to make it consistent with itself, and conformable to already-existing standards; and a help to those who should afterwards write in Scots (p 335).

His translation thus provides us with Smith's personal view of what constituted classical literary Modern Scots before the activities of MacDiarmid called all things into question.

If his language owes little to Waddell, Smith did copy from him some ideas about the book's format. It is set out in double columns like a standard English Bible of the day and he follows Waddell's practice of providing footnotes, chapter headings and page headings in Scots. These add their own element of moral, historical and editorial commentary and bring the translator's personality before our eyes. For instance, of Christ's statement that 'Gin Sautan rise up again his sel, and be twa, he canna staun, but comes till an end' (Mark 3:26) he writes that 'We wad a' like to see sic an end o' Sautan's pooer; but we maunna think Sautan his sel wad help it forrit!' and regarding Luke's report that Mary 'laid up a' thae things in her heart' (Luke 2:51) he asks 'What coud Mary's thochts be, a' thae years. She aiblins didna come to the fu' licht till aboot the time o' his death. And hoo did Luke ken sae mickle aboot her ponderins o' heart? Nae doot, frae hersel, in eftir days.'

As an example of the sort of Scots that could be easily understood not only by people in Scotland but by those familiar with Scots only through literature, Smith's work won a deserved popularity and was reprinted twice in full, with separate reprints of the four gospels following later in the century.

PATERSON'S PROVERBS (1917)

Thomas Whyte Paterson (d.1920) was a United Free Church minister at Roberton and then Mid-Calder. In 1915 Alexander Gardner of Paisley, the publisher of Cameron's Genesis, brought out Paterson's *Auld Saws in New Scots Songs*, a volume of poems illustrating selected Scots proverbs and others chosen from the Bible, and two years later the same publisher produced Paterson's *Wyse Sayin's o' Solomon*, a translation of Proverbs. The books of the Bible traditionally assigned to Solomon have played a prominent part in the Scots translations; this is the only Scots version of Proverbs but we have already noted the five versions of the Song of Solomon.

So far all the translations from poetic books of the Bible had been laid out on the page by their publishers in the traditional format of Bible printing and not as verse although the selections from the Psalms and Isaiah to be found in the selection of Waddell's works published just after his death were laid out as lines of poetry without verse numbers.[21] Apart from this posthumous and selective publication Paterson was the first of our translators to lay out a poetical book of the Bible as verse where this was appropriate. The straightforward proverbs are laid out in numbered verses but with ample space between them. Other parts are set out in poetic lines with the verse numbers grouped at the beginning. Paterson's model, as he tells us in his introduction (p viii), was Moulton's *Modern Reader's Bible* and one feels throughout this work that it has been printed with the needs of the modern Scots reader in mind. The layout allows the reader to recognise the poetic shape of the verse and reading is made easy and pleasant by a generous allowance of space so that this relatively short book of the Bible occupies a full one hundred and seventy pages of print.

Paterson tells us in his introduction that he has 'generally followed the text of the Revised Version throughout' (p vii). What he does not say, but what we might perhaps have expected from his earlier poems based on proverbs, is that this is a very free rendition, so much so that it is often impossible to determine what text he is in fact following at any particular point.

Paterson begins as he means to go on and the opening verses illustrate many features of his style of translation:

> To ken what's wyse an' what's guid guidin;
> To hae an inklin intil the words o' guid understaun'in;
> To get advisins intil the cannie dailins o' life,
> Intil richteousness, an' jidgment, an' even-doon weys;
> To gie pith to the feckless;
> To the growin laddie richt-kennin an' discreetness;
> That the man o' mense may speel the heicher,
> An' that ony body wi a pickle sense
> May be better kent, e'en yet,
> For his gleg, straucht-gaun coonsel:

> To ken for yer ainsel a wyse-sayin,
> An' to grup what may be the ettlin o't,
> Ye hae afore ye THE WORDS O' THE WYSE,
> An' their AULD SAWS,
> Weel worth an eident sairch (1:2–6).

The Revised Version, for example, reads thus:

> To know wisdom and instruction;
> To discern the words of understanding;
> To receive instruction in wise dealing,
> In righteousness and judgement and equity;
> To give subtilty to the simple,
> To the young man knowledge and discretion:
> That the wise man may hear, and increase in learning;
> And that the man of understanding may attain unto sound counsels:
> To understand a proverb, and a figure;
> The words of the wise, and their dark sayings.

Already we have evidence of his free rendering of the text, his tendency to expand and his use of very colloquial diction. *Speel the heicher* is a very free rendering of *increase in learning* and *may be better kent, e'en yet, For his gleg, straucht-gaun coonsel* is both a very loose rendition of *may attain unto good counsels* and also a considerable expansion of it. Paterson's amplification of the text is most strikingly illustrated in the last phrase *Weel worth an eident sairch* which has no counterpart at all in either the Authorised Version or the Revised Version and is simply an addition expressing his sense of the author's intentions. The phrase *his gleg, straucht-gaun coonsels* is a translation of either the Revised Version's *sound counsels* or the Authorised Version's *good counsels* or a conflation of both—it is impossible to say which—but the words *a wyse-sayin, An' to grup what may be the ettlin o't* is much closer in meaning to the Authorised Version's *a proverb and the interpretation* than the Revised Version's *a proverb, and a figure* or even its alternative reading *a proverb, and an interpretation*. In fact, Paterson quite often chooses to follow the Authorised Version reading. When the *ill-deedie woman* tries to lure the *young chiel, wi' nae muckle gumption* to his destruction she begins by saying *I hae offerins o' guid-wull wi' me* (7:14). This is very similar to the Authorised Version's *I have peace offerings with me* and departs from the Revised Version's *Sacrifices of peace offerings are with me* yet later in the same speech her *strippit cleedin frae Egypt itsel* (7:16) derives from the Revised Version's *striped cloths of the yarn of Egypt* and not from the Authorised Version's *with carved works, with fine linen of Egypt*.

The success of Paterson's expansions of the Revised Version varies. The well-known proverb *Hope deferred maketh the heart sick* is expressed quite differently but effectively as *Houps that are putten aff an' aff, Bring a dowie dwaum ower the hairt* (13:12). In rendering the verse *The king's wrath is as the roaring of a lion; But his favour is as dew upon the grass* Paterson fills out the second half considerably: *The anger o' the king is like the rampagin o' a lion; But his guid-will is sic-like as the saft, seeping dew on drouthie gress* (19:12). The image has been made more vivid but at some expense to the conciseness which we expect in proverbs. Amongst those of our translators who are working from particular English versions Paterson is undoubtedly the most willing to undertake radical recasting of his source's expressions. Some of the time he does this so as to adopt one of the forms typical of Scottish proverbs. A number of Scots proverbs begin with *ilka: Ilka corn has its shool, Ilka land has its ain land-law* and so on. With examples like these in mind Paterson reworks the Revised Version's *The heart knoweth its own bitterness* into *Ilka hairt kens best its ain wae* (14:10).

In Paterson we see the end-product of the process which began with Robson's tentative departures from the Authorised Version towards a more colloquial rendering of the Song of Solomon. Working, like Robson, from a text in archaic English, Paterson has been much more ruthless in expunging inappropriate diction and has achieved a much more thoroughly colloquial text. He shows none of the reluctance to change the familiar text which is so evident in the Bonaparte translators. Consequently he can adopt and maintain a consistently colloquial style. Like Robson, but much more frequently, he opts for colloquialisms even if it means bringing in English terms rather than purely Scots ones. Colloquial expressions common in English regularly appear: *tak pat-luck, share-an'-share alike* and so on. Purists like Waddell would have rejected these. Opting for colloquial language entails the replacement of much of the Revised Version's formal diction, something Paterson often achieves with a periphrasis, as when *his habitable earth* becomes *the yirth He made for His folks* (8:31). As part of the colloquial register, Paterson often employs reduplicated verbs like *dreep-dreepin* (19:13), *fraise-fraisin* (7:5) and *wink-winkin* (10:10) and we find the typically Scots use of continuous tenses. Colloquialisms work particularly well in vituperative passages like the following:

> A scabbit, capernoitit craitur,
> An ill-daein body—
> he strunts aboot wi' an impident gab (6:12)

although *forritsome* might have been more appropriate here than *impident*.

The type of language used by Paterson, modern and colloquial, allows no room for archaisms. The Revised Version's archaisms are removed and Paterson makes very little use of obsolete Scots. *Da* meaning 'doe' is one of his rare Scots archaisms. Paterson very rarely follows Waddell's lead in constructing his own new compounds and, of Waddell's own distinctive compounds, I have noted just one case of the use of *blythe-biddens* (22:9). In the opening verse he uses his own creation *richt-kennins* for 'knowledge' but this too is exceptional. Both Waddell and Cameron had created a colloquial register while using some archaic diction. Paterson, by contrast, uses only contemporary language. Not only this but he sticks to the better-known modern diction and does not search out current but rare words from particular dialects or from dictionaries. The result of all this is a text which is vividly worded and easy to read, a genuinely new version which shatters the mould of the Revised Version and becomes, to adapt Paterson's phrase, 'New Saws in an Auld Sang'.

CAMERON'S GENESIS (1921)

Henry Paterson Cameron was born in 1852, educated at Glasgow University and became minister of the parish of Milton in 1879. He was the translator of Theodor Storm's *Immensee* and the author of *Text Book for Communicants* which was in its third edition by the time he published his *History of the English Bible* in 1885. Cameron looked set for a promising career but his life had already been touched by tragedy with the early death of his only child a 'little flower' to whom the *History of the English Bible* ('hoc opusculum ad curam expellendam scriptum') is touchingly dedicated. Then in November of 1890 he was both deposed as minister and divorced by his wife. The whole direction of his life was changed and we next find him in 1896 in New South Wales running a private school in Parramatta. It does not seem that Cameron ever again became a minister and in the following years he moved about from place to place around Sydney until his death in 1921 at Liverpool near Sydney. Despite, or perhaps because of, the dramatic change in his life and his exile 'faur awa frae Bonnie Scotland' (as he puts it in the dedication of his *Genesis in Scots*), Cameron retained his interest in Scots. In 1912 he compiled an extensive glossary to the works of John Service, another Scottish writer living in New South Wales, and this appeared as an appendix to Service's *Robin Cummell* the following year. In the same year he published his translation into Scots of Thomas à Kempis's *Imitation of Christ*. The book had an enthusiastic reception in Scotland and elsewhere. It was called by the *United Free Church Record* 'a gowden buik in the mither tongue... weel worth perusin' in the quate o' the fireside' and was reprinted in 1917. Finally Cameron's long-standing interest in both the Bible and in Scots culminated in his *Genesis in Scots*, completed and published in the year of his death.

As is clear from his Prefatory Note, Cameron was conscious of the strangeness of working on a translation into Scots 'i' the Australian "bush"' but he claimed that 'still-and-on e'en mids the eldritch yowling o' the dingo, the rowtin o' nowte, the maein o' fe, and the schill crawin o' the "rooster," he haes hard athin his saul and abune them a' the "saft, couthie" müsick o' the Doric'. Yet Genesis, with all its emphasis on a people from elsewhere coming to settle and name a new land, was a natural choice for a Scot in Australia where these processes, in which his countrymen had played an important part, were still going on. Perhaps Genesis spoke to his heart about his own experiences as a settler in a new land.

With its frequent use of quotations from the Bible, the translation of Thomas à Kempis had already offered Cameron an opportunity to render parts of the Scripture into Scots. For the *Imitation* Cameron used the subtitle *Frae Latin intil Scots* which recalls the subtitles of Waddell's translations and there is indeed plenty of evidence of Waddell's influence on both this work and Cameron's Genesis but in his Genesis Cameron did not follow Waddell's example of translating direct from the Hebrew. Instead he based his translation on the Revised Version. Of this version he had written in his *History of the English Bible* that 'We venture...to think that it will not supersede the Authorised [Version]—at all events not in our own day' (p 178) but he no doubt chose it as the basis of his translation of Genesis into Scots because in its time it embodied the latest of Biblical scholarship.

We would expect the vigorous and innovative language of Waddell to influence later translators and in Cameron this influence comes out strongly. He has also studied Paterson's language. In his extensive glossary to *Genesis in Scots* Cameron occasionally cites his sources: he gives Paterson as his source for *bickerin* meaning 'strife' and *bidden* meaning 'command' and Waddell for *hame-bringin* 'deliverance', *kith-gettin* 'generation' and *neibor-kins* 'tribes'. In fact the extent of his indebtedness is greater than this. Paterson may also have given him *besturtit* 'disturbed' (45:3) and there is a string of words from Waddell. These include some highly characteristic Waddellian compounds like *blythe-bid* 'bless' (12:2), *godlowse* 'wicked' (18:25), *heal-ha'din* 'salvation' (49:18) and *richt-recht* 'judge' (30:6). Next there are words used by Waddell in special senses like *glock* meaning 'devour' (37:20), *ootcome* used to translate the Revised Version's *seed* (21:12) and *tryst* for the Revised Version's *covenant* (9:11). Finally there is Waddell's *wuth* meaning 'anger' (27:45) which we have already discussed as a possible borrowing by Waddell from German.

Yet if these words set Cameron firmly in the tradition of Waddell he is certainly no mere timid imitator. Many of these words occur only occasionally and he is also willing to use terms like *blessin* (27:12), *deleever't* (14:20), *jidgement* (18:19), and *sacrifeece* (31:54) which Waddell had taken great pains to avoid. Recognising the proper meaning of *thirl* 'a person bound in servitude', he uses Waddell's compound *thirlman* only when the Revised Version uses a term like *bondman* (43:18) by which some kind of servitude is implied: Waddell had also used it where the Authorised Version had *servant* but for the Revised Version's *servant* Cameron prefers *servitor* (18:5) or even *gillie* (18:7). As well as Paterson and Waddell he seems to have drawn on Riddell from whom he apparently had the otherwise unrecorded *smowe* 'to stink' (34:30: cf. Riddell's Ps. 38:5). In addition Cameron has a number of independent sources for providing appropriate diction. The sources cited in his glossary include Barbour, Burns, Gavin Douglas, Dunbar, Henryson, Hogg, Service, Shirrefs, Tennant, Wilson's *Noctes Ambrosianae* and Wyntoun. As this list demonstrates, Cameron draws vocabulary from Scots of all periods, although his basic vocabulary is taken from Modern Scots. As well as the words for which he gives sources, many other words are revived from earlier Scots. His revivals from Middle Scots include *mawngery* 'feast' (26:30), *thusgates* 'in this way' (45:9) and *waithman* 'hunter' (10:9) while his *yeid* as a past tense of *gae* (21:19) and *mowe* 'dust' (2:7) became obsolete during the eighteenth century. While he is clearly well acquainted with Scots literature he has also taken a number of words from one or other of the editions of Jamieson's Dictionary, words like *blinter* 'hasten' (18:6), *gad* 'travelling company' (37:25), *reibie* for the Revised Version's *leanfleshed* (41:4), *sibmen* 'kindred' (12:1) and *skultie* 'naked' (2:25). These are all rare and in some cases unknown except in Jamieson. The phantom word *smewy* meaning 'savoury' which arose from a misprint of the word *smervy* in the Glossary to Shirrefs' poems also turns up in Cameron's translation of the Revised Version's *savoury meat* (27:4). Either in Jamieson or directly in his source, Ruddiman's glossary to Gavin Douglas, Cameron discovered the phrase *gie him his muldemete* and used it to translate the Revised Version's *slay him* (37:18). This is how Ruddiman glossed it, taking *mulde-mete*, a combination of *muld* 'the earth of a graveyard' and *meat*, as 'the last food that a person eats before death'. More recently it has been re-interpreted as 'food sacrificed over a grave'. Lastly we may note that Cameron's eclecticism extends to place as well as time. From Aberdeen dialect he takes *buisty* 'bed' (49:4) and *repree* 'rebuke' (37:10) and from Shetland dialect *uplöse* 'reveal' (35:7).

All this produces a large and varied vocabulary, including both well-known and little-known Scots terms. The range of Cameron's vocabulary led W M Metcalfe, himself the author of a Supplement to Jamieson's Dictionary, to write in his Foreword to Cameron's *Imitation* that

> His acquaintance with [Scots] vocabulary and idioms, and his deftness in their use are remarkable. While reading the following pages, the present writer thought that, on several occasions, he had found the author nodding, using a wrong word or a wrong phrase, but on consulting the authorities he invariably found himself mistaken, and the impression which has been forced on him is that in his knowledge and mastery of the contents of 'Jamieson' or of Lowland Scots Mr Cameron has few equals (pp ix–x).

In both grammar and spelling Cameron is a pretty consistent scoticiser. The Revised Version's *thou* is generally replaced by the contemporary Scots *ye* but *thou* is retained for speech to God (18:23–5) and to intimates (12:11–13) where it is followed by the Scots *s* inflection. However Cameron avoids the stigmatised *s* inflection with plural subjects and introduces one mistaken form, the use of *I'se* for *I am*. This form began in the later eighteenth century as a misunderstanding of the use of *I'se* in the phrases like *I'se warrant* where *'se*, normally a future form, has the force of an emphatic present. Cameron's spelling exhibits a few personal quirks, like the use of *haes* and *haed* for 'has' and 'had', but generally he adheres to the conventions of the modern literary standard and avoids regional forms. Thus, although he notes in his glossary that *ae* and *ance* should be pronounced *yae* and *yince* (the Central and Southern Scots pronunciation), he retains the traditional spellings in the text. He aims to differentiate Scots from English as much as is possible within the conventions of Modern Scots spelling. Where he departs from these conventions he looks to Older Scots for authority; thus in the glossary he backs his use of *wes* rather than *was* by reference to Barbour. Overall, Cameron produces a consistent, standardised, literary Scots heavily dependent on written sources rather than the reproduction of actual speech of a particular place and time such as Murray had aimed at.

A reviewer in the *Glasgow Herald* wrote of Cameron's *Imitation of Christ* that 'His language is such as might have been written in the days of Knox or Buchanan'.[22] In fact Cameron's Scots includes many elements of vocabulary, spelling and grammar which are of more recent origin than the mid sixteenth century. But we could say that Cameron's language represents a guess at what Scots might have become if it had continued in the period after Knox and Buchanan to develop as an independent language separate from English. Unlike Riddell's, his language is not an uneasy mixture of past and present Scots and uncertain where it is heading. Rather it is Modern Scots enriched in its vocabulary by an infusion of earlier Scots. In fact this is very similar to the language of the poets of the twentieth-century Scottish Renaissance. Like Cameron, MacDiarmid and others took extra vocabulary from earlier Scots literature and from Jamieson. Cameron's language is a prose counterpart to MacDiarmid's attempts in verse to re-establish Scots as a literary language.

As a translator Cameron follows the Revised Version closely, indicating only once in a footnote that he has preferred the Authorised Version's reading (20:16). By and large he retains the Revised Version word order but opts as much as possible for distinctively Scots vocabulary and grammar. He replaces archaisms, as when *entreated* in the old sense of 'treated' becomes *guidit* (12:16), but his removal of formal terms, like when he replaces *abomination* with *scunner* (43:32), seems to be primarily a means of introducing distinctively Scots forms and diction rather than arising from an objection to formal terms as such since he is quite happy to introduce Scots formal terms like *commuved* (28:8), *decern* (41:32) and *obtempered* (28:7) or to retain the Revised Version's formal terms when they can be given a Scots form, as happens with the change of *continued* to *conteena'd* (40:4). The result is a rather formal style of Scots. Although there is an occasional, rather out of place, informal note like the use of *shankit aff* (Revised Version *made haste*, 43:30) and *gied hissel a scrape* (Revised Version *shaved himself*, 41:4), Cameron generally avoids homely, informal Scots preferring, for instance, to revive the Middle Scots *garth* for 'garden' (2:8) rather than using the Modern Scots *yaird* with its 'kailyard' associations even though he uses *yaird* in his glossary to define *garth*. The formality is increased by the frequent retention of the Revised Version word order and by the use of *quha* and *quhilk* rather than the colloquial *at*. This formal Scots serves his purposes well but it is sometimes inappropriate as when Rebekah's adjuration to her son to *onlie obtemper my vice* (27:13) is made quite unnaturally pompous by the use of the formal word *obtemper*.

Adopting the practice of the Revised Version, Cameron sets out the text in paragraphs, thus giving it the appearance of modern English versions like the New English Bible. Indeed, he goes further and omits the verse numbers. It reads, too, like a modern narrative. One reason for this is a notable feature of Cameron's style of translation, the diversification of the vocabulary. Many passages of the original and of the literal rendering in the Authorised and Revised Versions derive their effect from the repetition of key words and phrases. For instance, in cursing Cain the Lord says *a fugitive and a wanderer shalt thou be in the earth* and Cain repeats these same words in his reply. In Cameron's version the Lord's words are *a foyard and a waffinger sal ye be i' the erd* (4:12) but Cain's words are *I sal be a fugie and a land-louper i' the erd* (4:14). Earlier in the same chapter it is recorded that *Cain was very wroth, and his countenance fell* and the Lord then asks him *Why art thou wroth? and why is thy countenance fallen.* In Cameron this reads *Cain wes vera teenfu', and his cheir drappit* and *Whatfor are ye wrothy? and whatfor glumsh ye sae?* (4:5–6). The varying of the diction removes the primitive simplicity which is so characteristic of the original and makes the narrative much more modern in style. To achieve this Cameron has mainly drawn on Scots current in his lifetime (*fugie, glumsh, land-louper, waffinger*) but he has also used a rare word only otherwise recorded in Jamieson and which the *Scottish National Dictionary* considers 'perhaps not genuine' (*foyard*) as well as two nineteenth-century English archaisms (*cheer, wrothy*). Nevertheless his sense of tone is well developed and none of these words seems out of place in the context. Moreover, because the readers recognise the characteristic Hebraic balancing of synonyms, they can easily deduce the meaning of words that are unfamiliar to them.

Cameron's is one of the most successful of the Scots Bible translations. Like Waddell, he has created his own literary register of Scots, maintained it with only a few lapses in consistency, and used it with confidence. He keeps a good balance between basic, familiar Scots terms and exotic, less familiar ones. Unlike Waddell, he has opted for a slightly formal style rather than a very colloquial one and he has retained Latinate diction and revived earlier Scots vocabulary rather than inventing his own new compounds. The resulting text lacks the colloquial immediacy and passion of Waddell's translations but it has a stateliness which gives due solemnity to the events of the narrative even if it may not be much to the taste of some modern readers accustomed to more colloquial renditions. Readers of this text will not be enlightened about the features of modern spoken Scots as the readers of Murray's Ruth would be but they will read a well-told story in a fluent and accessible literary Scots.

Borrowman's Ruth (1979)

Alex Borrowman (d.1978), for many years a minister in the Church of Scotland, was also a poet writing in Scots and took an active part in the Lallans Society (later called the Scots Language Society). His *The Buik o Ruth and Ither Wark in Lallans* appeared posthumously in 1979 and, as Alexander Scott writes in his Poem to that work, 'Aa thae concerns, wi religion, wi the Scots leid, and wi the skeelie wyvin o words, hae come thegither i the blads prentit here'. In Borrowman's case, as in Smith's, we have the benefit of introductory comments by the author and they remind us forcibly that Borrowman is the first of our translators to postdate the Scottish Renaissance and all the effort that had been put into the revival of Scots as a literary language by MacDiarmid and others around him. Scots had certainly been given a new lease of life in poetry but, if it was to be fully revived as a literary language, it must come to be used in prose as well. The Lallans Society sought to encourage this development by, amongst other things, the journal *Lallans* which contains prose articles in Scots on a variety of subjects. That Borrowman shared this aim is clear and in his introduction he writes that 'We hae a wheen makars in Lallans . . . but we have a needcessity for mair screevers o prose'. Indeed the 'Ither Wark' includes not only selected passages in prose from other parts of the Bible but sermons, orders of service, a commentary on Ruth and verse translations of some of the Psalms, all in Scots. His Bible translations, then, were undertaken both to extend the amount of the Bible in Scots (he seems to have been unaware of Murray's version of Ruth—not surprisingly, when it is hidden away in *The Dialect of the Southern Counties of Scotland*) and also as examples of modern Scots prose.

In his introduction Borrowman lists the work of most of his predecessors. He praises the publications of Prince Louis as a 'guid ensample o the Auld Alliance' but, of the versions of the Song of Solomon, seems to know only Riddell's. He calls Waddell 'gie auld-fanglt' and mentions Paterson, Cameron, Nisbet and Smith but does not list Murray. But, while showing himself aware of what had come before, Borrowman breaks new ground by using, for the first time amongst our translators, an English version written in contemporary language as his foundation. For his Ruth he tells us that 'The found o the translation is the New English Bible. Ah hae taen a keek at the Authorised Version, alsweel Moffat's translation, in the by-gaun'. The short selections from other books, however, are generally based on the Authorised Version. This is the case, for instance, with the 'Aucht Portions for Yule' but he sometimes turns to the New English Bible as his basis as in verses 3 and 4 (but not verse 2) of Micah 5—presumably in this case because the meaning of the Authorised Version text is unusually obscure. In view of the different basis for the other translations it is best to consider his Ruth separately.

As a short, beautifully rounded and moving story, the Book of Ruth is, as Murray had already discovered, a perfect choice for a sample translation into Scots. It also has the advantage that it can be rendered in a straightforward style, neither too formal nor too colloquial, which does not make unreasonable demands on a language that is widely perceived as lacking a full formal register. Because he is working from a translation in contemporary English Borrowman has no problems with English archaisms left over from the Auth-orised or Revised Versions like many of his predecessors. He does, however, introduce at least one English archaism of his own, *deponent* 'witness' (4:9), which he uses instead of the Scots equivalent *deponer*. With a few exceptions like this he renders the text in fully developed Scots, not a hybrid of Scots and English, and achieves a consistent, appealing and readable style. As a product of the Scottish Renaissance, he is committed to an eclectic style of Scots and tells us 'Ma ain leid is a mixie-maxy, and nae wonner, for Ah hae dwalt in Stirling, Dumfries, Fife, Bute and Glesca! Ah hae eesit dictionars alsweel!' but few readers will have any trouble with his diction which is mostly well-known and commonly used in the last two centuries. Moreover he supplies both a glossary and detailed comments on words of special interest. There are, all the same, a few Scots archaisms and rare words. Like others before him, Borrowman has clearly searched both the highways and byways of Jamieson's dictionary and to it he probably owes such terms as the archaic *fruschit* meaning 'broken to pieces' (1:21) and rare words like *vaishle* 'maidservant' (2:13), mentioned only by Gregor in his 1866 book on Banffshire dialect and copied thence into later editions of Jamieson, and *wont-tae-be* 'custom' (4:7). Beyond doubt he has culled his use of *inger* (2:9) from its unique appearance in Jamieson. Attempting to explain the Lothian phrase *inger's pock* meaning 'a quantity of grain dried in a pot and ground into meal', Jamieson surmised that *inger* meant 'gleaner'. The *Scottish National Dictionary* calls this interpretation into question but Borrowman is happy to accept a word so useful for telling the story of Ruth's experiences in Boaz' fields. But Jamieson is not his only source of rare words: for *ayler*, a northeastern form of elder, the *SND* cites only one source, Watson's *Glimpses o' Auld Lang Syne* of 1905; either Watson or the *SND* itself seems to be Borrowman's source. The use of the Lothian *inger* and the northeastern *ayler* in the one text confirms Borrowman's description of his language as a 'mixie-maxy' of various areas as well as various times. It is a far cry from Murray's meticulous differentiation between dialects but Murray and Borrowman had quite different aims in mind.

In spelling Borrowman follows the modern practice of avoiding apostrophes, aiming to establish Scots in its own right and not as a variant of English, and he adopts a thoroughly Scots grammar, replacing the obsolete *thou* with *ye* and even scoticising the first person singular pronoun as *Ah*, a spelling justified by the pronunciation but not historical in Scots, as he points out in a note:

> Barbour in 'The Brus' and Harry the minstrel in 'Wallace' eese IC or IK for I. This is gie auldfanglt. Maist makars eese I. William Alexander in 'Johnny Gibb o Gushetneuk' eeses AW. Dr Purves in his blad anent orthographie eeses AU. Ah hae fun, in makin ma translation, that the Sudron I sets ill [misprinted *setsill*] on the blad, sae Ah cognosit for AH (p 40).

Borrowman's treatment of the New English Bible varies from close translation to free paraphrase. Just how freely he can handle the English text can be seen in his rendition of Naomi's speech to her daughters-in-law:

NEW ENGLISH BIBLE

> Go back, my daughters. Why should you go with me? Am I likely to bear any more sons to be husbands for you? Go back, my daughters, go. I am too old to marry again. But even if I could say that I had hope of a child, if I were to

marry this night and if I were to bear sons, would you then wait until they grew up? Would you then refrain from marrying? No, no, my daughters, my lot is more bitter than yours, because the LORD has been against me.

BORROWMAN

Gang hame, lasses, gang hame. Fou suld ye gang wi me? Amna Ah owre auld tae hae onie mair sons? Gang hame, lasses, gang hame. Ah'm owre auld tae merry a saicond time. Gif Ah were tae ligg in jizzen and hae sons wald ye bide till they were men-bodies? It waldna be wyce gif ye were tae nay-say anither merridge. Na, na, lasses. Ah hae a wersher weird than ye tae dree for the Lord has been agin me (1:11–13)

As can be seen, the first and last parts of this follow the New English Bible closely but the middle section is substantially reworked. Borrowman's paraphrase is much tighter and clearer then the awkward succession of conditional clauses which the New English Bible accurately carries over from the original text. While the liberties Borrowman takes with the text are greater here than is normal in his version, it shows how far he is willing to go to achieve a readable and coherent text. Where apropriate, too, he introduces a colloquial note into the dialogue: in the New English Bible Boaz' servant tells him that Ruth *has been on her feet with hardly a moment's rest from daybreak till now*; Borrowman renders this vividly as *She . . . hasna taen the wecht aff her fit frae skreigh o day till noo* (2:7).

The influence of the other texts into which Borrowman had 'taen a keek', the Authorised Version and Moffat, is not particularly striking although Moffat's use of *mantle* where New English Bible has *cloak* and the Authorised Version *vail* may have encouraged Borrowman to use *mantua* (3:15) on which he has a long note. More interesting is the transitory influence of Smith. In his translation of the Lord's Prayer Borrowman adopted Smith's rendition *needfu' fendin* where the Authorised Version has *daily bread* (Matt. 6:11). In Ruth the New English Bible simply tells us that the Lord had given 'food' to his people but Borrowman sees a chance to highlight a parallel with the New Testament text and freely renders it with this same phrase *needfu fendin* (1:6).

It is inevitable that we should compare this version with Murray's. It does not have the same determination to achieve pure spoken dialect but it nevertheless avoids sounding artificial. Murray's Ruth, Naomi and Boaz are made to sound like ordinary peasants from the Borders and there is an appropriateness about this—the original Hebrew story was concerned with a not totally dissimilar rural society. Nevertheless English versions have accustomed us to a style of translation without such strong connections with a particular group of speakers. Inevitably, too, Murray's language is very colloquial. When Scott commended a passage from Patrick Walker's life of Peden as being a 'simple, but very affecting, narrative', the style of which produced an effect similar to 'the beautiful book of Ruth',[23] he was no doubt thinking of the plain style of the Authorised Version which steers a middle line between the extremes of colloquialism and formality. Borrowman's version retains something of this quality.

Borrowman uses a very similar style of Scots in the translations based on the Authorised Version. The vocabulary is Modern Scots with a few archaisms like *athil*, a rare Middle Scots word meaning 'noble' for which Borrowman has adopted Jamieson's definition 'prince' (Isa. 9:6), *ensample* 'example' (Matt. 1:19), *nouvelles* 'tidings' (Luke 2:10), *roy* 'king' (Mic. 5:2) and *thesaury* 'treasury' (Matt. 2:11). These are exceptions: generally he does not use archaisms and the Authorised Version's own archaisms are removed. For instance, he sets aside the exclamation *behold*, replacing it with *ma certie* (Matt. 1:20), *aweel* (Luke 1:38) or Smith's phrase *Tak tent!* (Matt. 1:23) or omitting it altogether (Matt. 2:1; Luke 2:10). Similarly, *lo* is changed to *wow* (Luke 2:9). Borrowman aims to make his vocabulary as distinctively Scots as possible and discards shared English-Scots terms like *justice* and *saviour* in favour of his own creations *richt-daein* (Isa 9:7) and *Hainer* (Luke 2:11) but he avoids Waddell's rather excessive use of new creations. The grammar, too, is generally Scots but there is a tendency to carry over the word order of the Authorised Version as well as the occasional phrase of doubtful Scots currency like *ye sall caa his name JESUS* (Matt. 1:21). Rightly rejecting the Authorised Version's *on this wise*, he opts for another common and archaic Authorised Version phrase, *efter this mainner* (Matt. 1:18) which is Modern Scots only in its spelling. He also uses *wha* although Scots, when uninfluenced by English, prefers *at* or *that*. These are minor blemishes; for the most part these translations have the good qualities of Borrowman's Ruth.

Borrowman translated different parts of the Bible to Waddell and used a much less idiosyncratic style of Scots but the two are very similar in one respect: they impress us by the totality of their effort. Each wished to provide translations of key parts of the Bible but each also wished to place these translations in a wider setting. Waddell does this by surrounding them with a full scholarly apparatus; Borrowman does this as well, but to a lesser extent, and also surrounds his translations with all the other elements necessary for public worship: sermons, prayers and hymns. With both men the translations themselves are only part of a wider campaign to expand the use of Scots, a language they hold passionately dear.

LORIMER'S NEW TESTAMENT

William Laughton Lorimer (1885–1967) is almost the last and certainly the greatest of our translators. All the translators of the modern period played their part in the efforts to break free from the influence of English translations and to find a fitting form of Scots for biblical translation. In every respect Lorimer took their work a step further and his translation represents the culminating achievement and pinnacle of this endeavour.

Lorimer's father and grandfather were ministers of the Free Church. His mother belonged to an Anglo-Indian family and was brought up mainly in Edinburgh but she also travelled widely in Europe and came to speak several European languages fluently. Lorimer himself was born in his father's parish on the outskirts of Dundee, the seventh of eight children. His parents, his two elder brothers and his elder sister all demonstrated a strong interest in languages and Lorimer followed their lead, spending most of his life teaching Greek in the universities at St Andrews and Dundee and becoming Professor of Greek at St Andrews in 1953.

During his career as a university teacher he made important contributions to both Greek and Scots lexicography: between the two world wars he contributed to a revised edition of Liddell and Scott's Greek Lexicon and in 1946 he began contributing to the work of the *Scottish National Dictionary*, becoming Chairman of its Executive Committee in 1953. Yet all this work now seems merely a prelude to the great task of his life, the translation of the New Testament into Scots. This he undertook, in the confident hope that he would share his ancestors' longevity, in the years after he had reached seventy and retired. In the eight years from late 1957 he made a first draft of all of the New Testament; he then made final transcripts of about a quarter of this and a revision of the rest. Unable finally to continue, he handed over editorial control to his son, R L C Lorimer, who then undertook to prepare the final form of the text in accordance with his father's overall instructions. This was a considerable task but in 1983 *The New Testament in Scots* was finally published, the cost being financed mainly by public subscription. It was an immediate and spectacular success with 2,500 copies being sold in a fortnight. A reprint promptly followed and only two years later it was issued by Penguin in paperback. The result of Lorimer's years of hard work gained the reception it justly deserved.[24]

In coming to Lorimer's translation the most important thing to remember is that this is an entirely new translation from the original Greek and not a reworking of any previous English or Scots translation. Lorimer was aware of his predecessors: in particular, we can assume a thorough knowledge of the Authorised Version and he makes clear in his notes that he consulted Smith on occasions.[25] He also made use of the New English Bible which appeared in the same year as he began work on the Gospels. Yet these other translations have only minor influence on his own. A lifetime of teaching the translation of Greek texts had left him both with clear ideas about the kind of Greek used in the New Testament and with a willingness to search beyond the obvious and the traditional for the best possible translation. His originality and inventiveness as a translator shows up even with a relatively straightforward passage like the one from Matthew which we have used before in comparing different translations.

> Herod than caa'd the spaemen til him in hidlins, an whan he hed lairnt frae them the day an hour o the stairn's kythin, he sent them awà tae Bethlehem, biddin them gang their waas an seek out aa the speirins they coud win at anent the bairn: 'An whan ye hae fund him,' qo he, 'bring me back wurd, sae at I may gae an wurship him mysel.'
>
> They did een as the Kíng baud them, an tuik the gate; an, behaud, thair wis the stairn gaein on afore them, on an on, or it stappit abuin the houss whaur the bairn wis; an byous blythe war they tae see the stairn! Syne they gaed ben, an saw the bairn, wi Mary his mither: an they fell on their knees and wurshippit him, an apnin their treisur-kists, they laid gifts afore him—gowd, an frank-

incense, an myrrh. Than they fuir awà hame anither gate nor they hed come, sin they hed been warnished in a draim no tae gae back til Herod (Matt. 2:7–12).

Neither Purvey (working via the Vulgate) nor the Authorised Version depart from a fairly literal translation here although neither hesitates to make such minor changes as altering the Greek (and Latin) construction in verse 9 which means literally 'coming it stood' to it *came and stood* in order to give a more flowing English style. Nor do Nisbet (following Purvey) and Riddell and Henderson (following the Authorised Version) depart any further from the original text. Smith (following the Revised Version) is a little freer—for instance, he replaces the Revised Version's *they rejoiced with exceeding great joy* with *were blythe wi' unco blytheness*—but his version remains very close in word order and structure to the Greek. Lorimer opts for a much less literal approach. For example, he moves even further than Smith from the literal Greek in this particular phrase and renders it simply as *byous blythe war they* and what the Authorised Version translates literally as *Go and search diligently for the young child* he changes to indirect speech and renders, as we can see, with *gang their waas an seek out aa the speirins they coud win at anent the bairn*. Likewise, not content with the adequate but uninspired *it came and stood* for the Greek participial construction, he comes up with the much more interesting and colourful *on an on, or it stappit*. Altogether, even in this fairly pedestrian passage, Lorimer shows his ability to look behind the literal translation to a freer rendering which, while remaining accurate, gives a much more interesting narrative style.

This greater freedom in handling the Greek is by no means limited to this passage. One of his characteristic traits is to use two words where the Greek text has one. This can be particularly effective when he uses an alliterating phrase, either a traditional combination like *sturt an strife* (Matt. 10:35) or one of his own like *fairce an fierie* (Rev. 14:8). Indeed, alliteration is one of his favourite effects: what the New English Bible renders tamely as *deep roar* he turns into *dunnerin dinnle* (Rev. 14:2). Often, too, he will replace a single word with a rather longer phrase to bring out the full effect. Consider the following passage from Jude:

> They ar girners, thir men, ey channer-channerin at their faa; they airt their lives bi their desires; they ar ey blawin an blowstin, but will beck an beinge tae fowk, whan there is onie fore tae be gotten o'd (Jude 1:16)

Here *ey channer-channerin at their faa* and *beck and beinge* both expand single words and *blawin and blowstin* gives a suitably contemptuous tone to the phrase translated more literally by the Authorised Version as *their mouth speaketh great swelling words*. Similarly, in the words *warldlie kyauch an care an the chaitrie glaumour of walth smoors the Wurd* (Matt. 13:22), *kyauch an care* replaces one word and *the chaitrie glaumour o walth* expands words meaning simply 'the deceitfulness of riches' (as the Authorised Version puts it). Here Lorimer has taken a hint from the New English Bible which adopts a less literal approach than the Authorised Version and uses the words *the false glamour of wealth* but Lorimer has improved this with the vivid word *chaitrie*. This is only one case where Lorimer prefers a specific image to a general term. Compare, for instance, his *wi bruindin* ('blazing') *een* (Mark 3:5) with the Authorised Version's literal *with anger* or consider a more striking case mentioned by his son in his introduction (pp xx–xxi). Lorimer's final personal preference in translating 1 Corinthians 14:11 was for the rendering *I will be like a barbárian tae him an he will be like a barbárian tae me* but he had also experimented with various other renderings which expressed the underlying idea metaphorically. As his son notes the Greek word used here, $\beta \acute{\alpha} \rho \beta \alpha \rho o \varsigma$ means 'one who does not speak Greek' and 'in classical Greek, foreign languages were proverbially compared to the twittering of birds'. Taking this up, Lorimer considered various ways of expressing this image. From these his son, unwilling to 'collaborate with his scholarship in inhibiting his creativity', has chosen for the printed text the rendering *my speech will be like the cheepin o a spug tae him, an his will be like the chitterin o a swallow tae me*. Finally we may note that Lorimer does not hesitate to add an adjective to bring out the full tone of a passage: compare his *Think ye at I am some laundlowpin reiver, at ye hae come out wi swuirds an rungs tae fang me?* (Matt. 26:55) with the New English Bible's *Do you take me for a bandit . . . ?*

Arguably in these cases Lorimer has achieved a more accurate translation by his freedom from strict literalism and by searching for his own words rather than adopting those of previous translations. Elsewhere, on the other hand, he has been absolutely literal but nevertheless chosen an unusual but better word. For instance, the Authorised Version has Christ say to Peter *before the cock crow thou shalt deny me thrice*. The use of *deny* to mean 'disown' later became archaic as Riddell and Smith recognised by using *disown*; yet the New English Bible sticks to *deny*. Lorimer employs *disavou* (Matt. 26:34).

Lorimer also demonstrates his independence of other translations in his handling of proper names. All personal names are scoticised where possible even if this means no more than indicating a Scottish vowel. Hence we find: *Archeláus, Dauvit, Elshinder, Elspeth, Jeames, Jeremiah* and *Sautan*. Place-names are also scoticised, not just in the obvious ways like the use of *loch* in *Loch Gennesaret* (Luke 5:1) but also with more ingenious creations like *Jordanside* (Luke 3:3) and *the Laich o Tyre an Sídon* (Luke 6:17). All this shows that willingness to adopt new solutions to the problems of translating individual passages which makes this version such an act of creativity within the bounds of fidelity to the sacred text. But Lorimer's text is not just a new and independent translation, it is also a translation with a clear sense of where it is heading. Three ideas of Lorimer's inform this sense of direction. Firstly, he believed the New Testament was not written in Standard Greek. Secondly, he considered the different writers of the New Testament had varying styles of Greek. Thirdly, he hoped that a Scots translation of the New Testament could help revitalise the Scots language.

In one of this notebooks Lorimer wrote 'Jesus spakna Standard Aramaic— for ordnar oniegate—but guid ('braid') Galilee, an the New Testament isna written in Standard Greek, as the Kirk Faithers alloued'.[26] The implications of this are quite complex. Insofar as Scots is seen as a non-standard and dialectal form of English such a view obviously gives a special appropriateness to a translation into Scots. But there is another way of seeing this which I suspect might be closer to Lorimer's own. Scots can itself be seen as a standard language, an alternative standard to Standard English but one which follows in many cases the usages of everyday speech. Similarly, New Testament Greek had its own standard, departing from standard literary Greek towards the popular spoken language. In this sense Scots offers the opportunity to use a standard language with a high input from popular speech as the medium for translating another standard language strongly influenced by everyday spoken usage. Furthermore, the Koine of New Testament times was a conglomerate of various Greek dialects built on an Attic base. To parallel this Lorimer has not at any stage adopted a purely local and dialectal Scots, say Southern Scots or North-Eastern Scots, but has built on that ill-defined notion of a Standard Scots, based on Lothian Scots but drawing on other dialects, which we find in Burns and Scott. His language has a basic stock of words shared by the various Scots dialects but also includes words which are or were once current only in parts of Scotland, words like *bourached* (Luke 11:29), *hungrisome* (Matt. 4:2), *nochtifie* (John 8:48) and *toupachin* (Matt. 4:5). At the same time Lorimer recognised that Scots has never in the modern period possessed an absolutely fixed standard and, as we shall see, he allows certain carefully limited variations of spelling and grammar between the twelve different writers responsible for the New Testament.

The recognition of New Testament Greek as non-standard, or at least as not following the most prestigious standard, carries with it another important implication. Standard language tend towards the formal, non-standard towards the informal. What this means for Lorimer is that he can translate the New Testament into informal Scots and thus draw on one of the areas in which Scots has been most vital, the area of colloquial language. What makes Lorimer's work stand out against not only other Scots translations but also contemporary English ones is its colloquial vigour. It is full of lively colloquialisms like *the man said naither 'Eechie' nor 'Ochie'* meaning 'he was utterly silent' (Matt. 22:12) or *ye will flee hereawà thereawà* (John 16:32). Colloquial Scots has always been good at coining terms of a abuse and the vituperative language comes alive in a Lorimer in a way not paralleled in other modern translations. For instance, here is a passage from the Sermon on the Mount as translated in the Good News Bible (which is, by the standards of English version, very colloquial):

> whoever calls his brother 'You good-for-nothing' will be brought before the Council, and whoever calls his brother a worthless fool will be in danger of going to the fire of hell.

The final version in Lorimer is:

> 'Onie-ane at says til his brither, "Ye bee-heidit gowk!" maun thole an assize afore the Council. But I say: 'Onie-ane at says til his brither, "Ye muckle

sumph!'' maun thole an assize afore ane at can duim him til the lowes o hell'
(Matt. 5:22)

but Scots has no shortage of abusive terms and Lorimer had also considered
translating the first insult as *boss-heidit cuif* and the second as *muckle gomeril.*
Likewise the writer's scorn comes through loud and clear here:

> The rackless, wilyart sorras at they ar, thir men arna afeared tae miscaa the
> dwallers in glorie . . . . Gilravitchin in braid daylicht is the tap an wale o pleisur
> for them; an hou they gavaul an gilravitch, whan ye feast thegither, tae the
> skaith o your guid name, the fousome sorras! (2 Pet. 2:10, 13)

The accents of colloquial speech also come through in alliterative pairings of
words like *dule an dridder* (Matt. 26:37), *jamphin an jeerin* (Luke 16:14) and
ruggit an runched (Mark 1:26), in a fondness for diminutives like *grumphie* (2
Pet. 2:22), *lassie* (Luke 8:54) and *laudie* (Luke 15:31), in the use of reduplicated
verbs like *channer-channerin* (Jude 1:16), *jow-jowin* (Matt. 8:24) and *skelloch-
skellochin* (Matt. 15:23), in exclamations like *A-weill* (Luke 20:29), *Deed* (John
9:38), *na, na* (Luke 22:57), *ou, ay* (John 11:24) and *Trowth an atweill* (Luke
18:29) and in the use of intensives like *dooms* in *I am that dule—ay, nicht an
day sae dooms wae-hairtit* (Rom. 9:2).

The Greek of the New Testament is not Standard Greek but it is written
language and thus not the language of totally uneducated people. At the
same time, it does not conform to the usages of the most prestigious literary
models of the time. Hence it is important that Lorimer's language should
never sound too literary. This does not mean that a colloquial style is always
appropriate although it is clear that he felt that it was sometimes the only
appropriate style, as in the verse from Galatians which he translated *Sall, but
I wiss thae din-breeders amang ye may gang on an libb themsels* (5:12). In a note
he quoted an opinion that this verse was the climax of Paul's more than
usually 'vernacular' style in this book (Note 1). Much of the translation, then,
is in a more neutral style of Scots but on the few occasions where it is literary
and formal Lorimer seems to have made it deliberately pompous and affected
as if to show us the original writer is ill at ease with such formality, as in the
opening verses of 2 Peter:

> Symeon Peter, a servan an apostle o Jesus Christ, til them wham the richteous
> providence o our God an Sauviour Jesus Christ hes made our comburgesses i the
> Commonweill o Faith: Grace an saucht be gíen ye afouth throu the knawledge o
> God an Jesus our Lord!

The marks of a very conscious literary language here are the use of the
pompous word *comburgesses* and particularly the use of *wham,* followed up
by the use of *whilk* in the next few verses, since Lorimer's usual practice is to
use only *at* as a relative. Lorimer's note, quoting Moulton's description of the
language of 2 Peter as 'Greek which seems to have been learnt mainly from
books' and 'this artificial language', shows that his choice of this affected

literary style here is quite conscious although he also seems to have thought that the author adopted a more colloquial style later in the epistle.

Another consequence of generally avoiding literary language is that Lorimer does not go in for the kind of literary coinages that Waddell so favoured. Any coinages (and there are very few anyway) must be obvious and straightforward ones such as an ordinary everyday speaker of the language might spontaneously create, terms like *slave-lass* (Gal. 4:22). Nothing so conscious as Waddell's *heal-ha'din* or *kith-gettin* can be accepted. This means that Lorimer must use the Latinate terms Waddell avoided by creating new compounds, terms like *consecrate* (John 17:17), *glorified* (John 14:13), *redemption* (Luke 2:38), *resurrection* (1 Cor. 15:12) and *salvâtion* (Luke 19:9) which make up a large part of traditional biblical diction in Scotland and England. Lorimer, it seems, finds no problem in this; he clearly does not believe they are the 'lang-nebbit dictionar wurds whilk hae mair syllables nor sense' distrusted by the author of 2 Peter (2:18). He presumably recognised that even uneducated speakers can use the educated terms for which they have a need. Moreover, the writers of the New Testament were not entirely uneducated; if not educated to the highest standards of contemporary Greek culture, the writers of the New Testament were at least literate. They could write good, workmanlike Greek, using more formal terms where necessary. Like educated Scottish peasants they could handle the specialised diction of Christianity even when it took them beyond the bounds of colloquial speech. We see this in Scott's novels. Here is Davie Deans in *The Heart of Mid-Lothian*:

> What, sir, wad ye speak to me . . . about a man that has the blood of the saints at his fingers' ends? Didna his eme die and gang to his place wi' the name of the Bluidy Mackenyie? and winna he be kenned by that name sae lang as there's a Scots tongue to speak the word? If the life of the dear bairn that's under a suffering dispensation, and Jeanie's, and my ain, and a' mankind's, depended on my asking sic a slave o' Satan to speak a word for me or them, they should a' gae down the water thegither for Davie Deans (vol 1, ch 11).

Here a basically colloquial speech can accommodate more formal terms like *dispensation*. Consider, by way of comparison, how skillfully Lorimer sets the traditional biblical word *magnify* against the Scots *nochtifie* in *I am magnifíein my Faither, an ye ar nochtifíein me* (John 8:49).

All this about the colloquial element in Lorimer's language having been said, it must be recognised that Lorimer's Scots is itself a literary product, not in the sense of using a specialised literary register like Milton or the Middle Scots aureate makars, but in the sense of being something which is written and which is translating a written text, which has been thought about and worked on, which does not have the absolute spontaneity of speech. However, in creating this literary product, Lorimer has combined the language of written texts with the language of ordinary speech to build a unified new language which has the dignity of written language and the vigour of speech in a way that is reminiscent of Chaucer in his efforts to turn English into a fully functional literary tongue. This can be seen in a passage like the following from Paul:

> We ar fuils for our sairin o Christ, an ye are wysslike members o Christ; we ar
> sillie, and ye are strang; ye ar hauden in honour, an we ar hauden in scorn bi
> the warld. Tae this day we dree hunger an drouth; we haena a hap tae wir
> backs; we get aagate the baff an the blaffart; we hae nae bidin naewey; we
> maun ey be trauchlin awà, wurkin wi our nain haunds tae fend wir needs. We
> meet bannin wi blissin, persecution wi pâtience, ill-speakin wi the couthie wurd.
> We hae been like the dichtins o the yird, the outwale o mankind, an sae ar we
> eenou (1 Cor. 4:10–13).

Here the alliteration of *the baff and the blaffart* belongs to a traditional oral
register while the alliteration of *persecution wi pâtience* comes from literary
models yet both fuse happily together. This ensures that the Latinate diction,
although it has a place, does not dominate. As translated by Lorimer Paul
does indeed seem to 'preach the Gospel o the Cross, an no i the braw langage
o the wyss, at wad tak aa the fusion out o it' (1 Cor. 1:17).

Lorimer's second important point about the language of the New Testament
may be stated in his own words:

> I have deliberately refrained from writing in a uniform 'standard' Scots. On the
> contrary, I have made differences between different writers. In doing so, I have
> made the following units, which are intended to be *internally* consistent.[27]

He then lists these twelve units as Matthew, Mark (except 16. 9–20), Luke–
Acts, John (except 7:53–8: 11; 21), Paul, Pastorals, Hebrews, James, 1 Peter,
2 Peter, Jude and Revelation. The main differences between the units are in
spelling and morphology. In a notebook entitled 'N. T. Scotice: Orthographica
etc' Lorimer offered what is explicitly stated to be 'the final authority' both
on spellings to be used throughout the New Testament and on variations
between the various units. Here we find spelling variants such as *aisie* and
easie, *heicht* and *hicht*, *wame* and *wyme*. Interestingly, both *daith* and *deith* are
listed for use in the Gospel of John but Lorimer has used the variation to
distinguish between the main text (5:24) and the interpolated section by a
different writer (8:5). There are also morphological variants, such as four
possible past participles of *set: set, sutten, setten* and *sotten* and the two
equivalents of the English plural *shoes: shaes* and *shuin*. Altogether Lorimer
lists over one hundred words subject to variant forms in this way. By dividing
the whole corpus in different ways for each word Lorimer produced his set of
twelve slightly varied linguistic units.

Naturally, since Lorimer was using variants actually found in Scots, such
variation may not parallel any variation in the corresponding individual
Greek words. Similarly, he further differentiates his units by some variations
in diction even where the Greek has the same word, as with *michtier* (Matt.
3:11; Mark 1:7) and *stairker* (Luke 3:16). The whole question of these variations would repay further investigation but even at this stage one thing is
clear: Lorimer has not used these variants to produce for any unit a language
which can be wholly associated with a particular modern Scots dialect. Indeed

many of the variations are between forms that have both had widespread use throughout Scotland, like *dreidour* and *dridder, east* and *aist, saul* and *sowl*. What we have overall is a picture of a reasonably but not completely stabilised and standardised language with individual writers either adopting one of two accepted standard alternatives or introducing dialectal variants like the North-Eastern forms *ging, neipour* and *wyme* while generally accepting a standardised spelling. To have adopted a clear regional identity for each of his units would have been quite contrary to any aim of reflecting the Greek text—the New Testament may not be written in Standard Greek but neither is it written in a series of clearly differentiated regional dialects of Greek. The differentiation of the twelve authorial units remains one of the most interesting aspects of Lorimer's endeavours and, as far as I know, is unparalleled in any other Scots or English version.

According to Robin Lorimer

> it was while reading the neutral press in 1916–19 that [Lorimer] had first become keenly interested in the problems encountered by linguistic minorities in reviving or developing their languages. Before the beginning of the Second World War further study had convinced him that, if Scots was ever to be resuscitated and rehabilitated, two great works must first be produced: a good modern Scots dictionary, and a good modern Scots translation of the New Testament (p xiv).

As we have already remarked in discussing Borrowman, Hugh MacDiarmid and others had revived Scots verse but the effort had failed to carry over into prose. According to his son, Lorimer, in undertaking a translation of the New Testament, 'was well aware that . . . he would also be setting out to resuscitate and recreate Scots prose' (p xiv). Although there has been some addition to the vocabulary of Scots in the twentieth century it cannot be denied that its resources have been greatly depleted. However, Lorimer did not feel that he could follow the lead of MacDiarmid who had looked to Middle Scots and his own creations as a way of expanding contemporary Scots diction. It seems likely also that he was unwilling to use an avowedly artificial ('synthetic') Scots to translate the natural, ungarnished Greek of the New Testament. His solution was to confine his diction to words used in the Modern Scots period: in one of this notebooks he wrote that 'Some Older Scots has been used in Old Testament quotations and occasionally elsewhere for special reasons. Otherwise eighteenth and nineteenth century Scots'.[28] Moreover he normally used only words which are found in sources recording actual Scots speech; he eschewed any of the literary creations of writers like Waddell. This was, perhaps, a slowly evolving aspect of his scheme. In an early draft of James he used the word *steidfastness* but on the verso of the previous page recorded the alternative reading *langtholance*.[29] This word was not in normal spoken use but was created by Riddell as a translation of the Authorised Version's *longsuffering* (Ps. 86:15). In the final published text the reading is *pouer to thole aa ills* (Jas. 1:3). Perhaps he was at first willing to use such diction or perhaps it was only later that he realised the word was a literary creation.

Certainly, though not a Scots-speaker himself, he had from childhood an interest in the language of actual Scots-speakers, recording details in a note-book from the age of nine (p xiii). His son tells how Lorimer once noticed his housekeeper using a word that he had not heard before, *forfauchelt* meaning 'exhausted'. Typically he duly recorded it and transmitted it to the *Scottish National Dictionary* and then later used it in his New Testament. He also conned written texts where they were such as to provide evidence of spoken usage: using the word *allouance* meaning 'permission' (John 19:38), he notes that the word occurs in the record of a criminal trial (John, note 11). This is a record of spoken usage and gives him the authority to use it. By allowing himself to range over the whole of Modern Scots Lorimer introduced some terms which are now obsolete in speech but they are often ones that are easily understood in context, words like *foresaits* 'front seats' (Luke 11:43) and *hiremen* 'hired servants' (Luke 5:9). As his own note has already informed us, in translating quotations from the Old Testament he allowed himself a greater freedom and included some Older Scots words. Hence we find occasional words like *vailiet* from the sixteenth century Scots verbs *vail* 'to be worth' used in a passage quoting Zechariah (Matt. 27:9). As well as this, a few of the spelling variants in Lorimer's list are specifically intended to cater for Old Testament quotations: thus, while he usually has the spellings *proclaim* and *receive*, he uses *procleim* (Heb. 2:12) and *resave* (Heb. 12:6) in two such quotations.

Viewed as an example of Modern Scots prose, perhaps the most important aspect of Lorimer's vocabulary is his decision to retain the formal Latinate terms rejected by Waddell and, to a lesser extent, other translators. This ensures that his vocabulary has both an informal and a formal dimension, a basic requisite for a written prose language if it is to have any widespread use. All the same, he was able to give a Scottish character to many words shared with English, without, however, destroying their spelling links with Latin, by using a special form of the letter *a* in words like *revelation* and *ï* or *ÿ* in words like *hypocrite*. In the printed text these appear as *â, í* and *ý* so that we have spellings like *nâtion, salvâtion, mínister, perdítion* and *sýnagogue*. The advantage of an accent is that it merely marks a difference of pronunciation without making that pronunciation seem illiterate in the way that spellings like *naution, meenister* and *seenagogue* tend to do. Nevertheless, he did use a special spelling where an accent was not feasible, for instance in *maument* 'moment' (Luke 2:38). He also made full use of those Scots formal words of Latinate origin which have not just a different pronunciation but also a different form to that of English, words like *dictionar* (2 Pet. 2:18), *exeme* (Matt. 17:26) *exerce* (1 Cor. 9:12) and *glore* (Matt. 24:30) as well as such Scots legal terms as *compear* (Matt. 27:11) and *depone* (Matt. 27:12). On other occasions Scots itself offered him an alternative to these terms shared with English: examples are his use of *duimed* for *condemned* (Matt. 27:3), *forespeaker* for *advocate* (John 14:16) and the more colloquial *tuik the rue* for *repented* (Matt. 27:3).

It will be clear from what has just been said about some of Lorimer's diction that his spelling, too, was of a kind to enhance the status of Scots as a standard literary tongue. Leaving aside the relatively few words which vary in spelling and which perhaps amount to about as many as those distinguishing the two Standard English systems, the British and the American, Lorimer has adopted a consistent orthography. It is very much in the mould of much recent Scots writing which we have already seen reflected in Borrowman. Apostrophe spellings are almost totally absent so that the implication that Scots is merely English mispronounced is avoided. Where it is possible to differentiate the spelling from English but still retain the traditional Scots spelling, this is done; thus *ei, ch* and terminal *ie* are preferred to *ee, gh* and *y* but, where differentiation can only be achieved by adopting English spelling conventions, Lorimer prefers to retain the traditional Scots form; he writes *our* and *out* rather than *oor* and *oot* and *I* rather than *Ah*. Scots is thereby presented as a language with traditions, including a spelling tradition, not merely a spoken dialect written down according to the spelling rules of a standard language.

These efforts to differentiate Scots from English carry through to grammar as well. Only Murray in the modern period equals Lorimer in his determination to preserve distinctively Scots grammar. Most notable is Lorimer's consistent use of the *s* verbal ending, according to the rules discerned by Murray, not only in the third person singular (as in English) but also with plural subjects, either when the pronoun is separated from the verb as in *them at gíes me orders* (Matt. 8:9) and *ye at drees hunger* (Luke 6:21) or when the subject is a plural noun as in *John's disciples is ey fastin an prayin, an the Pharisees' disciples dis the same, but your disciples eats an drinks* (Luke 5:33). The *s* form also follows *thou* as in *thou hes* (John 17:2) although this inflection is rare in Lorimer since he follows the New English Bible practice of only using *thou* in direct address to God. Smith had been inconsistent in these usages as he was also in the handling of past participles ending in *ate* or *ute*. Here, too, Lorimer is absolutely consistent in usage, never adding an inflection: *Him at miscaas faither or mither lat him be execute tae the deid* (Mark 7:10), *What I wad hae waired on your throubeirin is aa dedicate tae God* (Matt. 15:5). Again, like Murray, Lorimer only uses the one relative pronoun, *at*. On the other hand Lorimer does not follow Murray in differentiating in spelling between present participles and verbal nouns/adjectives: both end with *in*. Already, in Murray's time, this was only a feature in Southern Scots and was thus unsuitable for the standard form of Scots that Lorimer was creating even though some modern Scots poets have revived the distinction on historical grounds.

By providing Scots with a consistent spelling and grammar (apart from a few clearly specified exceptions) Lorimer was, in every verse of his translation, asserting the independence of Scots from English. Scots becomes a language in its own right with its own rules, not a dialect subject to the constant intrusion of English grammar rules, as Smith had presented it. If a model is sought for a standard modern Scots, then Lorimer has provided it.

Lorimer stands head and shoulders above all the other translators of the Bible into Scots. Only Nisbet and Smith translated an equally large amount of the Scriptures but both of them set limits on how far they were willing to depart from the English versions on which they based their translations. Only

Lorimer and Waddell worked from the original texts but Lorimer's language never has the quaintness which sometimes detracts from the considerable virtues of Waddell's work. Lorimer shares with Murray a clear understanding of what he means by Scots and his complete consistency in following that understanding through but Lorimer applies it to a much bigger and more demanding text. Like Borrowman and Paterson he adopts a spelling that does not demean Scots but he adds to this spelling a consistent and distinctive Scots grammar, the other ingredient needed to revive Scots as a standard language. With Smith he welcomes the colloquial strengths of Scots but whereas Smith is always losing his nerve and mixing his colloquialisms with other, inappropriate language taken from the Authorised or Revised Versions, Lorimer sustains the colloquial register over lengthy passages. In all these respects Lorimer surpasses his predecessors but what really makes his work so important and successful is his creative ingenuity as a translator, his ability to find new and exciting ways of translating familiar passages, in short his ability to revitalise the text, to give it back its original power as the writings of ordinary people about an extraordinary man. This is not some scoticised reflection of a familiar English text but a genuinely new version with all the ability of a new version to make us see a well-known text in an entirely new light. Iain R Torrance in reviewing Lorimer wrote that it was 'Paul's letters that I most admired. Paul's argument, especially in the modern versions, can seem bloodless and hair-splitting. In Lorimer's version, with his graphic language, we feel again the living passion of a preacher'.[30] In my own experience this renewal of a familiar text applies to the whole of Lorimer's New Testament and is, I believe, its greatest quality.

STUART'S SELECTIONS FROM THE GOSPELS (1985)

Jamie Stuart's *Scots Gospel* is not a complete translation of the New Testament: it is a compilation of the gospel story with parts taken from each of the four evangelists. It is impossible to come to it without some sense of a letdown after the brilliance of Lorimer and it would be unfair to compare the two as equals. All the same Stuart's version has a number of interesting features. In one respect it differs from all the versions considered so far: it was first conceived as an actor's script. Stuart created the work as a piece of theatre and only after it had been presented by him at a number of different venues was it put into print in 1985.

Coming after a period of intense activity in Bible translation, Stuart has made a sensible use of some of the many translations available to him, both those in Scots (especially Smith but also Lorimer) and those in English (the Authorised Version, the New English Bible and possibly the Revised Standard Version). For the first time since the Bonaparte translations of the Song of Solomon we have a translator who is consistently making use of previous translations into Scots and, unlike them, he is also using more than one English version as well. Often he seems to be following Smith closely but always with interesting variations. Some of the similarity is no doubt due to their both using the Authorised Version (or in Smith's case the only slightly different Revised Version) but there can be no doubt for anyone comparing the two versions that Stuart has also made independent use of Smith. Stuart's reliance on Smith can be seen in a verse from the parable of the Prodigal Son where Stuart's translation reads:

> An a wheen o days efter, the young son gaithert aa his gear thegither an gaed awa frae hame til a far-awa laun; an thair he wastit his gear in ryatous livin (p 57).

The first part of this owes a strong debt to Smith:

> And, a wheen days eftir, the young son gaither't a' his gear thegither, and gaed awa frae hame till a far-awa lan', and thar sperfl't his gear in riotousness (Luke 15:13).

In this verse the Authorised Version (which is here closely followed by the Revised Version) reads:

> And not many days after the younger son gathered all together, and took his journey into a far country, and there wasted his substance with riotous living.

It will be seen that in the last part of the verse Stuart has reverted to using the Authorised Version as his source, presumably to avoid the unusual *sperfl't* and the clumsy *riotousness*. So, if Smith has a strong influence here (and elsewhere), Stuart is by no means slavishly following him. Wherever Smith's language is too archaic or formal, due often to its following the Authorised or Revised Version, Stuart adopts a much more colloquial idiom. For instance, where Smith retains their *entreat* (Luke 15:28), Stuart has *speired o him tae come ben* (p 58), and where Smith keeps *devoured your living with harlots* (Luke 15:30) Stuart reads *wastit yer fortune on hures* (p 58). Stuart also adopts distinctively Scots terms where Smith had used English terms or terms shared by English and Scots: *rejoice* (Luke 15:32) becomes *be blythe* (p 58) and *eatin* (Luke 15:16) becomes *gorbelin* (p 57). On the other hand he elsewhere prefers not to use some of Smith's more unusual words: where Smith has *gliff'd* (Luke 2:9, 10) he has *feart* and *frichtit* (p 21), and, rather than use the obsolete Scots *barrie-coat* like Smith (Luke 2:12), or, for that matter, Lorimer's *barrie*, he prefers to retain the Authorised Version's equally obsolete, but more familiar English term, scoticised as *swaddlin claes*. Stuart also retains the Authorised Version reading as *a michty famine in the laun* (p 57), feeling perhaps that its simplicity is appropriate to his own style, although Smith here has the rather effective *an awesome famine oot-throwe yon lan'* (Luke 15:14).

Lorimer's influence is not as continuous as Smith's but nevertheless significant. We often find Stuart adopting a distinctively Scots word from Lorimer where Smith uses a term shared with English or an entirely English term. Rather than Smith's *privately, warned* and *made sport o'* (Matt. 2:7, 12, 16), he adopts Lorimer's *in hidlins, warnisht* and *jouked* (p 23). Elsewhere he adopts Lorimer's word as being clearer in meaning: while Stuart's version of Luke 2:1 follows Smith closely, including the use of the obsolete *inhabiters*, he has replaced Smith's ambiguous *enrolled* with Lorimer's clearer *registrate* which also has the advantage of being distinctively Scots in form.

In other places modern English translations are behind his readings. While in the Sermon on the Mount he retains Smith's *gin the saut has tint its tang* (p 31: Matt. 5:13), he adopts the much clearer New English Bible's translation 'those who know their need of God' (Matt. 5:3), rendered as *thae wha ken thair need o God* (p 31), where Smith had offered *the spirits that are lown and cannie* as a gloss on the Authorised and Revised Versions' *the poor in spirit*. Earlier (p 19) the New English Bibles' colloquial *Who am I, that the mother of my Lord should visit me?* (Luke 1:43) suits Stuart's style better than Smith's rendering of the Authorised and Revised Versions' *whence is this to me that . . . ?* as *for what is this come to me that . . . ?*

Altogether then we might say that Stuart's work represents an intelligent and independent reworking of Smith's version which removes many of Smith's stylistic inconsistencies and creates a translation which is more up-to-date, more Scots and more colloquial. It would be unfair to object to his heavy reliance on Smith. Firstly, Bible translators have again and again over the centuries borrowed extensively from their predecessors. Secondly, Stuart is not primarily concerned with producing a new version but with carrying the Scots Bible into a new sphere, the stage. Finally one could argue he has successfully carried out what Smith aimed at and partly failed to do. One reason for this may be that Stuart's translation is intended for public performance where inappropriately formal language would quickly become apparent, whereas Smith saw his as for use in private study, as he made clear in his note 'To the Reader' in *The Gospel of Matthew in Broad Scotch*. It is also important to remember that the whole idea of a colloquial translation of the Bible was much more foreign in Smith's time than it is now.

Despite Stuart's general success in producing a stylistically consistent translation, he does, like Smith, but not to anything like the same degree, retain some expressions from the Authorised Version which are not appropriate in a context of Scots. Elspeth is said to be *weel stricken in years* (pp 17–18; Luke 1:18) although the same phrase had been nicely scoticised earlier, following Lorimer's example, as *weel up in years* (p 17; Luke 1:7) and the pharisees are described as having *murmered aganis the disciples* (p 28; Luke 5:30). *Murmered* here is an English archaism, or at least very old-fashioned, when used to mean what the New English Bible translates as *complained*. (The Scots idiom, latterly a legal usage, omits *against*). Stuart is unwilling here to use the relatively uncommon *yammer* or *channer* used by Smith and Lorimer. Also, by following Smith in using *wha*, he introduces what the *Concise Scots Dictionary* calls 'literary or formal anglicized usage' into an otherwise colloquial style. These are, however, minor departures from consistency of style; there is nothing like the degree of variation in style found in Smith.

Stuart's distinctively Scots vocabulary is perhaps somewhat less than Smith's and certainly less than Lorimer's. This is understandable in a version intended to be understood in live performance. While occasionally Stuart uses a Scots term which is used by neither Smith nor Lorimer in that context, like *gorbelin* (p 57; Luke 15:16), it is more common for him to use a term from the stock of words shared with English where Smith or Lorimer had made use of a purely Scots term. Compare, for instance, his *Let us no be testit* (p 33) with Lorimer's *sey-us-na sairlie* (Matt. 6:13). This no doubt says something about the decline in the use of purely Scots diction in this century. The diction Stuart does use is traditional; he makes no attempt to bring in twentieth century innovations in Scots vocabulary such as we find in many representations of Glasgow speech. He thus makes no use of a potential source of new diction which can partially offset the dying out of traditional terms. This may seem to contradict my earlier assertion that Stuart is more Scots than Smith. The point, however, is that Stuart, while making use of a smaller stock of distinctively Scots vocabulary than Smith, has at the same time used it more consistently and has more thoroughly avoided retaining English archaisms and English grammatical features from the Authorised Version (apart from the use of *wha*). In a 'Publisher's Note', prefixed to Stuart's translation, his language is described as 'a colloquial and modern Scots, but one rooted in the traditions of the past' (p 10). What this means in practice is that it is colloquial in style (though not as vividly colloquial as Lorimer) and modern in the sense of avoiding thoroughly obsolete terms but not in the sense of using recent innovations. Stuart's Scots is of a kind familiar to readers of eighteenth and nineteenth century Scots literature but with a diminished amount of distinctively Scots diction and grammar. It is clear, then, that his aim is not, like Lorimer's, to extend the lexical resources available for written Scots by reviving obsolete words and retaining obsolescent ones. The decline in familiarity with the traditional resources of Scots may also explain Stuart's occasional mistakes in usage, as in a phrase already mentioned, *speired o him tae come ben* (p 58), and in *Why gar ye aa this ado?* (p 47) and *mak redd the Passower supper* (p 68). In traditional Scots usage *speir* is not usually used of asking someone to do something, *gar* can only mean 'make' in the sense of 'cause to' and *redd* does not mean 'ready'. These seem to be unsuccessful attempts to improve on Lorimer's *priggit him tae come ben* (Luke 15:28), Smith's *Hoo mak ye a' this ado* (Mark 5:39) and Smith's *mak ready* or Lorimer's *mak reddie* (Luke 22:8). These may seem quibbling points but they are interesting indications of the encroaching influence of English. *Speir* and *gar* are extended to uses which are appropriate to their English counterparts, *ask* and *make*, but not to the Scots terms themselves while the choice of *gar* and *redd*, rather than *mak* and *reddie* which are shared with English, betrays a feeling that Scots must always differ from English to be truly Scots. Historically this is not the case but as soon as the identity of the Scots language becomes insecure this idea creeps in.

As regards spelling, Stuart follows Lorimer in avoiding apostrophes and in spelling both the participle and the verbal noun and adjective with *in*, but a desire to indicate what is generally seen as the most characteristically Scots vowel pronunciation prevails over historical considerations in his spelling of words like *noo* and *aboot*. While, therefore, his spelling is not as determinedly

Scots in heritage as Lorimer's, he avoids the implication of dialect status inherent both in Smith's use of the apostrophe and in his inconsistent reversion to English spellings for words he elsewhere spells in a Scots fashion. On the other hand, avoidance of dialect status is presumably not a particular concern of Stuart's since he is not trying to establish any standard of written Scots, unlike both Smith and Lorimer.

Stuart's grammar lacks a number of features found in Smith and Lorimer. While making consistent use of *na, ye* and the enclitic negative (except in addressing God) he has no cases of the use of *s* inflections with plural or first and second person singular subjects: for example where Smith has *Hoo's I to ken this* (Luke 1:18) Stuart reads *Hoo sall I ken this* (p 17). He also avoids the traditional future auxiliary, spelt *'se* by Smith and *s'* by Lorimer and uses *thae* but not *thir*. Like Smith he is inconsistent in his use of the *ate* ending in past participles: borrowing *registrate* (p 20) from Lorimer (Luke 2:1), he retains the uninflected form but, when he takes *incarcerate* from the same source (Mark 1:14), he inflects it as *incarceratit* (p 26).

With personal names Stuart follows Lorimer's more extensive scoticisation but, while he uses *Loch o Tiberias* (p 85), he omits some of the verses which contain the other place names for which Lorimer had found Scottish forms.

Overall, then, Stuart's language is Scots of a traditional kind but shows a weakening of the distinctively Scots elements of vocabulary and grammar such as we would expect in the latter half of this century except with a writer, like Lorimer, willing to treat all diction used in the past three centuries of Scots as potentially available for use or with a writer determined to use contemporary urban Scots. But this is to look at this work negatively. Not in the same class as Lorimer (but who is?), Stuart is still worthy of coming at the end of this story. His actor's text has become an attractive book offering the main events of the Gospels in a readable and lively Scots. He is indebted to those who came before him but has generally improved on his main source, Smith, and has borrowed sensibly from his other sources as well as adding elements of his own. For the ordinary reader he has provided an accessible and interesting text.

CONCLUSION

The story of the Scots translations from the Bible records some considerable achievements. Whether out of a religious conviction of the importance of providing a vernacular Bible or out of a secular interest in the Scots language or a combination of both, a number of writers have been led to undertake a very large volume of translation. Just as Scotland, whether independent or united with its southern neighbour, has always had to define itself against the greater power and prestige of England, so in this specific field the prestige of English translations cast its shadow over Scots versions. Both Nisbet and the earlier modern translators escaped only partly from this shadow, but the reasons for this in each case are quite different. Nisbet seems to have a clear sense of the identity of Scots and thus knows where he is heading: he is changing the spelling and grammar of an English translation according to clear and consistent rules and he is altering the vocabulary where necessary. His sense of the identity of Scots includes an acceptance that it shares a great deal with English—after all he probably called his own speech 'Inglis'. He feels no reluctance to use this shared language. The later translators live in an age when the identity of Scots is much more questionable. Its spelling is unfixed, its grammar subject to constant modification towards English rules and its distinctive vocabulary is seen as the preserve of peasants and is furthermore expected shortly to die out. The first modern translators react to this by sticking close to the Authorised Version. Unsure of the identity of the Scots towards which they are trying to head and accustomed to English as their religious language they venture only a short distance from the familiar text. Next comes Waddell. Determined to reassert the identity and sep-arateness of Scots, he over-reacts to its insecure identity and rejects a great deal that Scots has long and properly had in common with English. Eventu-ally, as some common notion of Scots spelling begins to re-emerge and after the identity of literary Scots has been reasserted and demonstrated in verse, later writers, especially Lorimer, seem to arrive at a firmer sense of the identity of Scots by recognising and accepting its links with English, like Nisbet had done, but asserting its differences in vocabulary, grammar and spelling.

The modern translators had another problem. Two centuries of dominance by the Authorised Version had established its style as the norm. This style was neutral in register rather than being strongly colloquial or strongly formal although it included many formal words. Looking around them the translators found contemporary Scots defined as a basically colloquial tongue. If they were to take full advantage of the strengths of Scots, which means its colloquial strengths, they would have to adopt a more colloquial register than that in the Authorised Version. This again was a difficult adjustment to make. Interestingly, Robson, one of the earliest modern translators, moved further in this direction than some later writers. Smith accepted the ideas but failed to carry it out in practice. Again it is Lorimer who seems to have finally accepted and carried through this shift to a more colloquial register.

Lastly, the Authorised Version's style included a strong element of archaic language. Modern Scots has no comparable tradition of archaism and this was perhaps the easiest feature of the Authorised Version's style to abandon. Nevertheless Riddell tried, at first, to retain some of the archaism by using the *ith* inflection and subsequent writers introduced occasional archaisms of diction. It was left to Lorimer to set a firm limit on this, to accept archaisms from Modern Scots but not from earlier.

Despite these difficulties in establishing a suitable register of Scots, these various translators have produced some notable work. Murray is the maver-ick, the only writer dedicated to a purely linguistic purpose and the only one to use his translation to present a specific, living, spoken dialect of Scots. Of the others, if Lorimer dominates by his sheer creative brilliance, Smith's version has many admirable passages. Even Lorimer does not outdo Waddell in the energy and urgency of his language. Cameron presents Genesis as a stirring narrative, Paterson makes Proverbs sound truly like proverbs,

Borrowman brings out the tenderness of the Book of Ruth and Stuart turns the gospels into a dramatic actor's script in familiar, easy to follow Scots. In short, amongst these translations there is much that does justice to the striking power and poetry of the original Greek and Hebrew texts.

NOTES

1   Throughout this introductory history references are to the editions cited in the bibliography with the exception of the cases described in note 2. Texts are quoted as they appear in the latest editions or impressions cited in the bibliography but they have been standardised to the extent that certain obsolete characters have been replaced by their modern equivalents, prose texts have been printed in paragraphs, verse numbers are omitted where they occur in the original texts and italicising of words not found in the original Hebrew or Greek texts has been removed.

2   John Hamilton's *Facile Traictise*, Archbishop Hamilton's Catechism and the works of Quintin Kennedy are cited from the notes to the STS edition of Nisbet which, in some cases, provides the only modern reprinting of the passages in the original text.

3   On this question see Ronald A Knox, *On Englishing the Bible* (London, 1949), p 21.

4   'Language Choice in the Reformation: The Scots Confession of 1560', in J Derrick McClure, ed, *Scotland and the Lowland Tongue* (Aberdeen, 1983), pp 59–78.

5   *The Letters of Sir Walter Scott*, H J C Grierson, ed (London, 1932–7), vii 83.

6   'Three Scottish Poems, with a Previous Dissertation on the Scoto-Saxon Dialect', *Transactions of the Society of Antiquaries of Scotland*, 1 (1792), 403.

7   For a discussion of the role of Scots in the early nineteenth century see Graham Tulloch, *The Language of Walter Scott: A Study of his Scottish and Period Language* (London, 1980), chs 5 and 8. For an examination of its subsequent role see Emma Letley's excellent study *From Galt to Douglas Brown: Nineteenth Century Fiction and Scots Language* (Edinburgh, 1988).

8   *A Catalogue of the Publications ... of the Late Prince Louis-Lucien Bonaparte* (Paris, 1902), p vi.

9   See the 'Memoir' by James Brydon prefixed to Riddell's *Poetical Works* (Glasgow, 1871), p lxvi.

10   The 'Notice to the General Reader' appears at the end of the volume and is separately numbered.

11   Alternatively Waddell may have been thinking of the Old English and Old Saxon *torn* and/or the Dutch *toorn*.

12   See the glossary to P H Waddell's *The Psalms in Scots* (Aberdeen, 1987).

13   Quoted from K M Elisabeth Murray, *Caught in the Web of Words: James Murray and the Oxford English Dictionary* (New Haven and London, 1977), p 51.

14   ibid.

15   ibid., p 80.

16   ibid., p 81.

17   For ease of comparison I have changed Murray's palæotype into conventional Scots spelling in the last two examples.

18   As the *Scottish National Dictionary* notes, *wean* originated in West Central Scots; it has now spread to East Central Scots but remains unusual in Southern and Northern Scots.

19   For a comparison of the work of Smith and Lorimer see my article 'The Language

of Two Scots Versions of the New Testament', in T L Burton and Jill Burton (eds) *Lexicographical and Linguistic Studies* (Cambridge, 1988), pp 91–102.

20   Quoted in James Veitch, *George Douglas Brown* (London, 1952), p 86.

21   See *Selections from the Published Writings of the Rev Dr Peter Hately Waddell* (Edinburgh, 1892), pp 300–46.

22   This quotation and that from the *United Free Church Record* on p 64 are cited from an advertisement in *Genesis in Scots* (p 173).

23   *Minstrelsy of the Scottish Border* (London, 1931), pp 278–9.

24   The introduction to *The New Testament in Scots* provides a good deal of information about the progress of Lorimer's work on his translation and the stage he had reached before his death and also about the considerable editorial effort required by his son to prepare it for publication.

25   See the notes to Mark 14:12.

26   The manuscripts of Lorimer's translation and various notebooks are deposited in the National Library of Scotland (Acc. 9052). This comment appears on the inside front cover of a notebook dated 'ii/1959' and beginning with a translation of Heb. 11:32–8. In this and other quotations from his notebooks I have expanded Lorimer's abbreviations. The various notebooks are not systematically numbered.

27   From a notebook entitled 'N. T. in Scots: Notes on Orthography & Pronunciation, etc.'.

28   Inside front cover of the notebook dated 'ii/1959' and beginning with a translation of Heb. 11:32–8.

29   In a notebook of first drafts beginning with the Epistle of James.

30   *Journal of Scottish Theology*, 37 (1984), 399.

NOTE ON THE TEXTS

This anthology of texts is intended to fulfil two purposes. Firstly, it illustrates the work of the various translators and secondly it provides a choice of Biblical texts for the reader interested in reading well-known parts of the Bible in Scots. I have tried therefore to choose passages which are sufficiently long to give an accurate impression of the translator's style and are also significant in their content. Where more than one translator has translated a particular book of the Bible I have also provided a number of translations of the same short passage to allow for a comparison. For the most part the texts are drawn only from translations of whole books of the Bible but there are two exceptions to this. Where a translator has translated a whole book and also translated isolated passages from other books I have made use of these extra passages and, for the sake of providing a comparison with the work of Nisbet, I have included a few short texts chosen from sixteenth century authors who cited passages from the Bible in their writings. The texts are printed as they stand in the latest impressions or editions cited in the bibliography but two minor changes have been made to achieve some uniformity of presentation while retaining the original translator's layout: verse numbers have been removed where they were included by the translator and obsolete letters have been replaced by their modern equivalents. The handling of quotation marks has also been standardised. James Murray uses the conventional alphabet to produce a phonetic transcript but it would be impossible to explain his system within the confines of this work; those who are interested should consult Murray's *Dialect of the Southern Counties of Scotland*. Similarly, the phonetic significance of Lorimer's careful spelling is explained in an Appendix to his text which is too lengthy to reproduce here. Words printed inside double square brackets in Lorimer's text were stigmatised in the translator's manuscript. It should be noted that in many texts italics are used to indicate a word with no direct equivalent in the original Greek or Hebrew but in Lorimer's text italics indicate an Old Testament quotation. Any marginal notes or footnotes by the translator have been omitted but where the translator supplies a descriptive heading to a passage this has been retained.

I have provided glosses of all except very common Scots words. In each case I have tried to discover the intended meaning of the translator which may not be the same as the meaning or meanings of the word when used by other writers. In doing this the *Scottish National Dictionary*, *Dictionary of the Older Scottish Tongue* and *Concise Scots Dictionary* have been invaluable but I have also fruitfully consulted Jamieson's *Etymological Dictionary of the Scottish Language* since this is the principal Scots dictionary that many modern Scots translators had access to. Some translators also provided glossaries or notes. Where I have cited longer notes by the translators themselves I have identified this by including the translator's initial after the note.

91

Selected Texts

GENESIS 1 (CAMERON)

The Schuppin o' the Warl

I'the ingang God schuppit the hevin and the erd. And the erd wes wust and vide; and the mirk happit the face o' the depe: and the Gheist o' God steerit apo' the face o' the watirs.

And quo' God, Lat thar be licht: and licht wes. And God saw the licht, that it wes guid: and God sinder't the licht frae the mirk. And God ca'd the licht Day, and the mirk He ca'd Nicht. And thar wes e'enin and thar wes mornin, ae day.

And quo' God, Lat thar be a lift i' the mids o' the watirs, and lat it sinder the watirs frae the watirs. And God schuppit the lift, and sinder't the watirs whilk war aneath the lift frae the watirs whilk war abune the lift: and it wes sae. And God ca'd the lift Hevin. And thar wes e'enin and thar wes mornin, a saicond day.

And quo' God, Lat the watirs ablow the hevin be gaither't thegither ontill ae bit, and lat the histie lan kythe: and it wes sae. And God ca'd the histie lan Erd: and the gaitherin thegither o' the watirs ca'd He Seas: and God saw that it wes guid. And quo' God, Lat the erd fesh furth gerss, yirb giean seid, and frute tree giean frute eftir its kin', whaurin is the seid o't, apo' the erd: and it wes sae. And the erd fotch furth gerss, yirb giean seid eftir its kin', and tree giean frute, whaurin is the seid o't, eftir its kin': and God saw that it wes guid. And thar wes e'enin and thar wes mornin, a thrid day.

And quo' God, Lat thar be lichts i' the lift o' the hevin till sinder the day frae the nicht; and lat thame be for witters and for saizzons and for days and yeir: and lat thame be for lichts i' the lift o' the hevin to gie licht apo' the erd: and it wes sae. And God made the twa muckle lichts, the muckler licht to rewl the day, and the wee'r licht to rewl the nicht: He made the starns als. And God set thame i' the lift o' the hevin till gie licht apo' the erd and till rewl owre the day and owre the nicht, and till sinder the licht frae the mirk: and God saw that it wes guid. And thar wes e'enin and thar wes mornin, a fowrt day.

And quo' God, Lat the watirs fesh furth rowthily the steerin craitur whilk haes life, and lat birds flee abune the erd i' the apen lift o' hevin. And God schuppit muckle whaals, and ilka leevin craitur that steers, whilk the watirs brang furth rowthily, eftir thair kin's, and ilka weengit bird eftir its kin': and God saw that it wes guid. And God sained thame, sayan, Be frutefu' and multiplie, and full the watirs i' the seas, and lat birds multiplie i' the erd. And thar was e'enin and thar wes mornin, a fyft day.

And quo' God, Lat the erd fesh furth the leevin craitur eftir its kin', nowte, and crowlin thing, and beiss o' the erd eftir its kin': and it wes sae. And God made the beiss eftir its kin', and the nowte eftir thair kin', and a'thing that crowls apo' the grun eftir its kin': and God saw that it wes guid. And quo' God, Lat us schupe man in oor maik, eftir oor seim: and lat thame hae gree owre the fysche o' the sea and owre the birds o' the lift, and owre the nowte, and owre a' the erd, and owre ilka crowlin haet whilk crowls apo' the erd. And God schuppit man in His ain maik, i' the maik o' God schuppit He him; lad and lass-bairn schuppit He thame. And God sained thame: and quo' God till thame, Be frutefu', and multiplie, and refull the erd, and cuddem it; and bear the gree owre the fysche o' the sea, and owre the birds o' the lift, and owre ilka leevin haet whilk steers apo' the erd. And quo' God, Behauld, I hiv gien ye ilka yirb giean seid, whilk is apo' the face o' a' the erd, and ilka tree, i' the whilk is the frute o' a tree giean seid; till yo it sal be for meit: and till ilka beiss o' the erd, and till ilka bird o' the lift, and till ilk haet that crowls apo' the erd, whaurin thar is life, I hiv gien ilka grene yirb for meit: and it wes sae. And God saw ilk haet that He haed made, and, lo, it wes vera guid. And thar wes e'enin and thar wes mornin, the saxt day.

ingang beginning   *schuppit* created   *wust* waste   *vide* empty   *mirk* darkness   *happit* covered
steerit stirred, moved   *lift* sky   *histie* dry   *kythe* appear   *yirb* herb   *witters* signs, tokens
rowthily abundantly   *nowte* cattle   *maik* image   *seim* likeness   *hael* thing   *cuddem* subdue
bear the gree have power

GENESIS 3:8–15 (BORROWMAN)

And they hard the voce o the Lord God, daunerin in the yaird in the lown time o the day, and Adam and his guidwife coorit doon amang the trees in the yaird, awa frae the sicht o God.

And the Lord God caad tae Adam, and said tae him, 'Whaur are ye?' Quo he, 'Ah heard yer voce in the yaird and Ah was feart for Ah was scuddy-nakit, sae Ah coorit awa'.

Quo He. 'Wha telt ye ye were scuddy-nakit? Hae ye prieit the tree whilk Ah telt ye no tae prie?'

Quo the man, 'The wumman ye gied tae be wi me, she gied me o the tree, and Ah hae etten'.

And the Lord God said tae the wumman. 'What hae ye dune?' Quo the wumman, 'The edder begowkit me and Ah hae etten'.

And the Lord God said tae the edder, 'Sin ye hae sae dune, Ah ban ye abune aa nowt, and abune aa beass o the rig; on yer wame sall ye gang and stour sall be yer vittle aa the days o yer life.

And Ah sall hae ill-wull pitten atween ye and the wumman, and atween yer cleckin and her weans: the weans sall ding yer heid, and ye sall brize their fit'.

daunerin strolling   *yaird* garden   *lown* calm   *coorit* cowered   *scuddy-nakit* naked   *prieit* tasted
begowkit tricked   *ban* curse   *nowt* cattle   *rig* 'used here for field' (B.)   *wame* belly   *stour* dust
cleckin brood   *ding* beat   *brize* bruise

GENESIS 3:8–15 (CAMERON)

And thay hard the vice o' the Lord God waukin i' the garth i' the cule o' the day: and Edie and his gudewife hade thairsels frae the sicht o' the Lord God mangs the trees o' the garth. And the Lord God ca'd ontill Edie, and quo' He till him, Whaur bestoo? And quo' he, I hard yer vice i' the garth, and I wes afeart, acause I wes nakit; and I scuggit mysel. And quo' He, Wha tauld ye that ye war nakit? Hae ye pree'd the tree, o' the whilk I tairge't ye that ye sudna eit? And quo Edie, The wumman wham ye gied to be wi' me, scho gae me o' the tree, and I eitit. And quo' the Lord God ontill the wumman, What is this whilk ye hiv dune? And quo' the wumman, The serpent begunkit me, and I eitit. And quo' the Lord God ontill the serpent, Acause ye hae dune this, banned are ye aboon a' nowte, and aboon ilka beiss o' the fiel; agrufe sal ye gang, and stoor sal ye eit a' the days o' yer life: and I'll pit feidom atween ye and the wumman, and atween yer seid and hir seid: it sal birze yer heid, and ye sal birze his heill.

garth garden   *bestoo* are you   *scuggit* hid   *pree'd* tasted   *tairge't* commanded   *begunkit*
fooled   *banned* cursed   *nowte* cattle   *agrufe* on your belly   *stoor* dust   *feidom* enmity   *birze*
bruise

GENESIS 22:1–19 (CAMERON)

Sacrifeece o' Izaak

And it cam aboot eftir thir things that God pruved Abraham, and said ontill him, Abraham; and quo' he, Heir am I. And quo' He, Tak noo yer son, yer ae son, wham ye loe, e'en Izaak, and gang intill the lan o' Moriah; and offer him thare for a brunt offran apon ane o' the heichts whilk I'll tell ye o'. And Abraham rase air morrow, and said l't his eizel, and tuik twa o' his callans, wi'm, and Izaak his son; and he chappit the wud for the brunt offran, and rase, and gaed intill the bit o' whilk God haed tell't him. O' the thrid day Abraham heized his een, and saw the bit a lang wey aff. And quo' Abraham ontill his callans, Stey ye heir wi' the eizel, and I and the bairn 'll gang yonner; and we'll wirschip, and come bak t' ye. And Abraham tuik the wud o' the brunt offran, and pat it apon Izaak his son; and he tuik in his haun the lowe and the whittle; and they fure baith o' thame thegither. And Izaak spak ontill Abraham his faither, and said, Faither: and quo' he, Heir am I, my bairn. And quo' he, Behauld, the lowe and the wud: bot whaur is the lam for a brunt offran? And quo' Abraham, God'll fend hissel a lam for a brunt offran, my bairn: sae thay yeid baith o' thame thegither. And thay cam to the bit whilk God tell't him o'; and Abraham biggit a cromlech thare, and saw till the wud, and bun Izaak his son, and streekit him o' the cromlech apo' the wud. And Abraham rax't forrit his haun, and tuik the whittle till slachter his son. And the eeran-rinner o' the Lord ca'd till 'm oot o' hevin, and said, Abraham, Abraham: and quo' he, Heir am I. And quo' He, Pit-na yer haun apo' the bairn, nouther dae ocht ontill him: for noo I ken that ye dreddour God, sin ye hivna wi'hauden yer son, yer ae son, frae Me. And Abraham liftit up his een, and luikit, and lo, ahint him a toop cotchan in a buss be his horns: and Abraham gaed and tuik the toop, and offer't him up for a brunt offran insteid o' his son. And Abraham ca'd the name o' that bit 'Jehovah-jireh': as it is said till enoo, I' the munt o' the Lord it sal be 'fendit.' And the eeran-rinner o' the Lord ca'd ontill Abraham a saicond time oot o' hevin, and said, Be Mysel hiv I swurn, quo' the Lord, sith ye hae dune this thing, and hivna wi'hauden yer son, yer ae son: that in sainin I wull sain ye, and in multipliean I wull multiplie yer ootcome as the starns o' the hevin, and as the saun whilk is apo' the rive; and yer ootcome sal bruik the yett o' his faes; and i' yer ootcome sal a' the natiouns o' the erd be sained; sith ye hiv obtemperit My voce. Sae Abraham gaed back to his callans, and thay rase up and fure thegither to Beer-sheba; and Abraham dwalt at Beer-sheba.

pruved tested   *air morrow* early on the next day   *eizel* ass   *callans* young men   *bit* place
heized raised   *lowe* fire   *whittle* knife   *fure* went   *fend* provide   *yeid* went   *biggit* built
cromlech altar   *streekit* stretched   *rax't* reached   *dreddour* fear   *toop* ram   *cotchan* caught
sainin blessing   *ootcome* descendants

Genesis 27:6–36 (Cameron)

Jakob Blythe-bidden

And it cam aboot, that whan Izaak wes auld, and his een war bleer't, sae that he cudna see, he ca'd Esau his auld son, and said to him, My son: and quo' he till him, Heir am I. And quo' he, Behauld noo, I'se auld, I kenna the day o' my dede. Noo tharfor tak, prethy, yer wappins, yer dorlach and yer bow, and gang oot to the fiel, and tak me venysoun; and mak me smewy meit, sic as I loe, and fesh it to me, that I mot eit; that my saul mot sain ye or I dee.

And Rebekah hard whan Izaak spak till Esau his son. And Esau gaed to the fiel till stauk for venysoun, and till fesh it. And Rebekah spak ontill Jakob hir son, sayan; Behauld, I hard yer faither speik ontill Esau yer brither, sayan, Fesh me venysoun, and mak me smewy meit, that I mot eit, and sain ye fornent the Lord afore my dede. Noo tharfor, my son, obtemper my vice conform to that whilk I commaun ye. Gae noo to the hirsle, and fesh me tharfra twa guid kids o' the gaits; and I'll mak thame smewy meit for yer faither, sic as he loes: and ye'se fesh it to yer faither, that he mot eit, sae that he mot sain ye afore his dede. And quo' Jakob till Rebekah his mither, Lo, Esau my brither is boozy, and I'se smeeth. Aiblins my faither'll fin' me, and I'se kythe till him as a swick; and I'se fesh a winze apon me and no a blessin. And quo' his mither till him, Apon me be yer winze, my son: onlie obtemper my vice, and gae fesh me thame. And he fure, and fush, and brang thame till his mither: and his mither made smewy meit sic as his faither loed. And Rebekah tuik the braw cleedin o' Esau hir auld son, whilk wes wi' hir i' the hoose, and pat thame apon Jakob hir young son: and sche pat the skins o' the kids o' the gaits apon his hauns, and apon the smeeth pairt o' his hals: and sche gied the smewy meit and the breid, which she haed preparit, intill the haun o' hir son Jakob.

And he cam till his faither, and said, My faither: and quo' he, Heir am I: wha are ye, my son? And quo' Jakob till his faither, I'se Esau yer ferstborn; I hiv dune conform to yer bidden: up, prethy, sit and eit o' my venysoun, that yer saul mot sain me. And quo' Izaak till his son, Hoo is't that ye hiv fun it sae radly, my son? And quo' he, Acause the Lord yer God brocht it till me. And quo' Isaak till Jakob, Come nar, prethy, that I mot fin' ye, my son, whither ye be my son Esau hissel or no. And Jakob gaed nar till Izaak his faither; and he fan him, and said. The vice is Jakob's vice, bot the hauns are the hauns o' Esau. And he tartl't him nane, sin his hauns war boozy, as his brither Esau's hauns: sae he sained him. And quo' he, Are ye akwally my son Esau? And quo' he, I am. And quo' he, Fesh it nar t'me, and I'se eit o' my son's venysoun, that my saul mot sain yo. And he fotch it nar till him, and he eitit: and he fotch him wyne, and he drank.

And his faither Izaak said ontill him, Come nar noo, and smoorich me, my son. And he cam nar and smoorich't him: and he felt the smell o' his claes, and sained him, and said:

See, the saur o' my son
  Is as the saur o' a fiel whilk the Lord has sained:
And God gie ye o' the techrys o' hevin,
And o' the mergh o' the erd,
  And rowth o' corn and wyne:

Lat peopils ser' ye,
  And natiouns boo doon t'ye:
Be laird owre yer brether,
  And lat yer mither's sons coorie t'ye:
Ban't be ilk ane that bans ye,
  And sained be ilk ane that sains ye.

And it cam aboot, as sune's Izaak haed fineist sainin Jakob, and Jakob was yit hardlies gane oot frae the praisence o' Izaak his faither, that Esau his brither cam in frae his staukin. And he als made smewy meat, and brocht it till his faither; and quo' he till his faither, Lat my faither get up, and eit o' his son's venysoun, that yer saul mot sain me. And quo' Izaak his faither till him, Wha are ye? And quo' he, I'se yer son, yer ferstborn, Esau. And Izaak trimml't uncolies, and said, Wha syne is he that haes taen venysoun, and fotchan it t'me, and I hiv etten o' a' or ye cam, and hiv sained him? aye, and he sal be sained. Whan Esau hard the wirds o' his faither, he loot an unco lood and waesum scraigh, and said to his faither, Sain me, e'en me als, O my faither. And quo' he, Is he no richtlie ca'd 'Jakob'? for he haes 'twiddl't' me thir twa times: he tuik awa my burthricht; and, lo, noo he haes taen awa my blythe-bidden.

smewy savoury   mot may   sain bless   fornent before   dede death   obtemper obey
boozy hairy   smeeth smooth-skinned   kythe appear   swick cheat   winze curse
fure went   cleedin clothes   auld elder   hals neck   radly quickly   fin' feel   tartl't recognised
smoorich kiss   saur smell   techrys dew   mergh fatness   rowth plenty   coorie bow down
ban't cursed   hardlies scarcely   syne then   twiddl't cheated   blythe-bidden blessing

GENESIS 27:6–14 (NISBET)

Rebecca said to hir sonn Jacob, I herd thi fader spekand with Esau thi bruther, and sayand to him, Bring thou to me of thi hunting, and mak thou metis that I ete, and that I blesse thee befoir the Lord, befoir that I dee. Now, tharfor, my sonn, assent to my consalis, And ga to the flock and bring to me the ij best kiddis, that I mak metis of tha to thi fader, quhilk he etis glaidlie; And that quhen thou has broucht in tha metis, and that he has etin, he blesse thee befoire that he dee. To quham Jacob ansuerd, Thou knawis that Esau my bruther is ane hairy man, alsa I am smothe. Gif my fader tuiches and felis me, I drede or perauentur he gesse that I wald scorn him, and or he bring in cursing on me for blessing. To quham the moder said, My sonn, this cursing be in me: aanly here thou my voce, and ga and bring that that I said.

yede went

Ruth 1:8–17 (Borrowman)

Than Naomi spak tae her two guid-dochters. 'Gang back, baith o ye tae yer mithers' hames. The Lord keep troth wi ye as ye hae keepit troth wi the deed and wi me: Ah howp He gies ye, ilk ane, a guid doonsettin in the hame o anither guid man'.

She kissit them and they grat sair.

Than said they tae her, 'We sall gang wi ye tae yer ain fowk'. But Naomi said, 'Gang hame, lasses, gang hame. Fou suld ye gang wi me? Amna Ah owre auld tae hae onie mair sons? Gang hame, lasses, gang hame. Ah'm owre auld tae merry a saicond time. Gif Ah were tae ligg in jizzen and hae sons wald ye bide till they were men-bodies? It waldna be wyce gif ye were tae nay-say anither merridge. Na, na, lasses. Ah hae a wersher weird than ye tae dree, for the Lord has been agin me'.

Than Orpah kissit her guidmither and airtit awa hame tae her ain fowk, but Ruth bidit wi Naomi.

'Atweel' quo Naomi, 'yer guidsister has gaen awa hame tae her ain fowk and her gods, gang ye wi her.'

'Dinna yoke on me tae gang and lat ye bide yer leelane' Ruth said. 'Whaur ye gang Ah sall gang and whaur ye bide Ah sall bide. Yer kin sall be ma kin, and yer God sall be ma God. Whaur ye dee Ah sall dee and thair sall Ah be yirdit. Ah tak ma aith afore the Lord yer God naething but daith sall gar us twine'.

---

guid-dochters daughters-in-law   *doonsettin* settlement   *grat* wept   *fou* why   *ligg* lie
jizzen childbed   *wersher* bitterer   *weird* fate   *dree* endure   *airtit* went   *guid sister* sister-in-law
yoke on assail   *yer leelane* on your own   *yirdit* buried   *twine* separate

Ruth 1:8–17 (Murray)

Thàn quo' Naaomi tui hyr tweae guid-dowchters, 'Gàng away! geae bàk ylk eäne o'ye tui (y)eir ayn muther's hooss! the Loard bey guid tui-ye, ǎz (y)ee've bein guid tui mey, an' tui thaim ǎt's geane. The Loard grànt ǎt (y)e mæ fynd ræst, ylkin o'ye ĭ (y)eir ayn hooss, wui a màn ŏ (y)eir ayn!' Thàn schui kysst them, an' thay beguid a-greitein lood an' sayr. An' thay said tyll'er 'Æh but! wey'll gàng heame wui yuw, tui (y)eir ayn fuok. But Naaomi said, 'Turn agean, ma dowchters! quhat wàd-ye gàng wui mey for? Ym aa gaand-a-hæ onie meae bairns tui bey mæn for-(y)e? Turn bàk, ma dowchters, gàng yeir ways, for aa'm ower aald tui hæ a màn. Yf aa wǎs tui say, Aa've huöpe, æy, an' yf aa'd a màn thys værra neycht, an' wǎs tui hæ bairns ǎs weil, wàd-(y)e wait òn-them quhyl thay greuw up, wàd-(y)e staye fræ hæin' mæn for thaim?

Naa! naa! ma dowchters, for aa 'm sayr væxt for yuwr seakes ăt the haand
ŏ the Loard hes geane seae agean us.' An' thay cryed oot lood, an' gràt
ageane, an' Orpah kysst hyr guid-muther, but Ruith hàng bey 'er. An' schui
said, 'Sey, (y)eir guid-syster's geane away heäme, tui her ayn fuok, an' tui
her gôds; geae 'way yuw tui, æfter (y)eir guid-syster.' An' Ruith said, 'O
dynna treit on-us tui leeve-(y)e, or tui gàng bàk fræ cumein æfter (y)e, for
quhayr-ever (y)ee gàng, aa'l gàng, an' quhayr (y)ee beyde, aa'l beyde; yoor
fuok 'll bey maa fuok, an' yoor Gòd maa Gôd. Quhayr (y)ee dey, aa'll dey, an'
bey laid î the greave theare aseyde-(y)e: the Loard dui-seae an' mayr tui
mey, yf owcht but death cum atwein yuw an' mey!'

guid-dowchters daughters-in-law   *a-greitein* crying   *gràt* wept   *treit* entreat

RUTH 2: (MURRAY)

An' Naaome hed a freind bey hyr guid-màn's seyde ŏ the hooss, a rowthie
màn duian' weil î the wòr'lt, an' eäne ŏ Eleimelek's kyn; an' thay caa'd 'ym
Boaz. An' Ruith the Moabeyte làss said tui Naaome, 'Læt's gàng oot òntui the
hærst-ryg neh, an' gæther the heids ŏ cuorn ahynt ònie ăt aa mæ fynd greace
î ther seycht.' An' schui said tyll'er, 'Gàng (y)eir ways, ma làssie.' An' schui
geade oot, an' càm an' beguid a gætherin' ònna the hærst-ryg ahynt the
scheirers, an' ăz hàp wad hæ'd, dyd-n' schui leycht on a byt ŏ the feild ăt
wăs Boaz's, hym ăt wăs eäne ŏ Eleimeleks ayn kyn.

Aweil thăn, Boaz càm oot fræ Bæthlem, an' says tui the scheirers, 'The
Loard bey wui-ye!' An' thay aansert bàk, 'The Loard blyss-(y)e!' Than Boaz
says tui the greive ăt wăs stàn'an' ower the scheirers, 'Quheae's auwcht thys
làss thăn?' An' the greive ăt stuid ower the scheirers tælld 'ym, an' said,
'Thàt's the Moabeyte làss, ăt càm bàck wui Naaome fræ the laand ŏ Moab;
an' schui àxt-us, "Aa bæg o'ye, læt-us gæther ahynt the scheirers, amàng
the stooks." Seae schui càm, an' hes bydden heir fræ the muornin' tyl duist
eenuw, ăt schui baid a wee quheyle î the hooss.' Thàn Boaz said tui Ruith,
'Heir (y)e, ma làss, dynna gàng tui gæther ynna ònie uther feild, nor gàng
away fræ heir avaa, but beyde heir cluoss aseyde maa maydens. Keip (y)eir
ein ònna the feild ăt thay're scheiran', an' gang ahynt-them; hæv-n' aa
chairget the laads nô tui fasch-(y)e; an' quhan (y)e're drye, gàng tui the càns,
an' teake a drynk ŏ quhatever the laads tuim oot.' Thàn schui fæll doon ònna
'er feace, an' buw'd 'ersel tui the grund, an' said, 'Huw ys't ăt aa've fund
greace î (y)eir seycht, for (y)e tui teake nuotice ŏ mey, syn aa'm eäne ŏ the
fræmd.' An' Boaz tælld-'er, an' said tyl-'er, 'Aa've bein luitten kæn the heäle
stuorie, aa' huw (y)ee've duin tui (y)eir guid-muther syn the deathe ŏ (y)eir
ayn màn, an' huw (y)e've læft (y)eir faither an' muther an' the laand ŏ (y)eir
byrth, an' cumd heir amàng a fuok ăt (y)e kænnd nowchts aboot afuore. Mæ

the Loard requeyte (y)eir dui ins an' a heäle rewaird bey gie'n-(y)e fræ the
Loard Gôd ŏ Ysrel, ăt (y)e've cumd tui lyppen (y)eirsel anunder'ys wyngs!'
Thàn schui said, 'Læt mey fynd fayver ynna (y)eir seycht, ma luord! for (y)e've
comfortit-us, an' spòken hærtsum wurds tui (y)eir haand-mayden, athoa
aa'm noa tui bey coontit leyke ònie eane ŏ (y)eir maydens.' An' Boaz tælld'er,
'At meale-teymes cum fòrrat, an' teake a beyte ŏ the breid, an' dyp (y)eir
peice ĭ the vynniegar.' An' schui sàt doon aseyde the scheirers, an' hey
raaxt'er bye ruostit cuorn, an' schui eitit 'er fyll an' geade 'er ways. An'
quhan schui'd rys'n up tui gæther, Boaz chairget the laads, an' said, 'Læt'er
gæther fòrrat amàng the scheives, an' dynna challinge 'er. An' læt faa' a
næffŭ nuw an' thàn wullantlie for 'er, an' dynna fynd faat wui'r.' Seae schui
gæthert òn ĭ the feild tyl neycht, an' schui thruisch oot quhat schui hed
gæthert, an' yt meade the fæck ŏ tweae haffuw ŏ baarlie.

   An' schui lyftit it up, an' geade 'er ways ynta the toon; an' 'er guid-muther
saa quhat schui hed gæthert, an' schui browcht oot an' gæ 'er quhat schui
hed læft ower, æfter schui hæd aneuwch. An' 'er guid-muther àxt 'er, 'Quhayr
hæ-ye bein gætheran' the-day? an' quhayr hæ-ye w'rowcht? Blyssins onna
hym ăt hæ teane nuotice o'ye.' An' schui luit hyr guid-muther kæn quheae
yt wàs ăt schui hed gæthert wui, an' says schui, 'Thay caa the màn Boaz ăt
aa was wurkan' wui the-day.' An' Naaomie said tui 'er guid-dowchter, 'Blyssins òn 'ym fræ the Loard, ăt hæs-na gie'n ower 'ys keyndness tui the leivan'
an' the deid.' An' Naaomie tælld'er, 'The màn's a nærr freind ŏ oor ayn, eäne
ŏ oor neist ŏ kyn.' An' Ruith said, 'Hey tælld-us tui, "(y)ee mæn beyde cluoss
aseyde maa laads, tyl thay 've duin wui aa' maa hærst."' An' Naaomie said
tui Ruith, hyr guid-dowchter, 'Yt's weill fòr-ye, ma dowchter, tui gang alàng
wui hyz maydens, ăt thay mæ no meit wui-ye yn ònie uther feild.' Seae schui
stàk cluoss be Boazis maydens, an' gæthert, tyl the baarlie hærst an' the
quheit hærst was beath duin. An' schui baid wui 'er guid-muther.

freind relative   *rowthie* prosperous   *hærst-ryg* harvest field   *beguid* began   *greive* overseer
quheae's auwcht thys làss who does this girl belong to   *fasch* bother   *tuim* pour
eäne o the fræmd a foreigner   *lyppen* entrust   *raaxt'er* passed her   *næffu* handful
wullantlie intentionally   *fæck* best part   *haffuw* half a bushel

RUTH 3 (BORROWMAN)

Ae day, Ruth's guidmither Naomi said tae her, 'Ma dochter, Ah suld be blythe
gin ye had a guid doonsettin. Noo, thair is our kinsman, Boaz: ye were wi his
lasses. The nicht he dichts bere at his threshie-flair. Whan ye hae wushen and
buskit yersel, pit on yer mantua, gang doon tae the threshie-flair, but dinna
mak yersel kent tae the man till he is by etten and drinkin. But whan he

liggs doon, tak tent o the bit whaur he liggs. Than, gang in, heize the cloak at his fit, and ligg doon. He sall tell ye what tae dae'.

'Ah sall dae strauchtlie what ye tell me', quo Ruth. Sae she gaed doon tae the threshie-flair, and did strauchtlie what her guidmither telt her.

When Boaz had etten and drunkan he was gie contentit wi the warld, and gaed awa tae ligg at the faur end o the bere bing. She cam in stownlins, heizit the cloak at his fit and liggit doon.

About midnicht some orra thing awaukent the sleepin man; he rowt owre, and, ma certes, wasna thair a wumman liggin at his fit!

'Wha are ye?' he speirt.

'Ah'm yer servin-lass Ruth' quo she. 'Noo, hap yer cloak owre yer frien, for ye are ma neist o kin'.

Quo he, 'The Lord has sainit ye, ma dochter. This last prief o yer lealty is faur mair nor the firsten; ye hinna socht efter onie callant, weel-aff or puir. Dinna fash yersel, ma dochter. Ah sall dae what is askit; for aa the neeborhood kens ye are an eident wumman. Are ye shair Ah'm the neist of kin? Thair's ane mair sib tae ye than Ah am. Bide here the nicht, and the morn, gin he is willin tae be yer neist o kin, weel and guid; gif he willna Ah sall dae it. Ah tak ma aith by the Lord. Noo, ligg doon till daydaw'.

Sae she liggit at his fit till daydaw, but awaukent air, afore onie docht ken wha she was; and he said, 'It winna dae for fowk tae ken a wumman has been tae the threshie-flair'. Than, quo he, 'rax me the mantua ye hae on, and haud it out'.

Sae she raxit her mantua, and he gied her sax gowpens o bere, and heizit it on her shoulder, and she gaed awa tae the brugh.

When she cam tae her guidmither, Naomi speirt, 'Hoo did it faa out wi ye ma dochter?'

Ruth telt her aa the man had dune for her. 'He gied me sax gowpens o bere', quo she, 'he waldna lat me come hame tae ma guidmither toom'. Quo Naomi, 'Bide a wee, ma dochter, till ye see what wull befaa. He sallna bide eith, till he has redd up the maitter the day'.

---

doonsettin settlement   *dichts bere* winnows barley   *buskit* dressed   *mantua* loose gown
liggs lies   *tent* notice   *bit* place   *heize* lift up   *strauchtlie* exactly, 'straightly' (B.)   *gie* very
bing heap   *stowlins* steathily   *some orra thing* something or other   *speirt* asked   *hap* cover
sainit blessed   *callant* young man   *fash yersel* worry   *eident* diligent   *sib* related
docht was able   *rax* pass   *gowpen* 'a double handful: here used for an unspecified amount' (B.)
toom empty-handed   *eith* easy   *redd up* fixed up

PSALM 13 (WADDELL)

The Lord's like till lose sight o' David; bot David maun ne'er lose sight o' the Lord.
   Till the sang-maister: ane height-lilt o' David's.

How lang, O LORD? Will ye mind me nae mair? How lang will ye hap yer face frae me?

How lang tak thought i' my saul maun I, *wi'* dule i' my heart daily? How lang sal my ill-willer rax abune me?

Tak tent *an'* hearken till me, LORD my God; enlighten my een, that I sleep-na the *sleep o'* dead:

That my ill-willer say-na, I hae waur'd him now! *or* my faes be fain an I be shukken.

Bot I'se lippen me a' till yer ain gude-gree; my heart sal be blythe i' yer ain heal-ha'din.

Na, I sal *e'en* gang lilt till the LORD; for he's wrought a' nieborlie for me.

mind remember   *hap* cover   *dule* sorrow   *ill-willer* enemy   *rax* stretch   *tent* notice
lippen entrust   *gude-gree* mercy   *heal-ha'din* salvation   *lilt* sing

PSALM 18 (WADDELL)

The Lord kens whan, wi' a bleeze frae the lift, till set his ain folk free frae a'
that wad steer them.

Till the sang-maister, till ser' the LORD: *ane* o' David's; whan he spak till the LORD ilk word o' this sang, i' the day the LORD redd him out frae the han' o' his ill-willers a', an' eke frae the han' o' Saul: an quo' he—

O LORD, my strenth, but I lo'e ye weel!

The LORD my rock, my hainin-towir, an' my to-fa'. my God, my craig; I maun lippen till himlane: my schild, the horn o' my heal-makin, *an'* my heigh-ha'.

I lilted fu' loud till the LORD; an' frae ill-willers a' I was setten free.

The dules o' dead dush'd me; an' spates o' mischieff fley'd me sair:

Dules o' the lang-hame fankit me about; girns o' dead war unco nar.

I' my strett *o' stretts* I scraigh't till the LORD; till God, my ain god, I sighet fu' sair. He hearken'd my scraigh, frae his halie howff, my bidden wan ben afore him, *it wan* till his vera lugs.

The yirth syne dinnl't, an' sheuk; the laighest neuks o' the hills trimml't an' steer'd, for He was angrie.

Reek raise in his angir, an' lowe licket afore him; coals kennl'd at his on-come:

An' he loutit the lift an' wan down; an mirk *was* aneth his feet:

An' he canter'd on a cherub, an' he flew; an' he raiket on the wings o' the win':

An' mirk he made a' for his howff about him; mirk o' spates, *an'* cluds o' the carrie.

Frae the light *was* afore him, his cluds wan awa; *wi'* hailstanes, an' *wi'* flaughts o' fire.

An' the LORD reel'd alang the lift; the Heighest lat his skreigh win but: hailstanes an' flaughts o' fire.

An' he lowsit his flanes, an' he sperfl't them; bleeze on bleeze, an' he dang them.

Syne war the wames o' the watirs seen, an' the growf o' the warld unhappit was; at sic wytan o' yer ain, O LORD; at the gluff o' the win' o' thine angir.

He rax't frae abune, he claught me; he harl'd me atowre frae a warld o' watirs:

He redd me frae my strang ill-willer, an' frae a' that wiss'd me ill; wha starker war nor me.

Me they o'er-gaed i' the day o' my down-gaen; bot the LORD was an out-gate till me.

An' he brought me atowre intil room; he redd me fu' right, for he liket me weel.

The LORD quat me even wi' my ain even-doen, an' contentit me weel for the cleanness o' my han's.

For I tentit ay sikker the gates o' the LORD; an' was nae ill-ganger frae my God:

For his right-rechtins a' *war* afore me; an' his biddens frae me I ne'er pat awa:

I was aefauld ay wi' himsel; an' wairded me weel frae my ain wrang-doen:

An' the LORD quat me right for my rightousness; for the cleanness o' my han's in his een.

Wi' the nieborlie man ye can be nieborlie, *LORD*; wi' the aefauld man, aefauld:

Wi' the weel-wushen man ye can sine yer han's; wi' the thraw-art carl ye can haud yer ain:

For down-dang folk yersel can saif; bot een owre heigh, ye can baise them a'.

For that light o' mine yerlane gar'd kennle; the LORD my God gar'd my mirkness lowe:

For, wi' yerlane, I raiket thro' a byke; an' wi' my God, I o'erlap a wa'.

For God, his gate 's aefauld; the word o' the LORD, it's pruif; a schild *is* he *ay*, till a' that lippen till himlane.

For wha *can be* Gude, an it be-na the LORD? or wha a stieve craig, an it be-na our ain God?

It's God himlane wha graiths me wi' might, an' straughts me fu' sikker the gate till gang:

Evenin my feet like the *cloots* o' the rae, an' stanan me stieve on my heighest roddins:

Ettlin my han's for facht, till ane airn-bow is flinder'd i' my arms.

An' the schild o' yer heal-ha'din ye hae gien till me; an' yer right han' has uphauden me; an' yer tholin made me unco great

My gate ye hae braided aneth me, that my fitsteds suld ne'er gae by.

I sal o'ertak my ill-willers; I sal fang them firm; I sal ne'er seek hame, till it's by wi' them.

I sal thring them thro', an' they sal ne'er man till rise; they sal gae down aneth my feet, *whar I stan'*.

For ye graith'd me wi' might for the stour; my gain-stan'ers a' ye hae whaml't aneth me

An' my faes ye 'gien me by the hals; my ill-willers eke, I hae sned them aff.

They sought, bot nae frien' *was thar*; till the LORD *they sought* bot he mindet them nane.

Syne I dang them like stoure afore the win'; like glaur ontil the heighroad, flang I them by.

Ye hae redd me frae the chauner o' the folk; ye hae setten me atowre the hethen; folk *that* I kent-na sal be loons o' mine.

Wi' loutit lugs sal they hearkèn till me; the sons o' the fremit sal kiss my caup.

The gangrel gang hae thowet awa; an' shukken wi' dread frae their benmaist ha'dins.

The LORD lives! an' blythe *be* my ha'din-height; heigh be the God o' my heal-makin:

The God wha wracks a' right for me, an' thirls the folk aneth my bidden:

Wha redds me atowre frae my ill-willers *a'*: na, ye hae liftit me heigh abune my gain-stan'ers; frae the ill-deedie carl, ye hae claught me awa.

Wharthro', amang the folk, I maun laud yerlane; an' lilt until thy name, O LORD:

Wha ettles sic health for his King: an' sic nieborlie gree for his Chrystit: for David, an' for his outcome, for evir an' ay.

---

hainin-towir tower of refuge   *to-fa'* support, refuge   *craig* rock   *lippen* trust
heal-makin salvation   *dules* sorrows   *dush'd* struck hard
fley'd frightened   *fankit* entangled   *girns* snares   *scraigh't* cried   *howff* dwelling place
bidden prayer   *lugs* ears   *dinnl't* shook   *steer'd* moved   *reek* smoke   *lowe* fire
loutit made to bow down   *mirk* darkness   *raiket* moved quickly   *carrie* sky
flaughts flashes   *flanes* arrows   *sperfl't* scattered   *dang* beat down   *growf* belly
unhappit uncovered   *wytan* rebuke   *gluff* gust   *rax't* stretched   *claught* grasped
harl'd pulled   *atowre* out   *redd* delivered   *starker* stronger   *out-gate* escape
redd right delivered   *quat* rewarded   *even-doen* uprightness   *tentit ey sikker* paid firm
heed to   *gates* ways   *right-rechtins* judgements   *ae fauld* honest   *sine* wash
thrawart crooked   *carl* man   *down-dang* oppressed   *baise* bring down   *lowe* blaze

byke swarm   *stieve* firm   *graiths* equips   *straughts* straightens   *cloots* hooves
roddins sheep-tracks   *ettlin* designing   *flinder'd* shattered   *heal-ha'din* salvation
tholin endurance, patience   *fitsteds* footprints   *fang* seize   *thring* thrust   *man* manage
stour battle   *whaml't* overthrown   *hals* neck   *eke* also   *sned* cut   *glaur* mud
chauner complaint   *loons* servants   *loutit* bowed   *the fremit* foreigners
thowet melted   *ha'din* height *stronghold*   *wracks* takes vengeance
thirls subjects   *redds* delivers   *ettles* intends   *outcome* descendants

PSALM 22 (WADDELL)

David foremaist, an' Chryst ahin him, baith maen fu' sair the mislipp'nin o'
God i' their ain day o' dule: mony wonner-wyss words i' the sang-makar's
mouthe anent this, an' till be weel tentit. For the lave, God himlane hauds
a' livin: nae man can haud himsel livin; they come a' an' they gang; bot
they're countit ay till the Lord for ane, for the Lord himsel maks a'.
Till the sang-maister on Aijeleth-Shahar; ane heigh-lilt o' David's.

My God, my God, whatfor hae ye mislippen'd me? Sae far *are ye* frae
helpin me, *an'* the words o' my waefu' wailin.

My God, I hae skreighit the leelang day, bot ye mind me nane; an'
the night *forby*, an' nae peace for me.

Bot ye are yerlane, an' weel fa' the leal lilts o' Israel.

Our faithers lippen'd till thee; they lippen'd, an' ye redd them hame.

They sigh't till yersel, an' wan weel awa; they lippen'd till thee, an'
war nane affrontit.

Bot 'am but a worm, an' nae man; a carl's sang, an' a geck o' the
peopil.

A' that see me laugh me by; they schute wi' the lip, they cave the
head;—*an'* quo' they,

He lippen'd the LORD; lat *the* LORD gar him gang: lat *the* LORD redd him
but, sen he liket him weel.

Bot yerlane redd me out frae the wame; ye mislippen'd me nane on
my mither's bosom.

On yersel was I cuisten frae the womb; frae my mither's bouk, ye
'been my God.

Be-na far frae me, LORD, for stretts are nar; for nane *but yerlane* can
mak sikker.

Droves o' nowte hae rinket me roun; stoor stirks o' Bashan hae fankit
me about.

They glaum'd abune me wi' their mouthes, *like* a rievan an' a roaran
lyoun.

'Am skail'd like watir; ilk bane o' me's lowse; my heart's nae better
nor wax, it's thow'd down laigh i' my bosom.

My bouk clang like a shaird, an' my tongue stak till my hals; an' ye brought me till the stoure o' dead.

For brachs hae forset me roun; the gath'ran o' ill-doers fankit me about; they drave thro my han's an' my feet.

I may count ilk bane *i' my bouk, for* they glaum *an'* glow'r at mysel:

They synder my cleedin amang them; an' fling for my vera manteele.

Bot yersel, O LORD, be-na far frae me: haste ye till help me, my strenth *an' a.*

Redd my saul atowre frae the swurd; *an'* the lave o' my *life* frae the grip o' the grew.

Redd me, LORD, frae the lyoun's glaum; ye hae heard me *or now*, frae the horns o' the reme.

I maun till o' yer name till my brether *ilk ane*; in mids o' the folk I maun lilt till thee.

Wha fear the LORD, ye suld laud him *a'*; a' Jakob's out-come, laud him heigh; an' the growthe o' Israel a', quauk ye afore him.

For he lightlied-na, nor grue'd at the dule o' the down-dang; nor happit his face frae him; bot hearken'd, whan he skreigh'd till himsel.

Frae yersel *comes* the sugh o' my sang; i' the gath'ran sae gran' I sal bide my trystes, afore them that fear him.

Lown-livin folk sal feed an' fen'; they sal lilt till the LORD, wha leuk for himsel: yer heart sal live as lang's *the lave.*

A' neuks o' the yirth sal hae min', an' sal turn their gate till the LORD; ilk kin o' the folk sal lout afore thee.

For the kingryk *'s* the LORD's: an' maister *is* he 'mang the natiouns.

The best on yirth sal feed an' fa'; wha gang till stoure, ilk ane maun lout afore him; for nae livin *wight* can ay thole livin.

Bot their out-come sal thole, *an'* be countit till the Lord for kith-gettin.

They sal come *i' their day*, an' gar his rightousness be ken'd to the niest-come kin, that himsel did *it.*

---

mislippen'd neglected *skreighet* cried *leelang* livelong *forby* as well *fa'* deserve
lippened trusted *redd hame* delivered *geck* object of scorn *cave* toss *tedd but* deliver
bouk body *sikker* safe *rinket* ringed *stoor* strong *stirks* young bulls
fankit entangled, ensnared *glaum'd* snatched at *rievan* ravening *skail'd* poured out
thow'd melted *clang* dried up *hals* throat *stoure* dust *brachs* hunting dogs *forset* beset
glaum stare *lave* rest *grew* greyhound *glaum* devouring *reme* 'Heb. some
heigh-gaen beiss, o' what kin' 's no ken'd: whiles ca'd *Unicorns'* (W.)
out-come descendants *lightlied* made light *grue'd* shuddered *dule* grief
down-dang oppressed *happit* hid *sugh* melody *bide* keep *trystes* vows
lown-livin humble *fen'* provide food for themselves *kingryk* kingdom *thole* endure
kith-gettin generation

Psalm 23 (Riddell)

Ane Psalm o' David.

The Lord is my shepherd; I sallna inlak.

He mak's me til lye doun in green an' baittle gangs; he leeds me aside the quæet waters

He refreschens my saul; he leeds me in the peths o' richteous-niss for his næme's sak'.

Yis, thouch I wauk throwe the vallie o' the skaddaw o' deæth, I wull feær nae ill: for thou art wi' me; thy cruik an' thy staffe thaye comfirt me.

Thou prepairist me ane tabel in the preesince o' mine enimies: thou anaintist my heæd wi' oolie; my cupp rins ower.

Shurelie guidniss an' mercie sall follo me a' the dayes o' my liffe; an' I wull dwall in the hous o' the Lord forevir.

inlak lack   *baittle gangs* rich pastures

Psalm 23 (Smith)

Dauvid is aye unreelin a pirn aboot Christ. Here he pents him as a Shepherd, and his sel as a silly bit lammie. It evens weel wi' the tenth o' John.

The Lord is my Shepherd; my wants are a' kent; the pastur I lie in is growthie and green.

I follow by the lip o' the watirs o' Peace.

He heals and sterklie hauds my saul: and airts me, for his ain name's sake, in a' the fit-roads o' his holiness.

Aye, and though I bude gang throwe the howe whaur the deid-shadows fa', I'se fear nae skaith nor ill, for that yersel is aye aside me; yere rod and yere cruik they defend me.

My table ye hae plenish't afore the een o' my faes; my heid ye hae chrystit wi' oyle; my cup is teemin fu'!

And certes, tenderness and mercie sal be my fa' to the end o' my days; and syne I'se bide i' the hoose o' the Lord, for evir and evir mair!

sterklie boldly   *airts* directs   *bude* had to   *howe* valley   *skaith* harm   *plenish't* stocked
chrystit anointed   *fa'* fate

PSALM 23 (WADDELL)

The sheep-keepin o' the Lord's kind an' canny, wi' a braw howff at lang last:
   David keeps his sheep; the Lord keeps David.
Ane heigh-lilt o' David's.

The LORD *is* my herd, nae want sal fa' me:
   He louts me till lie amang green-howes; he airts me atowre by the
lown watirs:
   He waukens my wa'-gaen saul; he weises me roun, for his ain name's
sake, intil right roddins.
   Na! tho' I gang thro' the dead-mirk-dail; *e'en thar,* sal I dread nae
skaithin: for yersel *are* nar-by me; yer stok an' yer stay haud me baith
fu' cheerie.
   My buird ye hae hansell'd in face o' my faes; ye hae drookit my head
wi' oyle; my bicker is *fu' an'* skailin.
   E'en sae, sal gude-guidin an' gude-gree gang wi' me, ilk day o' my
livin; an' evir mair syne, i' the LORD's ain howff, *at lang last,* sal I mak
bydan.

---

fa' befall   *louts* causes one to bow down   *howes* valleys   *airts* directs   *lown* quiet
wa'-gaen fainting   *weises* directs   *roddins* sheep-tracks   *skaithin* injury
buird table   *drookit* drenched   *bicker* cup   *skailin* over-flowing   *gude-gree* mercy
howff dwelling place

PSALM 38 (WADDELL)

David, in pitifu' plight, baith saul an' body, cries uncolie till the Lord till be
   gude till him an' help him.
Ane heigh-lilt o' David's, till keep *the Lord* in min'.

Wyte me na, LORD, i' yer lowan wuth; ding me na by i' yer bleezan
torne:
   For deep intil me yer flanes hae taen grip; an' sair ontil me is yer han'
down-borne.
   Nae feck i' my flesche, fornent yer angir; nae rest i' my banes, fornent
my sin.
   For my ain misdeeds hae gane owre my head; like some weary weight,
they're ill till carrie.
   My dulesome dints gang foich i' my folly;
   Twafauld am I, an' cruppen till naething; a' day lang, I gang dark
an' drearie.

For my lisk it's pang'd wi' some fusionless ill; an' nae soun'ness ava *is left* i' my body.

Feckless am I, an' forfochten sairly; I sigh wi' a sab frae the heart i' my *bosom*.

O LORD, afore thee *is* a' my yirn; an' my sighan, frae thee it has ne'er been happit.

My heart dwaums, my pith bides-na wi' me; na, the light o' my een, it's gane clean frae me.

My joes an' my frien's stan' atowre frae my breinge; an' my blude themsels haud far frae me.

Wha seek for my life hae girns till lay; wha ettle me ill speak a' mischieff, an' pingle on lies the hail day.

Bot I, like the deaf man, hearken'd nane; an' e'en like the dum, wha ne'er raxes his mouthe:

I was e'en as the man wha hears-na a sugh; an' ben i' whase gab *are* nae gainsayans.

For *a'* till yerlane I hae lippen'd, O LORD; ye maun speak till me lown, Lord God o' my ain.

For quo' I, Gin they 're fain till see me fa'; gin they haud themsels heigh an my fit slidder!

For likan till gang am I ay; an' my dule, it *'s* afore me evir.

For my sin I hae weel setten furth; on the wrang I hae dune, I tak thought wi' a swither.

Bot ill-willers on live, are *a'* fu' stark; an' mony are they, wha mislike me saikless:

Wha pay me wi' ill, for gude *till themsels*; wha seek me wi' wrang, for my ain weel-doen.

Dinna lea' me, O LORD, thou God o' my ain; nor bide frae me far, *as the lave are bydan*

Fy, haste ye till help me, O LORD, my heal-ha'din!

---

wyte reproach   *lowan* blazing   *wuth* anger   *ding* beat down   *torne* anger
flanes arrows   *feck* strength   *fornent* in the face of   *dulesome* painful
dints blows   *gang foich* stink   *twafauld* bent double   *lisk* groin   *pang'd* crammed
fusionless debilitating   *feckless* without strength   *forfochten* exhausted
happit hidden   *dwaums* grows faint   *joes* dear ones   *breinge* blow   *girns* snares
ettle intend   *pingle on* labour at   *raxes* stretches   *sugh* sound
gainsayans arguments   *lown* softly   *likan* likely, about to   *dule* sorrow
wi' a swither in a panic   *stark* strong   *saikless* innocent   *heal-ha'din* salvation

PSALM 39 (RIDDELL)

Til the chief musicien, een til Jeduthun, Ane Psalm o' David.

I said, I wull tak tent til my wayes, that I sinna wi' my tung:
I wull keep my mooth wi' ane brydle quhile the wicket is afore me.
I was dum wi' seelence; I helde my peece een frae guid; an' my sorra was sturret.
My hairt was het wuthin me; quhile I was muusin' the fire burnet: than spak I wi' my tung,
Lord, mak' me til ken mine en', an' the measur o' my dayes what it is, that I may ken howe bauch I am.
Behald thou hest mæde my dayes as ane han'sbreæthe, an' mine age is as naething afore thee: trewlie ilka man at his best stæte is a'thegither vainitie. Selah.
Shurelie ilka man gangs in ane vaine schaw: shurelie thaye ar wanrestet in vaine: he hotts up guids an' geer, an' kensna wha sall gether thame.
An' nowe, Lord, what waite I for? my houpe is in thee.
Free me frae a' my transgressiones; makna me the reproch o' the fulish.
I was dum; I openetna my mooth; becaus thou didist it.
Remuve thy straike awa frae me: I am consuumet bie the fluet o' thine han'.
Whan thou wi' rebuiks dest correck man for inequitie, thou makist his beutie til waiste awa like ane mæthe: shurelie ilka man is vainitie.
Heær my præyer, O LORD, an' gie ear untill my crye: haud-na thy peece at my teærs: for I am fremet wi' thee, an' ane sae-jurner, as a' my faethers wer.
O spare me, that I may gaine bak my pithe afore I gae hance an' be nae mair.

tak tent pay attention   *bauch* weak   *wanrestet* troubled   *hotts* heaps   *fluet* blow
fremet a stranger

PSALM 46 (RIDDELL)

Til the chief musicien, for the sons o' Korah; Ane Sang apon Alamoth.

God is our sang an' strencth, ane verra presint helpe in truble.
Therfor we wullna feær, thouch the yirth be remuvet, an' thouch the mountans be carryet intil the middle o' the se:

Thouch the waters o't rair, an' be trublet; thouch the mountans shog wi' the swallin' o' thame. Selah.

Ther is ane rivir whase rinners sall mak' gladsume the citie o' God, the haly plece o' the taabernakles o' the Maist Hie.

God is in the middle o' hir; she sallna be muvet: God sall helpe hir, an' that richt sune.

The heæthin frennet, the kingdooms wer comuvet: he uuteret his voyce, an' the yirth meltet.

The Lord o' hosts is wi' us; the God o' Jacob is our scug. Selah.

Cum, behald the warks o' the Lord, what desolationes he heth mæde in the yirth.

He mak's weir til cease untill the en's o' the yirth; he snegs the speer asinder; he burns the chariat in the fire.

Be quæit, an' ken that I am God: I wull be ræiset on hie amang the heæthin, I wull be mæde hie in the yirth.

The Lord o' hosts is wi' us; the God o' Jacob is our beild. Selah.

shog shake   *rinners* streams   *frennet* raged   *comuvet* moved   *scug* shelter
snegs chops   *beild* refuge

PSALM 65 (WADDELL)

Nae liltin o' laud at Zioun an God be na thar: narest till him, maun be blythest; but his gude-will's at-owre us a': the yirth hersel's fu' fain at his comin.
Till the sang-maister: ane heigh-lil: *an'* sang o' David's.

Thar's a whush for yersel, O God, i' the liltin o' laud at Zioun; till yersel sal the tryst be made-guid:

Till yersel, wha can hearken prayer, a' flesh be till airt its road.

Words wi' a faut, are owre mony for me; our deeds wi' a faut, ye sal dicht them by.

Blythe *abune a'* maun he be, ye wale an' tak hame wi' yersel; he sal bide i' yer faulds sae fine: *bot* we sal be stegh't wi' the gude o' yer houss, that halie biggen o' thine.

Sair wonners, O God, our heal-ha'din, in right ye hae gar'd us ken; tryste till a' ends o' the yirth, an' till them owre the sea that fen:

Rightin the hills in his strenth, graith't wi' nae end o' might:

Whushin the sugh o' the fludes, the sugh o' their waves, an' the peopil's sigh.

An' the dwallers on yonder-maist-yird, are fleyed at the trysts ye sen': the outgang o' mornin, *the hame*-come o' night, ye mak them *baith* liltin fain.

Ye win till the yirth, an' ye drook it; ye seep it fu' saft wi' the spring-tide o' God: ye lucken their corn i' the growin, whan sae ye hae ready'd the road.

Her furs ye swak wi' a spate-fu'; ye sloken her rigs wi' showers; her braird ye bring blythely awa.

Sae the year ye hae crown'd wi' yer gudeness; an' yer roun-gaens dreep rowth as they gang:

They dreep *on* the bawks i' the wustlan'; an' the knowes, they are graithit wi' sang:

The lea's, they are happit wi' fleeshes; an' the howes, they are theekit wi' corn: they skreigh wi' content o' pleasance; na, wi' joye they're *a'* liltin thrang.

whush silence *tryst* vow *airt* direct *dicht by* wipe away *wale* choose
stegh't crammed *biggen* building *heal-ha'din* salvation *tryste* someone to be trusted
fen fare *graith't* equipped *sugh* sound *fleyed* afraid *trysts* signs *drook* drench
seep soak *lucken* cause to grow and thrive *swak* soften *sloken* soak
braird first shoots of grain *rowth* abundance *bawks* unploughed land
knowes small hills *lea's* pastures *happit* covered *fleeshes* fleeces *howes* valleys
theekit covered *skreigh* cry out *thrang* busy

PSALM 74 (RIDDELL)

Maschil o' Asaph.

O God, wharefor hest thou casen us aff forevir? why deth thine angir reek agayne the sheepe o' thy heff-gang?

Mind thy congregatione, whilk thou hest coft o' auld; the rodd o' thine heirskep, whilk thou hest redeimet; this Muunt Zion, wharein thou hest dwalt.

Lift up thy feet untill the en'liss desolationes, een a' that the enemie heth dune wicketlie in the sanctuarie.

Thine enimies rair in the middle o' thy congregationes; thaye sete up thair ensygns for sygns.

Ance ane man was renommet akordin' as he had liftet up æxes apon the thick tries.

But nowe thaye brik doun the cervet wark thero' at ance wi' æxes an' hammirs.

Thaye hae thrawn fire intil thy sanctuarie; thaye hae fylet, bie thraw-ing doun the dwallin'-plece o' thy næme til the gruun'.

Thaye said in thair hairts, Let us destroye thame thegither; thaye hae brunt up a' the synigogues o' God in the lan'.

We seena our sygns; ther is nae mair onie prophit, næther is ther amang us onie that kens howe lang.

O God, howe lang sall the advarsarie speik dispichtfulie? sall the enimie blasfeme thy næme foraye?

Why haudist thou bak thy han', een thy richt han'? pu' it owt o' thy bozim.

For God is my King o' auld, wurkin' salvatione in the middle o' the yirth.

Thou didist cleefe the se bie thy strencth; thou didist brik the heæds o' the drægons in the waters.

Thou didist smatter the heæds o' leviathan intil flenders, an' gæfist him til be fude til the peeple habitatin' the wuldirniss.

Thou didist cleefe the fuuntan an' the flude: thou dryetist up michtie rivers.

The daye is thine, the nicht alsua is thine; thou hest prepairet the licht an' the sun.

Thou hest sete a' the boordirs o' the yirth: thou hest mæde simmir an' wintir.

Ae thing keep in mind, that the enimie hæs reprochet, O Lord, an' that the fulish peeple hae blasfemet thy næme.

O deliferna the saul o' thy turtle-dow untill the ferkishin' o' the wicket; forgetna the congregatione o' thy puir foraye.

Hae respeck untill the covenent; for the mirk pleces o' the yirth ar fu' o' the habitationes o' cruiltie.

O letna the oppresset cum bak doun o' mooth; let the puir an' needie prayse thy næme.

Ræise up, O God, pleed thine ain caus; beær in mind howe the fulish man reproches thee daylie.

Forgetna the voyce o' thine enimies: the throck an' dirdum o' thae that rise up agayne thee inkresses continwallie.

---

reek smoke   *heff-gang* pasture   *coft* bought   *renommet* famous
dispichtfulie maliciously, contemptuously   *flenders* fragments   *ferkishin'* crowd, mob
throck crowd, throng   *dirdum* uproar

PSALM 90 (WADDELL)

Man's like the gerss, an' his days like a tide: he comes an' he gangs, bot he canna bide.
Ane heart's bode o' Moses, the *ae* Man o' God.

Our hame Ye 'been ay, yerlane, O LORD; frae ae life's end till anither.

Or the heights war shot but, or the yirth an' the warld ye had schuppen; na, frae ae langsyne till anither, *hae* Ye *been* God.

Man ye fesh roun till naething; aye, ye say Hame again, Sons o' the yird!

For a thousan year i' yer sight, are the gliff o' a bygane day; or e'en as a steer i' the night.

Ye hae drookit them a' *in* a dwaum; i' the mornin are they, as the winnle-strae dwaffles:

I' the mornin, it braids an' it dwaffles; or night, it lies mawn an' winn.

For in yer angir, we're a' for-fochten; an' in yer wuth, are we dang clean dune.

Our fauts ye hae setten fornenst ye; our weel-happit *sins*, i' the glint o' yer glow'r.

For ilk day o' our ain drees by in yer angir; an' our years wear awa, like the sugh o' a sang.

The days o' our years, seeventy year o' them *a*'; or wi' meikle pith, aughty year they may gang: bot a weary warsle 's their feck wi' a'; for a gliff it gaes by, an' we flichter hame.

Wha daur mean the weight o' yer angir? e'en sae as ye're trystit, yer angir maun *be*.

Till count our days, gar *us* ken the better; an' airt *our* heart the gate o' *sic* lear.

Hame again, LORD, how lang *sal ye swither?* an' ay on yer thirlfolk rew the mair;

Stegh us fu' ere wi' *rowth* o' yer pitie; syne sal we lilt, an' be blythe a' our days.

Mak us blythe, for sae lang's ye hae dang us; an' the years we hae seen but ill:

Lat yer wark be but seen on yer thirlfolk; on their bairns, yer gudeli-heid *still*:

An' the will o' the LORD our God be amang us; an' the wark o' our han's, till oursels mak it guid: O the wark o' our han's, mak it guid till *oursel*.

shot but pushed out schuppen created *gliff* moment *steer* movement *drookit* steeped
dwaum daydream *windle-strae* tall, thin grass *dwaffles* grows limp *braids* springs up
winn dried out *forfochten* worn out *wuth* anger *dang* beaten *fornenst* in front of
happit hidden *glint* flashing light *drees* passes *sugh o' a sang* melody of a song
meikle pith great strength *warsle* fight *their feck* the most part of them *flichter* flutter
mean declare *airt* direct *gate* way *lear* learning *swither* hesitate *thirlfolk* servants
stegh cram *rowth* abundance

Psalm 100 (Murray)

Aa fuok ăt leeves, ònna the yerth, syng tui the Luord, wui a cheerfŭ voyce. Sær 'ym wui myrth, tæll furth 'yz prayse, cum ye afuore 'ym, ăn rejoyse! Kæn ye, the Luord yz Gôd yn trowth; hey meade us, wuthoot ònie hælp o' oors: wey're hyz hyrsel ăt hey feids, ăn hey teakes us for 'yz scheip. O cum yn, thăn, at 'yz yætts wui prayse, gàng fòrrat tui 'yz coorts wui joye: aiy prayse, an' lauwd, an' blyss 'yz neame, for yt's fàrrant tui dui seae. Quhat fòr? the Luord oor Gôd's guid; hez guidness is suir for aiy: hyz truith stuid sycker ăt aa teymes, ăn yt 'll læst fræ eage tui eage

hyrsel pasture   *yætts* gates   *fàrrant* wise   *sycker* firm

Psalm 100 (Riddell)

Ane Psalm o' prayse

Mak' ane joyfu' noyse untill the Lord, a' ye lan's.
   Ser' the Lord wi' gladsumeniss; cum afore his presince wi' singin'.
   Ken ye that the Lord he is God; it is he that heth mæde us, an' nat we oursel's; we ar his peeple, an' the scheep o' his heffgang.
   Entir intil his yettes wi' thanksgiein', an' intil his cuurts wi' prayse; be thankfu' untill him, an' bliss his næme.
   For the Lord is guid; his mercie is evirlestin', an' his trouth enduurs til a' ganæratians.

heff-gang sheep-walk

Psalm 100 (Waddell)

We're a' but the sheep o' God's lan', an' the flock o' God's han': a' livin folk, they suld laud him.
A lilt o' laud. [Ane o' Davids, quo' the LXX].

Skreigh till the Lord, the hail yirth, maun ye:
   Beck till the Lord wi' blytheheid an' a'; ben afore him, wi' a sang o' glee.

Ken ye fu' weel, the LORD he's God: himlane, *it was,* made us; oursel *made*-na we: his folk are we *syne,* an' eke o' his hirsel the fe.

Ben till his yetts wi' laud; till his faulds, wi' a lilt sae hie: lilt ye laud till himsel; *an'* that name o' his ain, bless ye.

For gude *is* the LORD; his gudewill *'s* for ay: an' frae ae life's en' till anither, that truth o' his ain, it *sal be.*

skreigh cry out   *beck* bow   *blytheheid* happiness   *hirsel* pasture

PSALM 121 (WADDELL)

David lippens till the heights abune Zioun; an' till him that's abune the heights.
A sang o' the Upgaens.

Till the heights, I maun cast my een; whar else can my help come frae?
My help *'s* frae the LORD himlane; wha made baith the lift an' the lan'.
Yer fit he winna lat steer; nor dover, wha hauds ye heal:
Na, he neither dovers nor sleeps, wha keeps waird upon Israel.
The LORD, he *'s* yer keeper an' a': the LORD *sal be* sconce till thee; on *yer* han', *on* yer ain right han'.
The sun sal-na blight ye by day; nor the mune, *as scho gangs* the night thro'
The LORD, he sal waird ye frae ilka ill; yer life, he sal waird it weel:
The LORD, he sal waird yer gaen-out an' gaen-in, for evir an' ay, frae the now!

lift sky   *steer* move   *dover* doze   *hauds ye heal* delivers you   *waird* guard
sconce shelter

PROVERBS 1: 20–33 (PATERSON)

Wisdom crackin wi' the fulish

Wisdom cries oot on the causey,
Athort the braid haudens o' men;
She's thrang ower-by at the merkets,
An' oot an' in by the entries.
An' a' through the toon,
She's cryin, an' sayin:—

'Hoo lang, ye saft, feckless craiturs,
Are ye gaun to be sae thowless—
Geckin at what's guid,
An', like the fules ye are,
Haudin aff frae richt-kennins?

Swee yersels roun', whan ye hear my repruif.

Tak tent! For I'm fain to gie ye my speerit,
An' mak my words weel-kent to ilk ane o' ye.

Ower an' ower again I've hoyit an' cry't,
But ye've a' been dour an' deif-luggit;
I've rax't oot my haun,
But ye fash't yersels nane;
The coonsel I spak, ye hae slichtit,
An' wadna hear ocht o' advisins.

But bide awee!
I'll hae the lauch
    In the day that ye're trauchl't;
I'll geck at you,
    Whan ye're chitt'rin wi' dreid;
Whan on comes yer fricht
    Like a blashin spate;
Whan doon comes yer skaith
    Like a swirlin blast;
Whan dule an' wae ye maun dree.'

Nae doobt, they'll speir for me then;
    But I'll answer them nane:
Seekin me then they wad be;
    But fin' me they'll no.

For didna they haud aff richt-kennins?
They waled-na the fear o' the Lord;
Ay! they'd herken to nae advisins;
They slichtit a' my repruif.

An' sae, they maun dree their ain weird,
An' be chokit wi' their ain ill-daeins,
Slippin back, an' gaun doon in their fecklessness,
An', like the fules, I tell ye, they are,
They'll be smoored 'neth the routh o' their ain fulishness.

But, whae'er wad herken weel to mysel,
A braw an' a couthie hauden he'll hae;
In a lown, lown howff he'll be happit ower
Wi' nae dreid o' ill ava.

causey street   *athort* across   *haudens* houses   *thrang* busy   *thowless* feeble
geckin scorning   *swee* swing   *trauchl't* overburdened   *spate* flood   *skaith* disaster
dule sorrow   *dree* suffer   *waled* chose   *weird* fate   *smoored* smothered
routh abundance   *couthie* pleasant   *lown* peaceful   *happit* covered

PROVERBS 7:6–23 (PATERSON)

For at the winnock o' my hoose
I keekit oot ayont the swee o't,
An' I saw amang the gawkie loon—
Little mair than callans they were—
I saw a young chiel,
Wi' nae muckle gumption.

He was gaun alang the causey near her corner;
He was takin the very airt o' her hoose,
In the gloamin,
At the e'enin hoor,
As the darklins o' the nicht were comin doon;
An' there was the hizzie to meet him,
The sleekie, ill-deedie wumman.

She's a licht-heidit, glaikit limmer;
She'll stey nane in her ain hoose;
Noo, she's oot on the causey;
Noo, she's alang by the merkets,
An' at ilka corner she's on the oot-look.

Sae she took him by the airms,
An' there she kiss't him;
An' wi' impidence, the heicht o't,
Glowerin in the face o' her,
Quo' she to the chiel:—

'I hae offerins o' guid-wull wi' me;
This very day I've been takin thocht o't:
Sae I cam oot to meet ye,
To see gin I could meet yersel,
An', noo, I've fand ye here

I've buskit the bink wi' braw graithin,
Wi strippit cleedin frae Egypt itsel;
An' I've strinkl't ower a'
The sweet-scentit fineries:
Come awa; swither nane;
Lat's hae love to oor likins till the mornin,
Lat's hae't to oor likens:
For the guid-man's awa frae hame;
He's gane aff to far-awa pairts;
He's taen a fu' wallet alang wi' him,
An' he'se no be back inside a month.'

Wi' her sliddry tongue
   She man's to come ower him;
Wi' the fraisin o' her mooth
   She gars him gie in.

He gangs eftir her at the meenit-
   Like the nowte till the slauchter-hoose,
   Or like the man that's sneckit in airns
   Wha *maun* herken to the blethers o' a fule-
Till a sherp flane dings through him.

Like a silly bit birdie
   He haps intil the girn,
An' the puir, thowless sumph
   Doesna ken that he's gaun to his daith.

winnock window   *keekit* peeped   *swee* casement   *callans* boys   *chiel* youth
glaikit thoughtless   *limmer* worthless woman   *buskit* adorned   *bink* bed
graithin covering   *swither* hesitate   *man's* manages   *nowte* cattle   *sneckit* locked
flane arrow   *dings* strikes   *girn* snare   *sumph* fool

PROVERBS 10:1–25 (PATERSON)

A laddie wi' a pickle gumption maks his faither rale prood o' him;
But a thochtless callan gies his mither mony a sair hairt.

Gear that's gether't by scafferie 'll bring blythe oot-come to naebody;
But richteousness 'll redd a man frae the grups o' daith itsel.

The Lord 'll ne'er lat ony o' His ain be sair scrimpit:
But He'll steek the door ticht against the ettlins o' the wicked.

The man that's slack in the haun 'll sune be toom in the purse;
But the haun that's eident is the haun that gethers the gear.

He's a sensible chiel, wha lays-by through the simmer;
But onybody, wha driddles in the hairst-time, 'll shame his ain folk by-
ord'nar.

Mony are the blessins that are strinkl't ower the heid o' the richteous;
But mony a sair clour 'll be clankit on the gab o' the wicked.

The memorie o' the guid is aye wi' us in a' its blythe-someness;
But the name o' the ill-doers 'll crine awa to naething.

A' the wyse at hairt tak tent to commauns gi'en them;
But a bletherin coof 'll come doon wi' a daiverin dunt some day.

Wha gangs uprichtly, gangs siccarlie;
Wha taks the crookit gate, 'll hae his name blabbit ower the hale pairish.

The man that's aye wink-winkin wi' his een, ettles muckle ill:
An' a lowse-tongued craitur 'll get a clarty tummle afore he's through
wi't.

The crack o' a guid man brings a gliff o' life;
But the crack o' the wicked is nocht but camsteerie clash.

Ill-wull steers up a' mainner o' rippets;
But, whaur there's love, mony bits o' mistaks are quaitly happit oot o'
sicht.

Wha has guid insicht, kens hoo to speak sense:
Wha wants gumption, wants a rung reislin on his back.

Men o' mense are aye gleg to pit an eik to what they ken already;
But fules, by their blether-bletherin, dae the warst for themsels.

The gear o' the rich man gairds him like a castle;
But the poortith o' the puir hauds him doon on his hunkers

The thrangness o' the richteous airts to life:
The thrangness o' the wicked airts to sin.

Wha gangs by guid advisins, hauds on the richt gate:
Wha gecks at repruif, waun'ers frae the straucht road.

Whae'er hides his ill-wull aneth a pretence o' guid-wull, is a leear:
An' whae'er keeps himsel thrang clypin clashes, is nae-thing but a coof.

Whaur there's a brattlin blether o' words, some o' them are like to be
ill;
Sae the man wi' a pickle sense taks care to keep a steek in his crack.

The crack o' the richteous is like siller—the very wale o't;
But that o' the wicked is no worth a broon bawbee.

The crack o' the richteous feeds an' fen's mony a life;
But silly sumphs dee for want o' guid understaun'in.

The blessin o' the Lord maks the puirest body bien,
An' there's nae back-draw o' dowieness gangs alang wi't.

A fule thinks it's daffin to mell wi' the wrang:
An', to the man o' the richt stamp,
Sic-like is the sairch eftir wisdom—
It's the brawest pleesur' o' ony!

What the wicked are frichtit for,
   Upon the wicked that'll fa':
What the richteous hae ettl't,
   That'll come their gate in the lang-run.

Whan the dirl o' the blast has gane by,
   The biggins o' the wicked are blawn clean oot o' sicht;
But tak a skance o' the haudens o' the richteous—
   They're foondit on a rock for evermair.

---

scafferie extortion   *redd* free   *ettlins* intentions   *toom* empty   *eident* diligent
driddles is lazy   *by-ord'nar* extraordinarily   *clour* blow   *crine* shrivel   *daiverin* stupifying
dunt blow   *siccarlie* securely   *clarty* filthy   *crack* conversation   *gliff o' life* a surprise
sensation, with the suggestion of a gleam; a glow (P.)   *camsteerie* wilful   *clash* gossip
rippets contentions   *rung* stick   *reislin* beating   *eik* addition
doon on his hunkers in poverty   *thrangness* activity   *clypin* gossiping   *coof* fool
brattlin noisily hurrying   *steek* restraint   *wale o't* choicest   *bawbee* halfpenny
bien comfortable   *dowieness* sadness   *daffin* a game   *mell* meddle
dirl vibrating force (P.)   *skance* glance

Song of Solomon 1:5–10 (Riddell)

   I am blak but bonnie O ye douchters o' Jerusalem, as the sheilins o'
Kedar, as the coortins o' Solomon.

Glowerna at me becaus I am blak, becaus the sun hes shaine on me: my mither's childer wer angrie wi' me; thaye mæde me keepir o' the vyneyairds, but mine ain vyneyaird I haena keepet.

Acquant me, O thou wham my saul loeist, wi' whare thou feedist, wi' whare thou mak'st thy hirsel til rest at nuun: for wharefor shud I be als ane that gangs danderin' agley efter the hirsels o' thy cumrades?

Gif thou kenna, O thou fairist amang wemen, gae thy wayes furth bie the fit-roddins o' the flok, an' feed thy kids alangs bie the sheep-herds' sheilins.

I hae lykenet thee, O my loefe, til ane cumpanie o' hors in Pharoah's chariats

Thy haffets ar wonsome wi' raws o' juils, thy nek wi' cheens o' gowd.

shielins tents *hirsel* flock *danderin'* roaming *agley* astray *fit-roddins* sheep-tracks
haffets cheeks *wonsome* pretty

Song of Solomon 2:1–14 (Henderson)

I am the rose o' Sharon, an' the lily o' the glens.

As the lily amang thorns, sae is my love amang the lasses

As the apple-tree amang the trees o' the wud, sae is my belovet amang the laddies. I sat doun aneath his shadow wi' muckle delicht, an' his fruit was sweet til my priein'.

He broucht me til the wassail-ha', an'his banner owre me was love.

Stay me wi' stowps, strengthen me wi' apples, for I am ill wi' love.

His left han' is aneath my head, an' his richt han' is roun' me

I rede ye, O ye dochters o' Jerusalem, by the raes, an' by the hin's o' the field, that ye dinna steer up, nar wauken my love, till he likes.

The voice o' my belovet! leuk! he comes loupin' on the hills, skippin' on the braes.

My belovet is like til a rae or a wee deer; behald, he stan's ahint our wa', he keeks out o' the winnock, shawin' himsel through the lattice-lozens.

My belovet spak', quo' he, Rise up, my love, my bonnie ane, an' come awa.

For, behald, the winter's awa, the rain is owre an' gane;

The flowers sproot out o' the grun'; the time o' the singin' o' burds is come, an' the cooin' o' the cushat is hear't in our lan':

The feg-tree pits out her green fegs, an' the vines wi' the wee grapes gie furth a nice smell. Rise up, my love, my bonnie ane, an' come awa

O my doo, whilk art in the rifts o' the rock, in the neuks o' the cliffs, let me hae a sicht o' thy face, let me hear thy voice; for thy voice is saft, an' thy face is winsome.

priein' taste   *wassail-ha'* banqueting hall   *stowps* flagons   *rede* advise   *loupin'* leaping
keeks peeps   *winnock* window   *cushat* ring-dove (here used for the AV's *turtle*)

SONG OF SOLOMON 3:1–8 (ANONYMOUS (1860))

By nicht on my bed I socht him wham my saul lu'es, I socht him, but fand na him.

I'll rise noo an' gang aboot the toon in the throo-gangs, an' in the braid ways I'll seek him wham my saul lu'es

The watchmen that gang aboot the toon fand me; Hae na ye seen him wham my saul lu'es, I speer't?

It was but a wee while I gaed frae them, whan I fand him wham my saul lu'es: I haudet him, an' wad na let him gang, tull I had brocht him intul my mither's hoose, an' intul the chamer o' hir that conceevet me.

I wairn ye, O ye dochters o' Jerusalem, by the raes an' by the hinds o' the field, that ye stir na up nor wauken my love tull he likes.

Wha is this that comes oot o' the wilderness like tooricks o' reek, scented wi' myrrh an' frankincense, wi' a' the poothers o' the mairchant?

Behauld his bed, whilk is Solomon's: threescore valient men are roond it, o' the valient o' Israel.

They a' haud swurds, bein' weel-skeelet in war; ilka man heth his swurd on his thie, because o' dreed in the nicht.

throo-gangs lanes   *speer't* asked   *tooricks* little towers   *reek* smoke
poothers powders

SONG OF SOLOMON 3:1–8 (HENDERSON)

By nicht on my bed I soucht him wham my saul lo'es, I soucht him, but I cudna fin' him.

I will rise up noo, an' gang about the toun in the throwgangs, an' in the braid roads I will seek him wham my saul lo'es: I soucht him, but I cudna fin' him.

The watchmen wha gang about the toun fand me: I spier't at them, Hae ye seen him wham my saul lo'es?

It was but a wee bit I had gane frae them, whan I fand him wham my saul lo'es: I grippet him, an' wadna let him gae, till I had broucht him intil my mither's house, an' intil the chammer o'her wha bure me.

I rede ye, O ye dochters o'Jerusalem, by the raes an' by the hin's o' the field, that ye dinna steer up, nar wauken my love, till he likes.

Wha is yon comin' out o' the muir like til lunts o' reek, smellin' o' myrrh an' frankincense, an' a' the powthers o' the merchan'?

Behald his bed, whilk is Solomon's; threescoore douchty chiels are roun' it, the maist douchty o' Israel.

They a' haud swerds, bein' weel skeellet in war: ilka chiel has his swerd on his theegh for fear in the nicht.

throwgangs lanes   *spier't* asked   *lunts* columns   *reek* smoke   *chiels* men

SONG OF SOLOMON 3:1–8 (RIDDELL)

Bie nicht on my bed I soucht him wham my saul loes: I soucht him, but fand him nat.

I wull ræise nowe, an' gae aboot the citie in the throwegangs, an' in the braid wayes I wull seek him wham my saul loes; I soucht him, but fin' him I couldna.

The wate-men that gae aboot the citie fand me, til wham I said, Saw ye him wham my saul loes?

It was but awee that I gaed frae thame, whan I fand him wham my saul loes; I haudet him, an' wadna let him gae, quhill I had brung him intil my mither's hous, an' intil the chammer o' hir that conceifet me.

I wærn yow, O ye douchters o' Jerusalem, bie the raes an' bie the hyn's o' the feeld, that ye sturna up nar awauken my loefe quhill he pleese.

Wha is this that cums owt o' the wuldirniss like towiricks o' reek, scentet wi' myrrh an' frankincense, wi' a' powdirs o' the mæchan'?

Behald his bed, whilk is Solomon's, thriescoore veilent men ar aboot it, o' the brafe o' Israel.

Thaye a' haud swerds, being wicht an' weel-skeelet in weir: ilka man hes his swerd apon his thie, becaus' o' dreædour in the nicht.

throwegangs lanes   *wate-men* watchmen   *quhill* until   *towiricks* little towers
reek smoke   *wicht* valiant   *dreædour* fear

Song of Solomon 3:1–8 (Robson)

By nicht on my couch I socht him wha my saul lo'es: I socht him, but I didna find him.

I'll get up the noo, an' gang awa' aboot the toon in the causeys, an' in the braid ways I'll seek him wha my saul lo'es; I socht him, but find him I coudna.

The waitmen that daunder aboot the toon fand me spierin'; quo' I, ha'e ye seed him wha my saul lo'es?

It was but a wee I had gaed frae them, when I fand him wha my saul lo'es; I grippet him fast, an' wadna' let him gang 'til I brung him til my mither's hoose, an' ben til the spence o' her that bore me.

I coonsel ye, O ye dochters o' Jerusalem, by the raes an' the hines o' the field, that ye stirna up nor wauken my love intil his ain pleesure.

Wha's yon comin' oot o' the wilderness like til lunts o' reek smellin' o' myrrh an' incense, wi' a' the pouthers o' the mairchan?

Do ye no see the bed o' Solomon wi' threescore braw chiels aboot it, the wale of the sojers o' Israel?

They a' bear swords, for they are unco' strang i' fecht; ilka chiel hes a blade upo' his theegh, on accoont o' the dreed hoor o' the nicht.

causeys streets   *waitmen* watchmen   *daunder* roam   *spierin'* asking   *spence* bedroom
lunts columns   *reek* smoke   *chiels* men   *wale* choicest

Song of Solomon 4:1–12 (Anonymous (1860))

Behauld, thoo airt fair, my love! behauld, thoo airt fair; thoo hest the een o' doos within thy lokes; thy hair is as ae hirsel o' gaits that kythe frae munt Gilead.

Thy teeth are as ae hirsel o' sheep that are snodlie clippet, whilk cam up frae the washin', whauro' ilka ane hes twuns, an' nane is kebbet amang them.

Thy lips are like ae threed o' scarlet, an' thy speech is winsome; thy forebroos are like ae piece o' pomgranate within thy lokes.

Thy neck is like the toor o' David, bigget for an airmorie, whauron hing ae thoosan' bucklers, a' shields o' dochtie men.

Thy twa breests are like twa young raes that are twuns, whilk feed amang the lillies.

Tull the day daw', an' the shaddies flee awa', I'll tak me t' the muntan o' myrrh, an' t' the hill o' frankincense.

Thoo airt a' fair, my love; there is nae spote in thee.

Come wi' me frae Lebanon, my bride, wi' me frae Lebanon: look frae the tap o' Amana, frae the tap o' Shenir an' Hermon, frae the lions' lairs, frae the muntans o' the lepperds.

Thoo hest reft my hert, my tittie, my bride; thoo hest reft my hert wi' ane o' thine een, wi' ae chine o' thy neck.

Hoo winsome is thy love, my tittie, my bride! hoo muckle better is thy love nor wine! an' the smell o' thy intments nor a' spices!

Thy lips, O my bride, drap as the hinnie-kame: hinnie an' mulk are anoonder thy tongue; an' the smell o' thy claes is like the smell o' Lebanon.

Ae gairden fenset is my tittie, my bride; ae spring steeket up, ae funtan sealet.

hirsel herd   *kythe* appear   *snodlie* smoothly   *kebbet* ewe with stillborn or soon dead offspring   *bigget* built   *reft* plundered or stolen   *tittie* sister   *steeket* shut

Song of Solomon 5:2–16 (Robson)

I sleep, but my hairt is wauken; it is the voice o' my lo'ed ane that tirls, quo' he, Open til me, my tittie, my love, my doo, my unfylet ane; for my heed is droucket wi' weet, an' my hair wi' the draps o' the nicht.

I ha'e putten aff my coat; hoo sall I pit it on? I ha'e washet my feet, hoo sall I fyle them?

My lo'ed ane pat in his haun' by the hole o' the door, an' my bowels yearnet for him.

I raise up til open til my lo'ed ane; an' my hauns drappet wi' myrrh, an' my fingers wi' the sweet-scented myrrh upo' the han'els o' the lock.

I open't til my lo'ed ane; but my lo'ed ane had taen hissel aff, an' was awa'; my saul swoonet as he spak'; I socht him, but I coudna find him; I ca't lood til him, but ansur he didna.

The waitmen gangin' roond the toon; they hat me, an' cut me badly; the wa'-keepers clicket awa' my veil frae me.

I coonsel ye, O dochters o' Jerusalem, gif ye find my lo'ed ane, ye sall say til him, that I'm forfairn wi' love.

What is thy love mair nor anither's love, O thou bonniest o' women? An' what is thy lo'ed ane mair nor anither's lo'ed ane, that thou keeps churmin' sae til us?

My lo'ed ane is fair an' rosy, the tap an' wale o' ten thoosan'.

His heed is like til the finest gowd; his locks are bushy, an' black as a corbie.

His een are like til the een o' doos by the rinlets o' waters, washt wi' milk an' bonnilie setten.

His cheeks are like til a bed o' spices, an' sweet flow'rs; his lips are like til lilies dreepin' wi' sweet smellin' myrrh.

His hauns are like til gowd rings set wi' beryl; his stamach is like til bricht ivory owercassen wi' sapphires.

His legs are like til columns o' marble stan'in' on sockets o' fine gowd; his coontenance like Lebanon, an' grand as the cedars.

His mou' is unco sweet; aye, he is a'thegither beautifu'. This is my ain love, an' this is my frien', O dochters o' Jerusalem.

tirls knocks   *unfylet* undefiled   *droucket* drenched   *clicket* snatched   *forfairn* faint
churmin' complaining   *tap an' wale* best   *corbie* crow

ISAIAH 5:1–7 (WADDELL)

Ill folk's like ane ill yaird; teel't as ye like, ye hae nae rewaird. Rack-rent and herriment, birlin an' bousin; liean an' swearin's a natioun's abusin: Hell gets a gowp o't, an' syne thar 's nae chusin.

An syne I maun sugh a bit sang, till ane I loe weel; the sang, it's my niebor himsel, an' the yaird he can teel. My niebor's a yaird o' his ain, on an unco growthy knowe:

An' he dykit it roun', an flang stanes out enew; an' he set it wi' stoks o' the wale'dest; an' he bigget a towir i' the mids o' the yaird, an' he howket a troch whar the wine maun be shair'd; an' he ettled it syne, till gie grapes in rewaird, bot it gie'd-na a grape but the wildest.

An' now a' ye folk i' Jerus'lem that fen'; an' o' Judah itsel, the lave o' the men; ye maun right atween me an' my vineyaird:

What mair 's till do wi' this yaird o' my ain, that I hae-na dune wi 't *till gar't carry?* whan I leukit syne it suld carry *me* grapes, what for brought it canker'd berries?

Come here awa syne, an' I'se gar yo ken what I ettle till do wi' my vineyaird: I'se out wi' its hedge, I'se down wi' its dyke; an' it 's baith be herried an' moul'ard:

I'se e'en mak it a' wust lan'; it sal neither be sned nor digget; bot the brier an' the thorn, they sal thig it: an' the cluds, I sal gie my commaun, that they dreep-na a drap till sloke it.

For JEHOVAH o' hosts, that vineyaird o' his, *it* 's the houss o' Isra'l; an' the stok he 's sae fain o', 's the men o' Judah: an' he leukit for right, bot ay it was wrang; an' for a' that was straught, bot ay the sugh o' sair tholin.

sugh sing   *teel* till   *knowe* knoll   *dykit* ditched   *wale'dest* choicest   *howket* dug out
shair'd separated from the skins?   *fen'* live   *right* judge   *ettle* intend   *dyke* wall

herried laid waste *moul'ard* allowed to moulder *sued* pruned *thig it* take it over *sugh* moan *tholin* suffering

ISAIAH 6 (WADDELL)

The feck o' God's might 's an unco sight; an' the Seer's tongue maun be tang'd, an he ettle till gang; e'en jimply syne, will folk hearken.

It was i' the year King Uzziah wan hame, I had a sight o' the LORD ontil a thron, uncolie heigh an' carried; an' the weight o' his cleedin, it boukit the temple.

Abune him stude the sax-wing'd seraphs, wi' their sax wings ilk ane: wi' twa *ilk* happit his face, an' wi' twa *ilk* happit his feet, an' wi' twa he couth flee.

Syne cry'd ane till anither, an' quo' he—Halie, Halie, Halie, is JEHOVAH o' hosts; the hail bouk o' yirth 's but the skance o' his glòiry!

An' the stoops o' the door dinnled at the sugh o' the seraph's skreigh; an' the biggin was bing'd wi' reek.

Syne quo' I, Wae's me, for 'am by! for 'am but a foul-lippit loon, an' I bide amang foul-lippit folk; for my een, they hae seen the King, JEHOVAH o' hosts.

Syne flew til me ane o' the seraphs, an' intil his han' a light-coal i' the tangs, he had taen frae atowre the altar.

An' he tang'd on my mouthe; an' quo' he: It's been tang'd on yer lips, an' yer ill's taen awa, an' yer slough's cuisten.

I heard syne the sugh o' the LORD, sayan:—Wha maun I sen'? an' wha is 't maun gang for oursel? An' quo'I, Siclike as I am, sen' me.

An' quo' he, Gang! an' say till this folk *as they fen'*; Ye sal hear like the lave, an' be nane the wysser; ye sal see like the lave, an' ken naething mair.

Mak the folk's heart dreigh, an' their lugs gar them theek, an' their een gar them steek; that they see-na wi' their een, an' wi' their lugs they hear nane, an' wi' their heart they suld-na ken; in case be they suld men', an' do fair.

Bot quo' I, LORD, how lang? An' quo' he, Till the towns be toom'd o' their loons, an' the biggins a' bare, wi' nane till bide thar; an' the yird has been utterlie soopit:

An' the LORD has flittit folk a' far awa, an' the mids o' the lan' has been scoopit.

An' e'en tho' a tent' suld be spared; gin it braird, it sal clean be roopit. Yet ay, like 's the arn an' the aik, whan they 're fell'd their pith 's no kill'd; sae a weel-hain'd seed, the stok o' the folk, sal be stoopit.

uncolie extremely   *boukit* filled   *happit* covered   *bouk* bulk   *skance* light   *stoops* pillars
dinnled shook   *sugh* sound   *skreigh* cry   *bing'd* filled   *reek* smoke
'am by I am finished, lost   *tang'd* touched   *lave* rest   *dreigh* dull   *theek* cover
steek shut   *toom'd* emptied   *biggins* houses   *soopit* swept, cleared   *flittit* moved
tent' tenth   *braird* sprout   *roopit* destroyed   *arn* alder   *hain'd* protected
stoopit supported

Isaiah 9:6,7 (Borrowman)

We hae gotten a bairn oot o jizzen and we hae gotten a son: and the
stere sall be upon his shouther: and his name sall be caad Wonnerfu.
Councillour, the Michty God, the aye-abidan Faither, Athil o Saught. O
the growin o his stere and saught there sall be nae end, upon the trone
o Dauvit, and upon his kinrick tae bigg it wi mense and wi richt-daein,
enoo and for evirmair; the ingine o the Lord o Osts sall hae it dune.

jizzen childbed   *stere* government   *athil* prince   *saught* peace   *kinrick* kingdom
mense intelligence   *ingine* ingenuity

Isaiah 9:6,7 (Gau)

Thair is bairne borne to vsz and thair is ane bairne giffine to wsz quhais
power is apone his schulders his nayme sal be callit wnderlie consalour
stark god fader of the wardil to cum prince of pece his impir sal be
multipleit.

stark strong   *wardil* world

Isaiah 9:6,7 (Nisbet)

For suth a litil child is born to vs, and a sonn is gevin to vs; and
princehede is made on his schuldir; and his name salbe callit Wonndir-
full, and Connsaler, God, Strenthie, a Fader of the warld to-cummand,
Prince of pece. His empire salbe multiplijt, and na end salbe of his pece;

he sal sitt on the sete of Dauid, and on the realme of him, that he conferme it, and mak stark in dome and richtfulnes, frahynfurth and till into withoutin end.

for suth truly *stark* strong

ISAIAH 9:6,7 (WADDELL)

For our Bairn, he's been born; our Son, he's come hame; and the right's like a gad on his shouthir: The Ferlie, the Wyss-redde, sal e'en be his name; the Mighty God, the Faither o' Time; the Laird o' Gudewill thegither.

Nae en' *sal be* till the growth *o' his* gree, an' his frienly gate wi' his neibor; ontil David's thron, an' his kingryk forby, till airt it an' mak it fu' sikker; wi' right an' right-rechtin, frae now an' for ay: lo's the will o' the Lord o' hosts, perfey, sic wark that sal wark the glegger!

right rule? *gad* good *ferlie* wonderful *wyss-redde* wise counsel *gree* supremacy
kingryck kingdom *forby* as well *airt* guide *sikker* secure *right-rechtin* justice
perfey truly *glegger* quicker

ISAIAH 40 (WADDELL)

The tryst-makin for the hame-gaen, an' the reddin o' the road frae Babel: The fleechin o' the LORD *atowre a' eidol gods, an' heart'nin syne for Jakob.*

Hearten ye weel, my folk; hearten ye weel, quo' your God.

Speak heart-healin words till Jerusalem; e'en gar her hear:—That her warsle's by; that her ill's forgien; that scho's doubled now, frae the loof o' the LORD, for a' her wrang-doens!

Quo' a sugh frae the wust sae braid: Redd up the gate o' JEHOVAH; straught owre the nieborless muir, a road for our God ye sal mak it.

Ilk howe maun be heighen'd; ilka knowe, an' ilk brae maun be laighen'd; an' the cruik maun come straught, an' the rough maun come even:

An' the gloir o' the LORD sal win but; an' a' flesch see siclike, that's livin: for the mouthe o' the LORD, it was, spak it.

Syne quo' the sugh, Speak: an' What sal I say? quo' I: A' flesch, it 's but gerss; an' its sheen, but the blum o' the fiel'.

The gerss, it maun gae, an' the blum winna stay; whan the drouth o' the LORD is blawin. O surely the folk, they're but haie!

The gerss, it maun gae, an' the blum winna stay; bot the word o' our God stan's, ay growin.

Up ti' the craig fu' hie, Dochtir wi' tidins till gie until Zioun! Up wi' yer tongue sae bauld; Dochtir, the news maun be tauld, till Jerusalem! Up, an' be nane affley'd; cry till the towns o' Judah *wide*, Leuk yer ain God, he 's comin!

Leuk, it's the LORD himsel; reddin the road wi' might, an' his arm rax't out atowre him. Leuk, for the darg's his ain; an' the worth o' his wark 's afore him.

Like the herd, he sal tent his fe: he sal oxter the lams himsel, an' his bosom sal fauld them fu' snod in; an' the yowes that are mithers till be, he sal cannily airt on the roddin.

Wha keppit the fludes in his loof, an' laid aff the lift wi' a span? an' streekit the stoure o' the yirth in a caup; an' weightit the heights on brods, an' bawkit the hills wi' *his han'*?

Wha ettled JEHOVAH's breath, or wyss-man o' his gied him lear?

Wha-wi' teuk he thought, made him wysser; or taught him right-rechtin till ware? or yet gied him gude understandin'; or airted him straughter till fuhre?

Na, the folk's but a drap i' the leglen; like stoure on the bawk, till his ee; an' the out-lyin folk on the watirs, he taks like a mote i' the sea!

No Lebanon's sel for a bleeze, nor its beiss for ane offran', wad stan': A' the folk syne fornenst him war nocht, an' like naething, or less, till his han'.

Till wham, syne, will ye liken God? or what draught o' yer ain will ye schupe him?

The founder, he cowps out a cast; an' the smith, he can cleed it wi' gowd, an' oop it wi' links o' siller.

Wha-sae canna fa' siclike, he wales a bit lastie timmer; some skeely han' maks an eidol o' that, sal stan' i' the neuk for evir.

Dinna ye ken? winna ye hear-ken? was't-na weel tell'd ye, ay frae the fore? Kenn'd ye na this, frae the yirth was in store?

Wha sits on the girth o' the yirth, an' its on-dwallers a' *are* but imoks afore him; wha streeks out the lift like a skift, an' raxes the *cluds* like a simmer-shielin:

Wha breinges the big folk till nought; wha maks lairds o' the yirth but a toom spailin:

They sal lea' neither soukir nor seed; their stok i' the grun sanna breed; on them gin he blaw, they sal wither awa; an' like stibble, the storm gar them skreed.

Till wham sal ye even me, than? or sal I be made like, quo' the Halie Ane, syne?

Rax up yer een, an' leuk: wha schupit a' the same? wha airts but their thrang ayont tellin, cryin ilk ane by his name? sae grit is his might an' his can-cracht, no ane o' them a' bides at hame.

What-for syne, cry ye, O Jakob? an' Isra'l, what-for do ye mene? My gate, frae the LORD it's been happit; an' my right, frae my God it's forlien!

Dinna ye ken? hae-na ye heard? that JEHOVAH's ay God himsel! the schaiper o' a' the outgaens o' yirth; that he's neither weak nor weary, an' his kennin's ayont a' tell!

Heart gies he till the dowie; an' the feckless, he stoops fu' weel:

Aye, young lads may swak an' weary; an' braw lads come down wi' a sweel;

Bot wha lippen ay till JEHOVAH, they sal eke out their strenth an' a'; they sal cleed them twice owre, like the aigle: they sal rin an' they sanna paingle; they sal gang, an' be nane forfoch'en ava!

---

warsle struggle   *scho's doubled* she has received double   *loof* hand   *sugh* voice
wust wilderness   *redd up* make clear   *howe* hollow   *cruik* crooked   *gloir* glory
win but come out   *affleyed* afraid   *reddin* clearing   *rax't* stretched   *atowre* away from
darg work   *tent* tend   *fe* sheep   *oxter* put under his arm   *snod* snug   *airt* guide
roddin sheep-track   *keppit* caught, contained   *loof* hand   *lift* sky
streekit measured out   *stoure* dust   *brods* scales   *baukit* weighed   *ettled* directed
lear instruction   *ware* dispense   *fuhre* go   *leglin* pail   *fornenst* in front of
cowps turns out   *oop* overlay   *fa'* obtain   *lastie* durable   *imoks* ants   *skift* curtain?
breinges dashes   *spailin* wood-shaving   *skreed* tear apart

ISAIAH 60 (WADDELL)

An Zioun's light war kennle'd right, an unco skance on the warld sal be: the gloam sal gang, an' the folk sal thrang, an' sal lout till the LORD on ilka knee.

Wauken an' light, for yer light's weel on; an' the gloir o' the LORD, it sal crown yo:

Aye, mirk it sal theek the yirth, an' gloam on the folk it sal lye syne; bot the LORD sal gang heigh, *wi' a bleeze*, owre yersel, an' his gloir sal be seen abune yo: an' the folk, they sal come till *the lowe o'* yer light, an' kings till the skance o' yer risin.

Rax yer een roun', an' see; they gather ilk ane, they come a' till thee:

frae far eneugh owre, yer sons they sal fuhre, an yer dochtirs aside them sal carried be. It's syne ye sal trimmle an' gang like a flude: an' yer heart it sal thole, an' rax the snood: whan sic a braw spate sal rowe yer ain gate, an' the feck o' the folk till yersel sal swee.

Droves o' camels sal theek yo thrang; dromedars frae Midian an' Ephah: the lave o' siclike frae Sheba sal gang; gowd an' spyse, they sal carry't alang; an' sal lilt out the laud o' JEHOVAH. Hail flocks frae Kedar sal gather till thee; the tups o' Nebaioth sal ser' yo fine: they sal gang for an offran till pleasur me; an' my howff sae braw I sal glorify syne.

An' wha can thae be, like a clud that flee, an' like dowis till their dookats abreid? *Wha* but the isles that's waitin on me, an' the schips o' Tarshish at their head? a' till fesh hame yer sons frae outowre, their siller an' gowd wi' themsels an' a'; till JEHOVAH's name, that's God o' yer ain, an' Isral's Halie Ane, for he made yo braw.

An' the sons o' the frem, they sal bigg yer dykes; an' their kings, they sal be at yer beck wi' a': for ance, i' my wuth, I raught yo reyks; bot wi' unco luve I sal tak yo a'. Syne wide eneugh ay, yer yetts they sal be; day nor night, they'se be steekit nane: for the feck o' the folk till win hame till thee; an' their kings, *in levee*, sal be airtit ben. For the folk an' reàle winna lout till yersel, frae the lave o' the warld they sal thowe awa; aye, folk siclike, wi' an unco reyk, sal be riv'n in twa.

Aye, Lebanon's crown, till yersel sal come roun'; the bright an' the tight, an' the straught thegither: my halie bit sae braw till fit; whar my feet maun stan', I sal mak it gran' like nae ither.

An' the sons o' wha wrang'd yo ance, they sal come an' sal cow'r till thee; an' sal lout till the soles o' yer feet, a' that ance lightlied yer plea: an' sal cry till yo syne, The LORD's ain town; the Zioun's sel, o' Him that's fu' lown intil Israel.

An' e'en's ye 'been skail'd an' misliket, wi' nane till gang thro' yo ava'; I'se mak yo nae en' o' blythe bidden, a joie till folk's outcome a':

An' ye'se pree o' the milk o' the hethen, an' thrive at the breist o' kings; an' ye 'se ken syne, mysel that's JEHOVAH, 's yer heal-hadder an' e'en yer hame-bringer, sae stieve intil Jakob *that rings*.

For brass, I sal e'en fesh the gowd; an' for airn, I 'se fesh siller an' a': for timmer, it's brass; an' for stanes, it 's airn I *sal ca'*: an' yer owre-leukers syne I 'se mak peace; an' yer tax-men, the best o' law. Nae mair sal stouthrief be heard i' yer lan'; wust nor wrang, intil a' yer marches: bot Salvatioun's sel, *till* yer dykes ye sal cry; an' Laud, ye sal cry, *till a'* yer arches. Nae mair sal the sun be yer day-light syne; nor the mune nae mair, be for sheen till guide yo: bot the LORD till yersel sal be light evir mair, an' that God o' yer ain be for gloir aside yo. Nae mair sal yer sun gang hame at night, nor yer mune ony mair be mendit: for the LORD, he sal e'en be yer lastin light; an' the days o' yer dule sal be endit.

Syne rightous eneugh, yer folk *sal be a'*; an' the lan', evir mair they sal haud it: the schute o' my sheughin, my ain han's makin, that sae I suld hae a' the laud o't.

Till a thousan', *or lang,* a nought sal growe; an' a wean, till a mighty natioun: mysel, that's the Lord, in time enow, for siclike I sal gie gude cautioun.

mirk darkness   *theek* cover   *lowe* flame   *skance* light   *thole* suffer
rax the snood break its bands?   *feck* greatest part   *swee* swing   *lave* rest   *tups* rams
howff dwelling place   *the frem* strangers   *dykes* walls   *wuth* anger
raught yo reyks struck you   *yetts* gates   *steekit* shut   *reàle* kingdom   *but* bow
thowe melt   *reyk* blow   *lightlied* slighted   *skailed* scattered   *blythe bidden* blessing
outcome descendants   *pree* taste   *heal-hadder* saviour   *stieve* strong   *rings* reigns
owre-leukers rulers   *stouthrief* violent robbery   *sheughin* planting   *or lang* before long
cautioun guarantee

Matthew 2:1–11 (Borrowman)

Noo, when Jesus was born in Bethlehem o Judaea in the days o Herod the Roy, there cam wyce men east-bye, tae Jerusalem.

Speirin, 'whaur is he wha is born Roy o the Jews? sin we hae gliskit his starn eassilt, and ettle tae worship him'.

Whan Herod the Roy was telt aboot it, he was fashit and aa Jerusalem wi him.

And when he had conveenit aa the Heigh Priests, and aa the Writers o the fowk thegither, he speirt at them whaur the native o Christ suld be.

And quo they tae him, 'In Bethlehem o Judaea, for sae it is screevit by the prophet.

And ye, Bethlehem in the kintra o Juda arena the peeriest amang the athils o Juda, for out o ye sall come a Capitane wha sall haud the stere owre ma fowk, Israel'

Than Herod, whan he spak in chaumer wi the wyce men, speirt at them eidentlie, whatna time the starn had been gliskit.

And he sent them awa tae Bethlehem, and quo he, 'Gang and speir eidentlie anent the wee laddie, and whan ye hae fun him, be shair and lat me ken, sin Ah maun come and worship him alsweel'.

Whan they had lippent tae the Roy, they tuik the gait and the starn whilk they saw eassilt gaed afore them, till it cam and stude owre whaur the bairn liggit.

Whan they saw the starn, they were unco blythe, aye, teemin owre wi joy. And when they cam intae the hoose they saw the bairnikin wi Mary his mither, and loutit doon, and worshipt him: and whan they had toomit their thesaury they gied him compliments; gowd, and frank-incense, and myrrh.

roy king   *east-bye* from the east   *speirin* asking   *gliskit* caught sight of
eassilt eastwards   *ettle* intend   *fashit* troubled   *native* birth-place
screevit written   *peeriest* smallest   *athils* princes   *stere* rule   *eidentlie* diligently
lippent attended to   *liggit* lay   *loutit* bowed   *toomit* emptied
thesaury supply of treasures   *compliments* presents

MATTHEW 5:3–13 (HENDERSON)

Blesset are the puir in spirit: for theirs is the kingdom o' heaven.
Blesset are they wha murn: for they sall be comfortet.
Blesset are the meek: for they sall inherit the yirth.
Blesset are they wha hunger an' thirst after richteousness: for they
sall be fillet.
Blesset are the mercifu': for they sall obteen mercy.
Blesset are the pure in hairt: for they sall see God.
Blesset are the peace-makers: for they sall be ca'd the childer o' God.
Blesset are they wha are persecutet for richteousness' sak': for theirs
is the kingdom o' heaven.
Blesset are ye, whan men sall misca' you, an' persecute you, an' sall
say a' kin'kind o' evil agayne you fausely, for my sak'.
Rejoice, an' be unco glad; for meikle is your reward in heaven: for
sae persecutet they the prophets wha were afore you.
Ye are the saut o' the yirth; but gif the saut hath tint its savour,
wharewi' sall it be sautet? it is thance-furth guid for naething, but to
be coost out, an' to be trampet under fit o' men.

misca' revile   *a' kin'kind* every kind   *meikle* great   *tint* lost

MATTHEW 5:3–13 (LORIMER)

Hou happie the puir at is hummle afore God,
    for theirs is the Kíngdom o heiven!
Hou happie the dowff an dowie,
    for they will be comfortit!
Hou happie the douce an cannie,
    for they will faa the yird!

Hou happie them at yaups an thrists for richteousness,
  for they will get their sairin!
Hou happie the mercifu,
  for they will win mercie!
Hou happie the clean o hairt,
  for they will see God!
Hou happie the redders o strow an strife,
  for they will be caa'd the childer o God!
Hou happie them at hes dree'd misgydin for richteousness' sake,
  for theirs is the Kíngdom o Heiven!

Hou happie ye, whan they tash an misgyde ye an say aathing ill o ye, líein on ye, for my sake! Blythe be ye an mirkie, for gryte is the rewaird bidin ye in heiven; it wis een sae they misgydit the Prophets afore ye.

  Ye ar the saut o the warld. But gin the saut gaes saurless, what will gíe it back its tang? There is nocht adae wi it mair but cast it outbye for fowk tae patter wi their feet.

dowff sad   *dowie* unhappy   *douce* quiet   *cannie* gentle   *faa* obtain   *yaups* hunger
sairin fill   *redders* peace-makers   *strow* commotion   *dree'd* endured
misgydin illtreatment   *tash* insult   *mirkie* cheerful   *saurless* tasteless   *adae* to do
patter trample

Matthew 5:3–13 (Nisbet)

Blessit be pure men in spirit: for the kingdom of heuenis is tharis. Blessit be myld men: for thai sal weld the erde. Blessit be thai that murnis: for thai salbe confortit. Blessit be thai that hungris and threstis richtwisnes: for thai salbe fulfillit. Blessit be merciful men: for thai sal get mercy. Blessit be thai that ar of clene hart: for thai sal se God. Blessit be peciabile men: for thai salbe callit Goddis childir. Blessit be thai that suffiris persecutioun for richtwisnes: for the kingdom of heuenis is tharis. Ye salbe blessit quhen men sal curse you, and sal persew you, and sal say al euil aganis you leand, for me. Joy ye, and be ye glaid; for your mede is plentuous in heuenis: for sa thai haue persewit alsa prophetis that war before you. Ye ar salt of the erde: that gif the salt vanyse away, quharein sal it be saltit? to nathing is it worthi ouer, but that it be castin out, and be defoulit of men.

weld rule   *leand* lying   *mede* reward

Matthew 5:3–13 (Riddell)

Blisset *ar* the puir in speerit: for theirs is the kingdoom o' heæven.

Blisset *ar* they that murn: for they sall be comfortet.

Blisset *ar* the meik: for they sall inherit the yirth.

Blisset *ar* they that do hunger an' thirst efter richtiousniss: for they sall be fillet.

Blisset *ar* the mercifu': for they sall obteen mercie.

Blisset *ar* the pure in hairt: for they sall see God.

Blisset *ar* the peace-makers: for they sall be ca't the childer o' God.

Blisset *ar* they whilk *ar* persecutet for richtiousniss' sak': for theirs is the kingdoom o' heæven.

Blisset *ar* ye whan men sall misca' yow, an' persecute yow, an' sall say a' kinkind o' ill agayne yow fauselie, for my sak'.

Rejoice an' be excessiv glad: for grit is your rewaird in heæven: for sae persecutet they the prophets whilk wer afore yow.

Ye ar the saut o' the yirth: but gif the saut has lost its savor, wharewi' sall it be sautet? it is frae that time furth guid for naething but til be casan out, an' trampet under fit o' men.

misca' revile   *a' kinkind* every sort

Matthew 5:3–13 (Smith)

Happy the spirits that are lown and cannie: for the kingdom o' Heeven is waitin for them!

Happy they wha are makin their maen; for they sal fin' comfort and peace.

Happy the lowly and meek o' the yirth: for the yirth sal be their ain haddin.

Happy they whase hunger and drouth are a' for holiness: for they sal be satisfy't!

Happy the pitfu': for they sal win pitie theirsels!

Happy the pure-heartit: for their een sal dwal upon God!

Happy the makkers-up o' strife: for they sal be coontit for bairns o' God!

Happy the ill-treatit anes for the sake o' gude: for they'se hae the kingdom o' God!

Happy sal ye be when folk sal misca' ye, and ill-treat ye, and say a' things again ye wrangouslie for my sake!

Joy ye, and be blythe! for yere meed is great in Heeven! for e'en sae did they to the prophets afore ye!

The saut o' the yirth are ye: but gin the saut hae tint its tang, hoo's it to be sautit? Is it no clean useless? to be cuisten oot, and trauchl't under folk's feet.

lown quiet *cannie* gentle *haddin* possession *pitfu'* misprint for *pitifu'?* *misca'* revile
meed reward *tint* lost *trauchl't* trampled

MATTHEW 5:3–13 (STUART)

Blythe are they wha ken thair need o God; for the Kingdom o Hevin is waitin for them.

Blythe are they wha are sorrowfu; for they sall find comfort an peace.

Blythe are the lowly an meek o the erthe; for they sall inherit the erthe.

Blythe are they whase hunger an drowth are aa for haliness; for they sall be satisfyit.

Blythe are the pitifu; for they sal win pitie thairsels.

Blythe are the pure o hert; for thair een sall dwell apon God.

Blythe are the peace-makers; for they sall be coontit as bairns o God.

Blythe are the ill-treatit anes for the sake o guid; for they sall hae the Kingdom o God.

Blythe sall ye be whan folk sall mis-caa ye, an persecute ye, an say things aganis ye fause, for ma sake. Be blythe an hae joy, for yer rewaird is grete in Hevin; for e'en so did they tae the prophets afore ye.

The saut o the erthe ye are, but gin the saut has tint its tang, hoo's it tae be sautit? It is wi'oot use but tae be cast away an tramplit under the feet o folk.

tint lost

MATTHEW 5:43–48; 6:1–23 (NISBET)

Ye haue herd that it was said to aldmen, Thou sal lufe thi nechbour, and hate thin ennimy: Bot I say to you, lufe your ennimyes, do ye wele to thame that hates you, and pray ye for thame that persewis and sclandiris you; That ye be the sonnis of your fadir that is in heuenis: that makis his sonne to rise vponn gude and euil men, and raynis on just and vniust men. For gif ye lufe thame that luvis you, quhat mede sal ye haue? quhethir gif publicanis dois nocht this? And gif ye salus your brethir anlie, quhat sald ye do maire? quhethir gif hethinmen dois nocht this? Tharfor be ye perfite, as your heuenlie fadir is perfite.

Takis hede that ye do nocht your richtwisnes befor men, to be sene of thame; ellis ye sal haue na mede at your fadir that is in heuenis. Tharfor, quhen thou dois almes, will thou nocht blaw trumpet befor thee, as ypocritis dois in synagogis and stretis, that thai be wirschipit of men. Suthlie I say to you, thai haue ressauet thar mede. Bot quhen thou dois almes, know nocht thi left hand quhat thi richt hande dois; That thin almes be in hidlis: and thi fadir that seis in hidlis sal quite thee. And quhen ye pray, ye sal nocht be as ypocritis: that luvis to pray standand in synagogis and newkis of stretis, to be sene of men. Trewlie I say to you, thai haue ressauet thar mede. Bot quhen thou sal pray, entir into thi cubicile, and quhen the dure is closit, pray thi fadir in hidlis; and thi fader that seis in hidlis sal yeld to thee. Bot in praying, wil ye nocht speke mekile, as hethin men dois: for thai wene that thai ar herde in thar mekile speche. Tharfor wil ye nocht be made like to thame: for your fader wate quhat is nedeful to you befor that ye ask him. And thus ye sal pray: Our fader that art in heuenis, hallewit be thi name. Thi kingdom cum to. Thi wil be done in erde, as in heuen. Gefe to vs this day our breid ouer vthir substance. And forgif to vs our dettis, as we forgef to our dettouris. And leid vs nocht into temptatioun, bot deliuer vs fra euile. Amen. For gif ye forgefe to men thar synnis, your heuenlie fader sal forgefe to you your trespassis: Suthlie gif ye forgeve nocht to men, nouthir your fader sal forgeue to you your synnis. Bot quhen ye fast, wil ye nocht be made as ypocritis soroufull: for thai deface thameself, to seme fastand to men. Trewlie I say to you, thai haue ressauet thar mede. Bot quhen thou fastis, anoynt thi heid, and wesch thi face; That thou be nocht sene fastand to men, bot to thi fader that is in hidlis: and thi fader, that seis in priuee, sal yeld to thee.

Will ye nocht tresoure to you tresouris in erde, quhar roust and mouris destroyis, and quhar thevis delues out and steles. Bot gader to you tresouris in heuen, quhar nouthir roust nor mowris destroyis, and quhar thevis deluis nocht out nore steilis: For quhare thi tresour is, thar alsa thin hart is. The lannterne of thi body is thin e: gif thin e be sympile, al thi body salbe lichtfull. Bot gif thin e be waywart, al thi body salbe mirk. Gif than the licht that is in thee be mirknessis, how gret sal thailk mirknessis be!

---

aldmen men in the past   *mede* reward   *quhethir gif publicanis dois nocht this* do not tax-gatherers do this?   *salus* greet   *suthlie* truly   *hidlis* secret   *quite* repay *yeld to* reward   *mekile* much, big   *wate* knows   *mouris* ants   *delves* dig   *e* eye *sympile* innocent, honest   *thailk* that same

MATTHEW 6:9–13 (BORROWMAN)

Faither o us aa, bidan Abune! Thy name be holie! Lat Thy reign begin!
Lat thy wull be dune, on the yirth as in the Lift. Gie us ilka day our
needfu fendin. And forgie us aa our ill deeds, as we forgie thae wha did
us ill. And lat us no be siftit; but save us frae aa ill. For the croun is
Thine ain, and the micht and the glorie, for evir and evir, AMEN.

lift Heaven   *fendin* provisions   *siftit* tested

MATTHEW 6:9–13 (HENDERSON)

Our Father wha art in heaven, Hallowet be thy name.
Thy kingdom come. Thy will be dune in yirth as it is in heaven.
Gie us this day our daily bread.
An' forgie us our debts, as we forgie our debtors:
An' lead us na intil temptation, but deliver us frae evil; for thine is
the kingdom, an' the power, an' the glory, for ever. Amen.

MATTHEW 6:9–13 (LORIMER)

Our Faither in heiven,
  hallowt be thy name;
  thy Kíngdom come;
  thy will be dune
on the yird, as in heiven.

Gíe us our breid for this incomin day;
forgíe us the wrangs we hae wrocht,
  as we hae forgíen the wrangs we hae dree'd;
an sey-us-na sairlie, but sauf us
  frae the Ill Ane.

dree'd suffered   *sey-us-na* do not test us

MATTHEW 6:9–13 (RIDDELL)

Our Faether whilk art in heæven. Hallowet be thy name.
Thy kingdoom come. Thy wull be dune in yirth, as *it is* in heæven.
Gie us this day our daily breæd.
An' forgie us our dets as we forgie our detters:
An' leed-us-na intill temptatione, but deliver us frae ill: for thine is
the kingdoom, an' the power, an' the glorie, for evir. Saebeid.

MATTHEW 6:9–13 (SMITH)

Faither o' us a', bidin Aboon! Thy name be holie!
Lat thy reign begin! Lat thy wull be dune, on the Yirth as in Heeven!
Gie us ilka day oor needfu' fendin.
And forgie us a' oor ill deeds, as we e'en forgae thae wha did us ill:
And lat us no be siftit; but save us frae the Ill-Ane! For the croon is
thine ain, and the micht and the glorie, for evir and evir, Amen!

fendin provisions   *siftit* tested

MATTHEW 6:9–13 (STUART)

Faither o us aa, bidin abune,
Thy name be halie.
Let thy reign begin,
Thy Will be dune,
On the erthe, as it is in Hevin.

Gie us ilka day oor needfu fendin,
An forgie us aa oor ill-deeds,
E'en as we forgie thae wha dae us ill.
An lat us no be testit,
But sauf us frae the Ill-Ane:

For the croon is thine ain,
An the micht,
An the glorie;
For iver an iver,
Amen.

fendin provisions

MATTHEW 14:15–33 (HENDERSON)

An' whan it was the gloamin' his disciples cam' til him, sayin', This is a muirland place, an' the time is now gane by; sen' the thrang awa, that they may gae intil the clachans, an' coff themsels victuals.

But Jesus said until them, They needna gang awa: gie ye them to eat.

An' they say until him, We hae here but five laives an' twa fishes.

He said, Bring them here til me.

An' he commaundet the thrang to sit doun on the gerse, an' teuk the five laives an' the twa fishes, an' leukin' up til heaven, he blesset, an' brak, an' gied the laives til his disciples, an' the disciples til the thrang.

An' they did a' eat, an' were satisfiet: an' they teuk up o' the orra bits whilk were left twal creels-fu'.

An' they that had eaten were about five thousan' men, forbye women an' bairns.

An' straughtway Jesus gar't his disciples get intil a ship, an' gae afore him until the tither side, while he sendet the thrang awa.

An' whan he had sendet the thrang awa, he gaed up intil a mountain by himsel to pray: and whan the gloamin' was come he was there alane.

But the ship was now in the middle o' the sea, tosset wi' waves; for the win' was contrair.

An' in the fourt' watch o' the nicht Jesus gaed until them, gangin' on the sea.

An' whan the disciples saw him gangin' on the sea, they were fleyed, sayin', It is a wraith; an' they screighet out for fear.

But straughtway Jesus spak' until them, sayin', Be o' guid cheer; it is me; binna fleyed.

An' Peter answer't him, an' said, Lord, gin it be thou, bid me come until thee on the water.

An' he said, Come. An' whan Peter was come doun out o' the ship he gaed on the water to gang til Jesus.

But whan he saw the win' gousty, he was afear't, an', beginnin' to sink, he criet, sayin', Lord, saufe me.

An' at ance Jesus raught furth his han', an' teuk haud o' him, an' said until him, O thou o' little faith, wharefore didst thou doubt?

An' whan they were come intil the ship, the win' ceaset.

Syne they wha were in the ship cam' an' worshippet him, sayin', Verament thou art the Son o' God.

clachans villages   *coff* buy   *gang* go   *orra* extra   *creels* baskets   *forbye* besides
gar't made   *fleyed* afraid   *screighet* screeched   *verament* truly

MATTHEW 22:1–14 (RIDDELL)

An' Jesus answiret an' spak' untill them agane in parables, an' said,

The kingdoom o' heæven is like untill ane certain king, whilk made ane bridal for his son,

An' sendet furth his servents til ca' them that wer bidden til the waddin': an' they wadna come.

Agane he sendet furth ither servents, sayin', Tell them whilk ar bidden, Behald, I hae prepairet my denner; my ousen an my fatlins *ar* killet, an' a' things *ar* readie: come til the bridal.

But they made licht o't, an' gaed their wayes, ane til his mailin, anither til his merchentdes.

An' the lave tuik his servents, an' treetet them despightfullie an' sleyet them.

But whan the king heard *o't*, he was verra angrie: an' he sendet furth his bands o' weir, an' destroyet thae murderars, an' brunt up their citie.

Than saith he til his servents, The waddin' is readie, but they whilk wer budden werna wurdy.

Gang ye therfor intill the hiewayes, an' as mony as ye sall fin', bid them til the bridal.

Sae thae servents gaed out intill the hiewayes, an' getheret thegither a' as mony as they fand, baith bad an' guid: an' the waddin' was fittet out wi' gests.

An' whan the king cam' in til see the gests, he saw ther ane man whilk hadna ane waddin' garmint:

An' he saith untill him, Frien', how camest thou in hidder, nat haein' ane waddin' garmint? An' he was dumfoun'eret.

Than said the king til the servents, Bin' him han' an' fit, an' tak' him awa, an' cast him intill outter derkness: there sall be greetin' an' cherkin' o' teeth.

For mony ar ca't, but few *ar* chosin.

ousen oxen   *fatlins* fattened animals   *mailin* farm   *lave* rest   *despightfullie* cruelly
greetin' weeping   *cherkin'* gnashing

MATTHEW 24, 25 (LORIMER)

Jesus nou quat the Temple; an, as he gaed alang, the disciples cam up an baud him luik up at the Temple biggins.

'Ye see aa that?' qo he. 'Atweill, I tell ye, no ae stane o them aa will be left abuin anither: the haill Temple will be but a rickle.'

Efterhin, whan he wis sittin his lane on the Hill o Olives, the disciples cam up an said til him, 'Whan is thae things tae be? An whattan taiken will we hae at your back-comin an the hinnerend o the praisent warld is naurhaund?'

Jesus answert, 'Tak tent at nae man leads ye agley! For monie-ane will kythe, takkin my name an threapin, "I am the Christ"; an monie feck they will lead agley. Ye will hear tell o wars an souchs o war, but be ye nane flichtert. Siccan things maun een be, but that isna the end. For fowk will mak war on fowk, an kinrick on kinrick; an faimins there will be an yirdquauks in orra pairts. Aa thae things is but the onfaa o the birth-thraws.

Than will they haund ye owre tae them at will sair ill-gyde ye an kill ye, an in ilka laund ye will be hatit because ye beir my name. Monie will tyne their faith i thae days an betray ilk ither for hate. Monie fauss prophets will kythe an lead monie agley, an wi the wickitness lairge in ilka place the luve o the maist feck will grow cauld. But him at hauds out till the end will be saufed. Mairatowre, this Gospel o the Kingdom will first be preached out-throu the haill warld an made kent til the haithen aagate, an syne the end will come.

Whan, therefore, ye see the *Deidlie Ugsome Thing* at the Prophet Daniel spak o staundin *i the Halie Place*'—ye at reads this, tak tent!—'them at wons in Judaea maun tak the hills. Him at is up on his houss-heid maunna gae doun intil the houss tae lift his gear, an him at is afield maunna gang back hame tae fesh his coat. Wae's me for weimen at is big wi bairn or gíein souk i thae days! Pray at your flicht faasna in wintertime, or on the Sabbath, for the *dule an dree* o that time will be *sic as there hesna been the like o frae the beginnin o the warld till nou*, nor nivermair will be. Gin thae days hedna been shortent, nae-ane avà wad be left tae the fore: but shortent they will be for the sake o the Eleck. Gin onie-ane says tae ye than, "Luik, here's the Christ", or "See, yonder's the Christ", lippen-him-na. For monie fauss Christs an fauss prophets will kythe an wurk míracles an ferlies tae gar een the Eleck gae will, coud sic a thing be. Mind, nou, I hae wairned ye! Gin they say tae ye than, "He's thereout i the muirs", gang-ye-na furth; or gin they tell ye, "He's ben the houss in ane o the chaumers", lippen-them-na. For as the fireflaucht lowps leamin athort the lift frae the aist tae the wast, een sae will be the comin o the Son o Man. Whaur the carcage liggs, thair the vulturs forgethers.

As shune as thae days o dule an dree is by,

> The sun will be mirkit,
>   an the muin winna gíe her licht;
> the stairns will faa frae the carrie,
>   an the pouers i the lift will be dinnelt.

Than will the sign o the Son o Man kythe i the lift, an aa the clans o the yird will murn an baet their breists; an they will see the Son o Man comin on the clouds o the lift wi unco micht an glore. Wi a dunnerin blast o the horn he will send furth his angels; an they will gether his Eleck frae the fowr airts, frae the tae end o the lift tae the tither.

Tak a lesson o the feg-tree. Whan its ryss grows sappie an saft, an the leafs onfaulds, ye ken at the simmer is naur. Siclike, whan ye see aa thir things happnin, ye maun ken at the end is naur—ay, at your verra doors!

Atweill, I tell ye, this generâtion winna pass awà or aa thir things hes happent. The lift an the yird will pass awà, but my wurds winna pass awà. But the day an the hour nae-ane kens, no een the angels in heiven, nor the Son: na, nane but the Faither alane!

At the comin o the Son o Man it will be the same wey as it wis i the days o Noah. I thae days afore the Fluid fowk wis thrang aitin an drinkin, mairriein an gíein in mairrage, richt up tae the time whan Noah gaed intil the Airk; an naething jaloused they, or the Fluid cam an soopit them aa awà. That is the wey it will be at the comin o the Son o Man. Twa men will be wurkin thegither i the field—ane o them will be taen, an the tither left ahent; twa weimen will be caain a haundmill thegither—ane o them will be taen, an the tither left ahent. Haud ye ey wauken, than, for ye kenna what day your Maister is comin. But o this ye may be shair: gin the guidman hed kent at what hour of the nicht the thíef wis tae come, he wad hae bidden waukin, an no latten his houss be brakken intil. Sae ye, tae, maun ey be reddie, sin the Son o Man will come at an hour whan ye'r bodin him nane.

Wha's the wysslike an faithfu servan at his maister lippent wi the owrance o the lave, an seein at they war maitit raiglar? Happie man, at his maister, whan he comes hame, finnds daein the wark he wis gíen tae dae! He'll gíe him the gydin o aa he is aucht, I s' warran ye. But gin he is an ill-set bleck, yon servan, an says til himsel, "He's lang o comin, the Maister", an faas tae lounderin the ither servans an gilravagin wi the dribblin-core, syne, on a day he bodesna, an at an hour he kensna, the maister o that servan will come hame, an will hag him in píeces an assign him his dail wi the hýpocrítes; an it is there at the yaumer an the chirkin o teeth will be!

Here is whatlike it will be wi the Kíngdom o Heiven, whan that day comes. The' wis aince ten deames gaed out tae meet the bridegroom an the bride at a waddin, takkin their bouets wi them. Five o them wis glaikit lassies, an five wis wysslike queyns. The glaikit anes tuik their bouets, but they tuik nae orra oil wi them: but the wysslike anes tuik baith their bouets an oil-pouries forbyes.

The bridegroom wis lang o comin, an the lassies aa dovert an fell owre. At midnicht the cry wis raised: "Here's the bridegroom; come out an meet him!" The din waukent the lassies, an they rase an fettelt up their bouets.

The glaikit anes said tae the wyss anes, "Lat see a twa-three draps oil: our bouets is gaein out!"

"Nae fears!" the wyss anes answert. "We haena what wad sair ye an hiz baith belike. Better gae tae the chops an buy yoursels some." Sae aff they gaed tae buy their oil.

I the mids o the meantime the bridegroom cam, an the lassies at wis reddie gaed inbye wi him tae the waddin-brakfast, an the door wis steikit. A whilie efter, the ither lassies cam an begoud cryin, "Pleise, sir, apen the door til us!" But he answert, "Atweill, I hae nae kennin o ye avà!" Haud ye ey wauken, than; for ye ken naither the day nor the hour.

Or again, it is like this. A man at wis gaein out o the kintra caa'd up his servans an haundit his haudin owre tae them tae gyde. He lippent ane wi five talents, anither wi twa, an a third wi ane—ilkane wi the soum confeirin til his capacitie. Syne he gaed his waas out o the kintra. The man at hed gotten the five talents gaed strecht awà an yuised them sae weill in tredd at he made ither five talents; an siclike him at hed gotten the twa talents wan ither twa talents. But him at hed gotten the ae talent gaed awà an howkit a hole i the grund an hade his maister's siller intil it.

Efter a lang time, the maister o thae servans cam hame an huid a racknin wi them. Him at hed gotten the five talents cam forrit wi ither five talents forbye an said, "Maister, ye lippent me wi five talents: see, here's ither five talents I hae made."

"Weill dune, guid an leal servan!" said his maister til him. "Ye hae been leal wi the gydin o little, I s' gíe ye the gydin o muckle. Awà in tae your Maister's banqet!"

Syne him at hed gotten the twa talents cam forrit an said, "Maister, ye lippent me wi twa talents: see, here's ither twa talents I hae made."

"Weill dune, guid an leal servan!" said his maister. "Ye hae been leal wi the gydin o little, I s' gíe ye the gydin o muckle. Awà in tae your Maister's banqet!"

Lest, him at gat the ae talent cam forrit an said, "Maister, I kent ye for a dour man an a stour, at maws whar he hesna sawn, an shears whaur he hesna seedit; sae I wis feared, an gaed awà an hade your talent i the grund: here it is back tae ye."

"Ye sweird wratch o a servan!" said his maister. "Ye kent at I maw whaur I haena sawn, an shear whaur I haena seedit—ye kent that, na? A-weill, than, ye suid hae pitten my siller i the Bank, an syne I wad hae gotten it back wi annualrent at my hamecome. Tak his talent awà frae him, an gíe it til him at hes the ten talents:

> For til havers mair is gíen,
> > till it faur outgangs their need:
> frae not-havers is taen
> > een what they hae.

An cast yon wanwurdie servan intil the mirk outbye." It is there at the yaumer an the chirkin o teeth will be!

Whan the Son o Man comes in his glorie, an aa his angels wi him, he will sit him doun on his throne o glorie; an aa the fowks o the yird will be gethert afore him, an he will shed them intil twa hirsels, as a herd sheds the sheep frae the gaits; an the sheep he will hirsel on his richt haund, an the gaits on his cair haund.

Than the Kíng will say til them on his richt haund, "Come your waas, ye at hes my Faither's blissin, an tak possession o your heirskip, the Kíngdom prepared for ye frae the founds o the warld wis laid. For I wis yaup, an ye gae me mait; I wis thristie, an ye gae me drink; I wis an outlan, an ye gae me bed an bicker; I wis nakit, an ye cleadit me; I wis síck, an ye tentit me; I wis in jyle, an ye cam inbye tae me."

Syne the richteous will answer, "Lord, whan saw we ye yaup, an gae ye mait? Or thristie, an gae ye drink? Whan saw we ye an outlan, an gae ye bed an bicker? Or nakit, an cleadit ye? Whan saw we ye síck or in jyle, an gaed inbye til ye?"

Syne the Kíng will say til them, "Atweill, I tell ye, oniething at ye did til ane o thir hummle brithers o mine, ye did it til me."

Than will he say til them on his cair haund, "Awà wi ye out o my sicht, ye curst anes, awà til the iverlestin fire prepared for the Deivil an his angels! For I wis yaup, an ye gae-me-na mait; I wis thristie, an ye gae-me-na drink; I wis an outlan, an ye gae-me-na bed an bicker; I wis nakit, an ye cleadit-me-na; I wis síck an in jyle, an ye tentit-me-na."

Syne they, tae, will answer, "Lord, whan saw we ye yaup, or thristie, or an outlan, or nakit, or síck, or in jyle, an wadna dae ocht for ye?"

An he will say tae them, "Atweill, I tell ye, oniething at ye did no dae til ane o thir hummle anes, ye did no dae it tae me." An thir will gang awà til iverlestin punishment, but the richteous will gang til iverlestin life.'

---

biggins buildings   *rickle* heap (of stones)   *his lane* on his own   *hinnerend* end   *agley* astray
kythe appear   *threapin* vehemently asserting   *monie feck* a great many   *souchs* rumours
flichtert afraid   *kinrick* kingdom   *onfaa* beginning   *birth-thraws* contractions of labour
ill-gyde mistreat   *tyne* lose   *maist feck* majority   *mairatowre* besides   *aagate* everywhere
ugsome horrible   *wons* live   *dule an dree* grief and misfortune   *tae the fore* alive
lippen believe   *ferlies* marvels   *will* astray   *ben* inside   *fireflaucht* lightning
leamin flashing   *liggs* lies   *mirkit* darkened   *carrie* sky   *lift* sky   *dinnelt* shaken
dunnerin thundering   *ryss* branch   *thrang* busy   *jaloused* suspected   *soopit* swept
ahent behind   *caain* working   *bodin* waiting for   *owrance* superintendance   *lave* rest
he is aucht he possesses   *ill-set* wicked   *bleck* scoundrel   *lounderin* beating
gilravagin carousing   *dribbling-core* drunkards   *hag* hack   *dail* portion   *yaumer* howling
chirkin gnashing   *deames* young married women   *bouets* lanterns   *glaikit* irresponsible
queyns young unmarried women   *orra* extra   *oil-pouries* oil-flasks   *forbyes* as well
dovert dozed   *fell owre* fell asleep   *fettelt up* saw to   *lat see* give us   *belike* probably
chops shops   *steikit* shut   *begoud* began   *haudin* possessions   *gyde* look after
confeirin corresponding   *howkit* dug   *hade* hid   *siller* money   *huid* held   *stour* stern
sweird lazy   *annualrent* interest   *wanwurdie* unworthy   *shed* divide   *hirsels* flocks   *cair* left
heirskip inheritance   *yaup* hungry   *outlan* stranger   *bicker* food   *cleadit* clothed
tentit took care of

MARK 5: 21–25, 27–42 (STUART)

Jairus' Dochter

Whan Jesus gaed back til the ither side o the loch, a grete thrang o folk gaithert aboot him. Noo, tak tent, thair kythit a man caa'd Jairus wha wis ruler o the Synagogue. He lowtit doon at Jesus' feet an socht o him tae come til his hoose. 'Ma dochter is at daith's door,' he cried. 'Gin thou wid but come an lay yer hauns ower her, she wid be sauvit, an she wid live'. Jesus gaed wi him, an monie folk followit an thrangit him.

Amang them wis a wumman wha had suffert frae a rin o bluid for twal year. Whan she heard of the things aboot Jesus, she cam up frae ahint in the crood an touched the hem o his coat, kennin that she wid be hailed. The fountain o her bluid wis stemmed at aince, an she kent in hersel that she wish deliverit frae that ill.

But Jesus, takin tent o the poo'er gaun oot frae him, turned aboot in the thrang an speired, 'Wha touched me?' The disciples quo, 'Ye see the thrang pressin on ye an ye ask, "Wha touched me"?' Syne Jesus luikit weel roon tae see wha had dune this thing. An the wumman, trimmlin wi fear, kennin whit wis dune tae her, cam forrit an fell doon afore him, an telt him aa the trowth. Jesus said tae her, 'Dochter, yer faith has gart ye hale; gang in peace an be lowsit frae yer trubill'.

While he yit spak, thair cam a message frae the ruler o the Synagogue's hoose: 'Yer dochter has dee'd. Why suld ye fash the Maister onie mair?' But at aince Jesus, owerhearin whit wis said, spak tae the messenger, 'Dinna be feart: onlie believe'.

As Jesus cam til the hoose, he fund a grete stramash, wi lood greetin an wailin. Jesus said tae them, 'Why gar ye aa this ado? The lassie isna deid. She is sleepin'. They leuchit at him, so Jesus tuik the faither an mither intil the room whar the bairn wis liggin. Takin her haun, he said tae her, *'talitha cumi'*, whilk means, 'Ma bairn, rise up'. At aince the lass, wha wis onlie twal year auld, rase up an walked.

kythit appeared *lowtit* bowed *gart* made *fash* bother *stramash* uproar *leuchit* laughed
liggin lying

MARK 12:1–11, 28–34 (NISBET)

Ande Jesus began to speke to tham in parabilis. A man plantit a wynyard, and set a hege about it, and deluet a lake, and biggit a toure, and set it in hyre to teelaris, and past furth in pilgrimage. And he send to the teelaris in tyme a seruand, to resaue of the erdteelars of the fruit of the wyneyard. And thai tuke him, and strake him, and left him void. And eftsone he send to thame ane vther seruand; and thai woundit him in the heid, and turmentit him. And eftsone he send ane vthir; and thai slew him, and vthir mony; striking sum, and slaing vthere. Bot yit he had a maast dereworthe sonn, and he sent him last to thame, and said, Perauentur thai will drede my sonn. Bot the erdtelars said togiddir, This is the aire; cum ye, sla we him, and the heretage sal be ouris. And thai tuke him, and slew him, and kest out without the wyneyarde. Tharfore quhat sal the lord of the wyneyarde do? He sal cum and he sal tyne the teelars, and geue the wyneyarde to vtheris. Quhethir ye haue nocht redd this scripture; The staan quhilk the biggars has reprevit, this is made in the heid of the connye: This thing is done of the Lorde, and it is wonnderful in oure een? . . . And aan of the scribes that had herd thame disputing togiddire, come neire, and saw that Jesus had wele ansuerd to thame, and askit him, Quhilk was the first mandment of al? And Jesus ansuerd to him, That the first mandment of all is, Here thou, Israel; Thi Lord God is a God: And thou sal lufe thi Lord God of al thi hart, and of all thi saule, and of al thi mynd, and of al thi mycht. This is the first mandment. And the secund is liik to this, Thou sal lufe thi nechbour as thi self. Thare is naan vthir mandment gretare than thir. Ande the scribe said to him, Maister, in treuth thou has wele said; for a God is, and thare is naan vthir out tak him. That he be luvit of al the hart, and of al the mynd, and of all the vndirstanding, and of all the saule, and of all the strenthe, and to lufe the nechbour as himself, is greatare than al brint offringis and sacrificis. And Jesus, seand that he had ansuerd wisely, said to him, Thou art nocht ferr fra the kingdome of God. And than na man durst ask him maire ony thing.

deluet dug out   *teelaris* farmers   *erdteelars* farmers   *void* empty-handed   *dereworthe* precious
tyne destroy   *Quhethir ye haue* Have you   *reprevit* condemned
mandment commandment   *out tak* except   *brint* burnt

MARK 14:1–50 (LORIMER)

It wantit but twa days or the Passowre an the Feast o Barmless Breid, an the Heid-Priests an Doctors o the Law wis castin owre hou they micht git their haunds on Jesus bi some prat an pit him tae deith. 'But no throu the Feast,' said they, 'or we'r like tae hae the fowk raisin a stramash!'

Ae day, whan he wis lyin at the buird i the houss o Símon the Lipper at Bethanie, a wuman cam in wi a stowp o dairthfu uilie o rael nard in her haund an, brakkin aff the tap o the stowp, tuimed the uilie owre his heid.

Some o them at wis there wis sair ill-pleised an said til ither, 'What for's this waistrie o guid nard? It micht hae been sauld for three hunder white shillins an mair, an the siller gíen tae the puir!' Syne they turned an yokit on the wuman.

But Jesus said, 'Lat her abee; what cause hae ye tae fash her? It wis braw an weill dune o her, this at she hes dune for me. The puir ye hae ey wi ye, an ye can dae them kindness whaniver ye will, but me ye s' no hae ey wi ye. She hes dune aa at wis in her pouer tae dae; she hes anointit my bodie for my buiral afore the day. Atweill, I tell ye, whauriver the Gospel is preached i the haill warld her storie will be tauld, sae as she s' ne'er be forgot.'

Syne Judas Iscariot, ane o the Twal, gaed awà til the Heid-Priests tae offer tae betray him intil their haunds. Whan he tauld them what he hed comed for, they war fair liftit up an shored him a soum o siller, an he begoud tae luik out for a guid opportunitie o betrayin him.

On the first day o the Feast, whan the Jews wis in yuiss tae fell the Passowre Lamb, the disciples speired at Jesus whaur it wis his will they suid ging an mak fore-redd for him tae ait his Passowre. Sae he sent aff twa o them wi thir orders: 'Ging intil the toun,' he tauld them, 'an there ye'll forgether wi a man wi a watter-kit cairriein. Fallow him; an whan he gaes intil a houss, say til the guidman o the same, "The Maister baud us ax ye whaur is the chaumer trystit for him an his disciples tae ait the Passowre in." The man will tak ye up the stair an shaw ye a muckle chaumer wi couches weill spreid up, an aathing in order. That is whaur ye ar tae mak fore-redd for us.' Sae the twasome tuik the gate an cam intil the toun, whaur they faund aathing as Jesus hed tauld them; an they made reddie for the Passowre.

Whan it wis weirin late, Jesus cam til the place wi the Twal. As they lay at the buird takkin their sipper, he said, 'Atweill, I tell ye, ane o ye is tae betray me, ane o ye at is here *at the buird wi me.*'

Dule war they tae hear him, an they said til him, ane efter anither, 'No me, shairlie?'

'It is ane o the Twal,' qo he, 'ane at is dippin his píece i the bicker wi me. The Son o Man maun een gae the gate at Scriptur foretells for him: but waesucks for the man at is tae betray him! Better wad it been for that man, gin he hed ne'er been born.'

Whan they war ey at the buird, Jesus tuik a laif an, efter he hed axed a blissin, brak it an gíed it til them, sayin, 'Tak ye this, it is my bodie.'

Syne he tuik a caup, gae thenks tae God, an raxed it til them, an ilkane o them drank frae it, an he said til them, 'This is my Bluid o the Covenant, whilk is skailed for monie. Atweill, I tell ye, I winna lip the bree o the grape again or the day tae come whan I drink a new wine i the Kíngdom o God.'

Whan they hed sung the Passowre Psaum, they gaed out an awà til the Hill o Olives. Belyve Jesus said tae them, 'Ye will aa turn fauss an faithless, for it is written in Scriptur:

"I will ding the herd,
an the hirsel will be sparpelt abreid."

But efter I hae risen frae the deid, I will ging on afore ye tae Galilee.'

Peter said til him, 'Lat ithers be fauss an faithless, Peter will ey haud leal an true!'

Jesus answert, 'Atweill, I tell ye, nae later nor this day's nicht, or the cock craws twice, ye will disavou me thrice.'

But Peter threapit the mair, 'Thou I buid díe wi ye, I winna disavou ye nane, at winna I!' An siclike said the haill o them.

Syne they cam til a dail caa'd Gethsemanè, an he said til his disciples, 'Sit ye here, till I ging an pray.'

Sae they bade there, but he gaed on wi Peter an Jeames an John. An nou an unco dridder cam owre him, an he said til them, 'My saul is likin tae díe for wae; bide ye here an haud ye wauken.'

Syne he gaed forrit a bittock an cuist himsel on the grund an prayed at, gin it coud be, the hour o dree micht ging by him. '*Abba*, Faither,' he prayed, 'nocht is abuin thy pouer, hain me this caup: yit no as my will, but as thy will, is.'

Syne he cam back an faund them asleep, an he said til Peter, 'Asleep, Símon, asleep? Docht-ye-na bide waukin ae hour? Bide ye aa waukin, an haud at the prayin, at ye haena tae dree nae sair seyal. Tho the spírit be freck, the flesh is feckless.'

Again he gaed awà an prayed the same prayer as afore. Syne he cam back aince mair an faund them asleep, for their een wis hivvie wi tire; an they kentna what answer tae gíe him.

Yit a third time he cam back, an nou he said til them, 'Ey sleepin? Ey takkin your rest? Lang eneuch hae ye sleepit. The hour is comed: see, the Son o Man is eenou tae be betrayed intil the haunds o sinners! Rise ye up, an lat us gae meet them: ay, here he comes, my betrayer.'

The wurds wisna aff his tung afore Judas—ane o the Twal!—cam up, an wi him a thrang o fowk airmed wi whingers an rungs, at hed been sent bi the Heid-Príests, Doctors o the Law, an Elders. The traitor hed gree'd a taiken wi them: 'Him at I kiss is the man ye'r seekin,' he hed sayen: 'grip him, an tak him awà under siccar gaird.' Sae, nou he wis at the bit, he gaed strecht up til him an caa'd him 'Maister' an kissed him; an than the ithers laid haunds on him an huid him siccar.

Ane o the staunders-by drew his whinger an lent the Heid-Príes's servan a straik at sneddit aff his lug. Jesus than tuik speech in haund: 'Am I some reiver,' qo he, 'at ye needs come out wi whingers an rungs for tae fang me? Day an dailie I wis in amang ye teachin i the Temple, an ye laidna a haund on me. But Scriptur buid be fulfilled, I trew.'

Syne the haill o his disciples forhoued him an scoured awà.

---

barmless unleavened   *prat* trick   *stramash* uproar   *buird* table   *stowp* container
dairthfu expensive   *tuimed* emptied   *white* silver   *siller* money

yokit on scolded severely   *fash* trouble   *braw an* very   *ey* always   *shored* offered
in yuiss tae accustomed   *fell* kill   *speired* asked   *ging* go   *fore-redd* advance preparations
watter-kit bucket   *trystit* reserved   *spreid up* covered   *gate* way   *dule* sorrowful   *bicker* bowl
raxed handed   *skailed* poured out, shed   *lip* taste   *bree* juice   *ding* strike   *hirsel* flock
sparpelt scattered   *threapit* insisted   *buid* had to   *dail* piece of land   *dridder* fear   *likin* ready
bittock little   *dree* suffering   *hain* spare   *docht* could   *seyal* test   *freck* eager
feckless weak   *whingers* short swords   *rungs* cudgels   *siccar* secure   *bit* place   *lent* gave
sneddit cut   *lug* ear   *reiver* robber   *fang* seize   *day an dailie* day after day   *trew* believe
forhoued abandoned   *scoured* scattered

LUKE 7:1–23, 36–50 (STUART)

A Sodger's Faith

Jesus gaed intil Capernaum aince mair, an a certane centurion's servan, wha wis thocht unco weel o by him, wis ill an like tae dee. The centurion, hearin aboot Jesus, sent til him elders o the Jews wha besocht him that he wid come an sauf his servin-man. Whan they cam til Jesus, they besocht him, sayin, 'The centurion is wurdie, for he luves oor nation an has biggit us a synagogue!'

Jesus stertit oot wi them, but no bein faur frae the hoose, the centurion sent freends, sayin, 'Lord, dinna fash yersel, for I am-na wurdie that ye suld come neath ma ruif. An so naither thocht I ma-sel wurdie tae come til ye; but gie ye the comman an I ken ma servin-man sall be gart weel. For e'en I ma-sel am ane wi authoritie, an hae neath me sodgers, an I say tae ane, "Gang!", an he gangs an tae anither, "Come!", and he comes; an til ma servan, I say, "Dae this!", an he dis it'.

Whan Jesus heard thae wurds he had wunner at the centurion, an turnin tae the thrang wha followit him, said, 'I say t'ye, I hae fund nae gretir faith nor this. Nae, no in aa Israel'. An they wha war sent noo gaed back til the hoose, an fund the servan in guid hail.

The Weedow's Son

An it cam tae pass that Jesus gaed intil a toun caa'd, Nain, wi monie o his disciples wi him, an a grete thrang o folk. As they cam til the yett o the toun, they met wi a funeral. The deid man wis the onlie son o his mither, an she wis a weedow-wumman.

Whan the Lord saw her, he had unco pitie on her, an said tae her, 'Dinna greet'. He cam an laid his haun on the coffin, an the bearers stappit. 'Laddie,' he said, 'I say onto thee, arise!' The deid man sat up an beguid tae speak. Jesus led him ower til his mither. An dreid fell apon them aa, an they praised

God, cryin oot, 'A grete prophet has rase up amang us!' and 'God has veesitit his folk!'

'Are Ye The Ane?'

Meantime the disciples o John the Bapteezer telt him aa that wis gaun on. John sent twa o his disciples til Jesus, sayin, 'Are ye the ane whilk suld come, or are we tae luik for anither ane?' At that verra hour Jesus hailed monie folk o thair diseases, pestrations an ill-speerits; an onto monie wha war blin, he gied sicht.

Than Jesus answert them; 'Gang yer wey an cairry wurd til John o whit ye hae seen an heard: hoo the blin win thair sicht an the lame gang aboot, hoo lepers are gart clean, the deif can hear, the deid are risen, and the puir hae the joyfu message preached tae them. Blissit is the man wha sall hae faith in me!'

An Ill-doer's Sins Forgien

An a certane ane o the Pharisees bid Jesus tae eat wi him; an gaun intil the hoose o the Pharisee, Jesus sat doon tae mait. An see! a wumman o the toun, wha wis an ill-doer, brocht oot an alabaster box o ointment. An staunin afore Jesus, she lowtit doon an beguid tae wet his feet wi her tears. An she dichtit the tears aff wi her hair, an wis kissin his feet, an anointin them wi the perfume.

Whan his host, the Pharisee, saw this, he spak tae his-sel, sayin, 'This man, gin he wis a prophet, wid hae taen tent wha an whitna sort this wumman is wha lays hauns on him; that she is an ill-doer'. Jesus, answerin his thocht, said tae him, 'Simon, I hae ane thing tae say tae ye'. Simon answert, 'Maister, say on'.

Jesus gaed on: 'Thair wis a certane creditor wi twa debtors; the ane owed five-hunner merk, an the ither fiftie. An whan they had nocht tae pey wi, he forgied them baith. Whilk ane a them noo will luve him mair?'

Simon answert, 'I wid trow he tae wham he forgied the maist'. 'Ye hae judged richt,' quo Jesus. Syne turnin tae the wumman, he said tae Simon, 'See ye this wumman? I cam intil yer hoose, ye gied me nae watter for ma feet; but she wet ma feet wi her tears, an dichtit them wi her hair. Ye gied me nae kiss; but she kissed ma feet. Ye didna anoint ma heid; but she, wi perfume, anointit ma feet.

'Whaurfore, I say tae ye, her monie sins hae been forgien for she luvit much. But he tae wham little is forgien, luves but little'. Jesus turned til the wumman an said tae her, 'yer faith has sauvit ye. Gang in peace'.

---

biggit built   fash trouble   hail health   greet weep   pestrations plagues   win get   gart made
lowtit bent   dichtit wiped   tent notice

Luke 15:1–32 (Smith)

The sheep forwander't. The siller tint. The wastrel son comes hame. Tak ye tent o' the Lord's meanin!

And thar war comin till him a' the tax men and the ill-deedie anes to hear him.

And baith the Writers and the Pharisees war yammerin at him, 'This ane taks in ill-leevin folk, and eats meat wi' them!'

And he spak to them this parable sayin,

'Whatna man amang ye, haein a hunner sheep, gin he tine ane frae amang them, disna lea' the ninety-and-nine i' the muirs, and gang awa eftir the forwander't ane, til he lichts on it?

And, fa'in in wi't, he heizes it on his shouther, rejoicin;

And, comin hame, he sen's for his freends and neebors; sayin to them, "Be blythe wi' me! for I hae fun' my sheep! the ane that forwander't!"

I say t'ye, that in siclike sal thar be joy in heeven ower ae sinner repentin, mair nor ower ninety-and-nine gude o' the folk wha needit nae repentance.

Or whatna wumman, haein ten siller-pennies, gin aiblins she tine ane o' them, disna licht a crusie, soop her hoose, and seek wi' tentie care, til whatna time she lichts on it?

And, lichtin on't, she brings thegither her freends and neebors, sayin, "Be ye glad wi' me! for I fund the siller-penny I tint!"

E'en sae, I say t'ye, sal thar be joy amang the Angels o' God ower ae sinner repentin.'

He said, forby, 'A particular man had twa sons;

And the young son said till his faither, "Faither! gie me my portion that wad fa' to me o' a' the gear!" And he portioned oot till them his leevin.

And, a wheen days efter, the young son gaither't a' his gear thegither, and gaed awa frae hame till a far-awa lan'; and thar sperfl't his gear in riotousness.

But mair: whan a' was gane thar cam up an awesome famine oot-throwe yon lan'; and he begude to be wantin.

And he gaed awa, and was sornin on ane o' the men o' that lan': and he sent him oot-by to herd swine.

And he fain wad fill't his sel wi' the hools the swine war eatin; and nae ane gied them till him.

But, comin' till his richt min', quo' he, "Hoo mony are the fee'd servants o' my faither, wha hae rowth o' breid, and on ower-come; while I, here, dee o' hung'er!

I wull rise and gang tae my faither, and wull say till him, My faither! I hae dune wrang, again Heeven, and afore you;

Nae mair am I fit to be ca'd yere son; mak me like till ane o' the fee'd servants!" And, sae risin, he cam awa till his faither.

But, while he was yet haudin far-awa, his faither spy't him, and was fu' o' compassion; and rinnin, he fell on his neck, and begude kissin him.

And the son said till him, "My faither! I did wrang again Heeven, and afore you: I am nae mair wordie to be ca'd yere son!"

But the faither said to the servants, "Waste nae time! bring oot a robe—the first and best ane—and pit it on him; and gie a ring for his fing'er, and shoon for his feet;

And bring oot the stall'd cauf, and kill it; that we may eat and be joyfu'! For he my son, was deid, and cam to life again; he had been tint, and is fund again!" And they begude to be joyfu'.

But his auld brither was i' the field: and, as he cam in, he drew nar the hoose, and heard music and dancin.

And, beckonin till him ane o' the fee'd folk, he speir't what aiblins a' this micht mean?

And he said till him. "Yere brither has come back again; and yere faither has kill't the stall'd cauf, for that he gat him hame again a' safe and soun'."

But he was fu' o' ang'er, and wadna gang in. His faither, tho', cam oot, and was entreatin him.

But he answerin him, said till his faither, "See! a' thir years hae I ser't ye; and never did I gang ayont yere commauns; and at nae time did ye gie me e'en a kid, that I micht mak a feast for my freends;

But whane'er this yere son, wha has devoor't yere leevin wi' harlots, cam, ye killed the stall'd cauf!"

But he said till him, "Bairn! thou art aye wi' me! and a' that is mine is thine!

But it was richt we soud mak merry and rejoice; for he, thy brither, was deid, and cam back to life again; he had been tint, and was fund!" '

yammerin complaining   _tine_ lose   _forwander't_ strayed away   _heizes_ lifts   _gin_ if
aiblins perhaps   _crusie_ lamp   _soop_ sweep   _tentie_ attentive   _young_ younger
sperfl't squandered   _sornin_ spongeing   _oot-by_ out in the fields   _hools_ husks
fee'd hired   _rowth_ plenty   _ower-come_ surplus   _stall'd_ fattened   _tint_ lost   _speir't_ asked

LUKE 16:19–31 (SMITH)

'A particular man was rich, and cleedit his sel wi' purple and fine linen, and enjoy'd his sel uncolie, ilka day.

And a particular beggar-man, ca'd Lazarus, was sutten doon by his yetts, fu' o' sairs.

And he was sair wussin he micht eat the mools that fell frae the rich man's buird; aye! e'en the dowgs cam and lickit his sairs.

Noo, it cam aboot that the beggar-man dee't, and was carry't awa by the Angels, and laid in Abram's bosom. And forby, the rich man, too, dee't and was bury't.

And in hell he raised his een, bein noo in torments, and sees Abra'm far awa, and Lazarus in his bosom.

And he, cryin oot, said "Faither Abra'm! hae mercie on me, and send ye Lazarus, sae as he may pit the tip o' his fing'er in watir, and cule my tongue; for I am in anguish in this lowe!"

But Abra'm said, "Bairn! ca' ye to min' that ye gat a' yere gude things i' yere lifetime; and Lazarus the ill things: and noo he is at rest, and ye are in sair pyne.

And forby, atween us and you an unco void has been set; that thae wha wad gang ower frae here to you, canna be able; nor thae frae you till us canna come ben!"

Than he said, "I entreat ye than, faither! that ye wad send him to my faither's hoose;

For I hae fyve brethren; that he may bear testimonie to them, that they come-na intil this place o' dool!"

Abra'm says till him, "They hae Moses and the Prophets; lat them hear them!"

But he says, "Na, faither Abra'm! but gin ane gaed to them frae the deid, they wull repent them!"

But he said till him, "Gif to Moses and the Prophets they tak nae tent, naither wull they be perswadit e'en by ane that raise frae the deid!" '

cleedit clothed   *uncolie* greatly   *ilka* every   *yetts* gates   *mools* crumbs   *buird* table
forby besides   *lowe* flame   *ben* in   *dool* sorrow

LUKE 23:26–49 (LORIMER)

As they led him awà, they claucht hauds o Símon, a man frae Cyrenè, at wis comin in frae the kintra, an gart him gang ahent Jesus cairriein his cross on his shuither.

A fell thrang o fowk fallowt him, amang them some weimen at wis baetin their breists an makkin a maen for him. Jesus turnt tae them an said, 'Murn-na for me, dauchters o Jerusalem: murn for yoursels an your childer; for, tent my wurds, the days is comin whan they will be sayin, "Happie the wuman at is barren, ay! happie the wame at ne'er buir bairn an the breists at ne'er gae milk." Than, tae, they will begin

> tae say tae the hills,
>   "Faa on abuin us",
> an tae the knowes,
>   "Kivver us owre."

For gif they dae siclike wi the tree at is green an growthie, what will be dune wi the tree at is wallowt an deid?'

Ither twa wis led out tae be execute for crimes alang wi him; an whan they cam tae the place caa'd the Hairn-Pan, they crucifíed him there, an wi him the twa ill-daers, the tane on his richt, an the tither on his left. Jesus said, 'Faither, forgíe them, for they kenna what they ar daein.' Syne the sodgers *cuist caivels* an *haufed his cleadin amang them.*

The fowk stuid by *luikin on,* an een the Councillors *geckit* at him: 'He saufed ithers,' said they; 'lat him sauf himsel, gif he is God's Messíah, the Choised Ane!' The sodgers, tae, hed their jamph at him, comin up an offerin him *sour wine,* an sayin, 'Gif ye ar the King o Jews, sauf yoursel!' There wis a plaicard abuin his heid wi the wurds:

THIS IS
THE KING
O JEWS

Ane o the ill-daers at hang there jeered him, sayin, 'Arna ye the Christ? A-weill, sauf yoursel, an hiz forbye!' But the ither ill-daer challenged him: 'Ar ye no fleyed een o God,' said he, 'whan ye ar dreein the same duim as him? An a juist duim it is for hiz twa, at is but gettin our sairin for things at we hae dune: but this ane hesna dune ocht wrang!'

Syne he said tae Jesus, 'Hae mind on me, Jesus, whan ye come intil your Kingdom'; an Jesus answert, 'Atweill, I tell ye, this day ye s' be wi' me in Paradise.'

It wis about twal hours, an the licht o the sun failed, an it mirkit owre the haill laund till the mids o the efternuin, at whilk hour the courtain i the Temple screidit atwà. Than Jesus cried wi a loud stevven, 'Faither, *intil thy haunds I commit my spírit';* an wi that he souched awà.

Whan the captain o the gaird saw what hed happent, he gae glorie tae God, an said, 'Trowth an atweill, yon wis a guid man!'

Aa the crouds o fowk at hed come thegither tae see the sicht, nou at aathing wis by, gaed their waas hame, strickin themsels on their breists for dule. But aa his fríends, an the weimen at hed fallowt him frae Galilee, bade staundin whaur they war, a guid gate aff, luikin on at aathing.

claucht seized *gart* made *fell* great *tent* take heed of *wame* womb *knowes* hills
wallowt withered *hairn-pan* skull *caivels* lots *cleadin* clothes *geckit* jeered *jamph* jeer
hiz us *forbye* as well *fleyed* afraid *dreein* suffering *duim* judgement *sairin* deserts
mirkit grew dark *screidit* tore *atwa* in two *souched awa* breathed his last *dule* sorrow

JOHN 3:1–21 (SMITH)

The man that cam i' the mirk, and gaed awa i' the licht. Christ maun wax, John maun wane.

Thar was ane o' the Pharisees, by name Nicodemus; and in authoritie amang the Jews.

An he cam i' the mirk o' the nicht to Jesus, and quo' he, 'Maister! we a' ken ye are a Teacher frae God; for nane coud do sic wunner-works as ye do, gin God warna wi' him!'

Jesus said till him, 'Truly say I t'ye, gin a man be-na born again, his e'en sal never see God's Kingdom!'

Quo' Nicodemus, 'But hoo's a man to born in eild? Maun he return till his mither's womb, and be born ower again?'

But Jesus spak: 'Truly, truly say I t'ye, Gin a man be-na watir-born and Spirit-born, he'se no come intil God's Kingdom!

And aye that whilk is born o' the flesh is itsel flesh, and that whilk is born o' the Spirit is spirit.

Mak nae ferlie o' my words, "Ye maun be born again!"

The wind blaws whaur it wull, and ye hear the sough o't, but canna ken whaur it comes frae, nor whaur it gangs tae: sae is ti wi' ane born o' the Spirit.'

Nicodemus says till him, 'Hoo can siccan a thing be?'

Quo' Jesus till him, 'Can ye be a Maister o' Isra'l, and ken-na thir things?

Truly, truly say I t'ye, we speak what we ken, and bear witness o' oor ain een; and ye winna hear us.

Gin I hae tauld ye things o' the yirth, and ye winna hae them, wull ye lippen my word anent things o' Heeven?

And nae man has e'er gane up Aboon, but he that cam doon frae Aboon—the Son o' Man, wha bides Aboon.

And like as Moses i' the wilderness heized up the serpent, sae maun the Son o' Man be liftit heigh;

That a' wha lippen till him soudna dee, but hae Life for aye!

For God sae lived the warld as to gie his Son, the Only-Begotten Ane, that ilka ane wha lippens till him sudna dee, but hae Life for aye.

For God sent-na his Son intil the warld to bring condemnation on't, but that raither the warld micht be saved by him.

And ane that lippens him isna hauden guilty; but ane wha winna lippen him is judged guilty e'en noo; for he hasna lippened to the Son o' God, the only-begotten Ane.

And here is the sentence he drees: that licht beams on the warld, and men lo'e the mirk and no the licht; for that their deeds are wrang.

For ilka ane that follows ill hates the licht, and comes-na till't; jalousin that his ill deeds wull be seen.

But the man wha has the truth seeks the licht, that a' his deeds may be plainly seen, that they are dune i' the pooer o' God.'

mirk darkness   *eild* old age   *mak nae ferlie o'* do not marvel at   *sough* sound
lippen trust   *heized* lifted   *drees* suffers   *jalousin* suspecting

JOHN 11:1, 3, 11–12, 14, 17, 19, 21–29, 31–36, 38–44 (STUART)

Lazarus Frae Bethanie

Syne Lazarus, the brither o Mary an Martha, failed badly, an his sisters sent wurd tae Jesus. Efter twa days, Jesus said tae his disciples, 'Oor freend Lazarus sleeps; I maun gang an wauken him oot o his sleep!' Than quo the disciples, 'Lord, gin he sleeps, he maun be on the mend!' But Jesus telt them straucht-forrit, 'Lazarus is deid. Nane-the-less, let us gang til him'.

Whan Jesus cam, he fund that Lazarus had been i' the tomb for fower days. An monie o the Jews had come oot til Martha an Mary tae condole wi them ower thair brither. Martha said tae Jesus, 'Lord, gin ye had been here, ma brither widna hae dee'd. An e'en yit I ken that whitiver ye will speir o God, God will gie ye'.

Jesus said tae her, 'Yer brither sall rise aince mair!' Martha quo tae him, 'I ken hoo he sall rise agin at the resurrection on the hindmaist day'. Jesus telt her, 'I am the resurrection an the life! Wha lippens on me sall dee nae mair. Dae ye trow this?' 'Aye Lord,' she said tae him, 'I trow ye are God's son, wha wis tae come intil the warld.'

Whan she had said this, she caa'd her sister Mary, sayin, 'The Maister is here an is seekin ye!' Whan Mary heard this she rase wi haste an gaed til him. The Jews wha war in the hoose tae condole wi her, followit efter, sayin amang thairsels, 'She gangs til the tomb tae murn'.

Syne Mary cam til whaur Jesus wis an lowtit doon at his feet, sayin tae him, 'Lord, gin ye had been here ma brither widna hae dee'd'. Whan Jesus saw her greetin, an the Jews wha cam wi her aa weepin sair, he had unco pitie in his hert an wis fu' o distress.

'Whaur hae ye laid him doon?' he speired, an they said tae him, 'Lord, come awa an see!' Jesus beguid tae weep. The Jews saw this an said, 'See hoo he luvit Lazarus'. Than Jesus cam til the tomb an a grete stane wis thair ower it. But Jesus said, 'Tak ye awa that stane!' Martha minded him, 'Lord, by noo the corp will be foul an stinkin, for he has been fower days in the tomb!'

Jesus said, 'Did I no say tae ye that gin ye wid trow in me, ye wid see the glorie o God?' So they tuik awa the stane an Jesus liftit up his een tae Hevin an said, 'Faither! I thank ye that ye did hear me. I ken that ye aye hear me; but it wis for the sake o aa the folk staunin here that I said it, so that they micht ken that ye did send me'.

Whan he said this, he cried oot wi a lood voice, 'Lazarus! Come furth!' The deid man cam furth, bund haun an fit in graif-claes, an his face bund roon wi a claith. Jesus said, 'Lowsen him an lat him gang hame'.

syne than   *speir* ask   *lippens* believes   *trow* believe   *lowtit* bowed   *greetin* weeping

JOHN 18:12–19:16 (LORIMER)

The sodgers o the garrison, wi their Cornel an the Jewish Temple Gairds, nou grippit Jesus, siccart his haunds, an tuik him til Annas. They brocht him til Annas first, because he wis guid-faither tae Caiaphas, the Heid-Priest that year—the same Caiaphas at hed counselt the Jews it wad sair them best at ae man suid díe for the haill fowk.

Jesus wis fallowt bi Símon Peter an anither disciple. This disciple wis acquant wi the Heid-Príest, an he gaed intil the yaird o the pailace alang wi Jesus, but Peter bade staundin thereout at the door. Belyve the ither disciple, him at wis acquant wi the Heid-Príest, gaed out an, efter twa-three wurds wi the janitress, brocht Peter inbye. The servan-lass—the janitress, like— said tae Peter, 'Ye'll no be ane o this man's disciples, tae, na?'

'No me,' said he.

The servans an Temple Gairds hed kennelt an ingle an war staundin beikin forenent it, for it wis cauldrif; an Peter stuid wi them an beikit an aa.

The Heid-Príest quastint Jesus anent his disciples an his teachin. 'I hae spokken fair out tae the haill warld,' Jesus answert: 'aa my teachin hes been in sýnagogues an the Temple; ne'er said I ocht in hidlins. What for div ye speir at me? Speir at them at hes hard me what I tellt them; they ken what I said.'

Whan he said that, ane o the Temple Gairds lent him a haffit wi his luif, sayin, 'Wad ye answer the Heid-Príest that gate?'

'Gin I spak ill the nou,' said Jesus, 'tell the Court what ill I said: but gin I spak weill, what for div ye clour me?' Annas than sent him awà, ey bund, tae Caiaphas the Heid-Príest.

Símon Peter wis ey staundin outbye beikin himsel at the fire. Sae they said til him, 'Ye'll be ane o his disciples, tae, na?'

But he disavoued him: 'No me,' said he.

Ane o the Heid-Príest's servans at wis sib tae the man at Peter sneddit his lug said, 'Did I no see ye i the gairden wi him?'

But Peter disavoued him aince mair; an straucht a cock crew.

I the first o the day they cairriet Jesus frae Caiaphas tae the Governor's Pailace. But they gaedna inbye themsels, for that wad fyled them an hendert them tae eat the Passowre. Sae Pílate cam out tae them.

'What chairge hae ye again this man?' he speired.

'An he wisna a fautor,' they answert, 'we wadna haundit him owre tae ye.'

'Tak him yoursels, an try him bi your ain Law,'said Pílate.

But the Jews answert, 'It is no leisome for us tae pit onie-ane tae daith.' Sae answert they because what Jesus hed said anent the daith he wis tae díe buid come true.

Pílate than gaed back intil the Pailace an gart bring Jesus afore him. 'Ar ye the King of Jews?' he speired at him.

'Ar ye sayin that at your ain haund,' said Jesus, 'or hae they spokken tae ye anent me?'

'Am I a Jew?' said Pílate. 'It is your ain kintramen an the Heid-Príests at hes haundit ye owre tae me. What hae ye dune?'

'My Kindgom,' Jesus answert, 'isna o this warld. Gin my Kingdom hed been o this warld, my sodgers wad be fechtin tae haud me out o the grips o the Jews. But na, my Kingdom belangsna this warld.'

'A-weill, ye ar a king, than?' said Pílate.

'Ye hae said it,' Jesus answert. 'It wis een for this I wis born an cam intil the warld—tae beir witness tae the trowth.'

'What is trowth?' said Pílate. An wi that he gaed outbye again tae the Jews an said tae them, 'I finnd nae faut in him. Ye hae a custom at I suid líberate ae man for ye at the Passowre. Is it your will at I suid líberate the King o Jews?' But they raired out again, 'No him! BarAbbas!' BarAbbas wis a reiver.

Pílate nou tuik Jesus an gart leash him. The sodgers than plettit a wreathe wi thorn-rysses an pat it on his heid an cled him in a purpie mantílle, efter whilk they made a ploy o coming up til him wi a 'Hail, the King o Jews', an syne lendin him a haffit wi their luifs. Belyve Pílate gaed out aince mair an said tae them, 'Luik, I am bringin him out tae ye tae lat ye see I finnd nae faut in him.'

Jesus than cam out, weirin the wreathe o thorn-rysses an the purpie mantílle, an Pílate said, 'See, here he is!'

At the sicht o him the Heid-Príests an Temple Gairds raired out, 'Tae the cross, tae the cross wi him!'

'Tak him an crucifíe him yoursels,' said Pílate; 'I finnd nae faut in him.'

'We hae our ain Law,' the Jews answert, 'an bi hit he suid be pitten tae daith for haudin out tae be the Son o God.'

Whan Pílate hard them say that, he wis the mair afeared, an he gaed back intil the Pailace an said tae Jesus, 'Wha ar ye?' But Jesus answert him nane.

'Will ye no speak tae me?' said Pílate. 'Div ye no ken I hae the pouer tae líberate ye, an the pouer tae cause crucifíe ye?'

'Ye wadna hae nae pouer owre me avà,' said Jesus, 'an ye hedna been gíen it frae abuin, an that maks him at pat me intil your haunds mair tae wyte nor ye ar.'

Efter that Pílate wis for settin him free, but the Jews raired an better raired, 'Gin ye set this man free, ye ar nae fríend o Caesar's; ilkane at hauds out tae be a king is settin himsel up again Caesar!'

Whan he hard what they war sayin, Pílate brang Jesus furth an sat doun on the juidgement-sait i the place caa'd 'The Plainstanes'—Gabbatha, i the Aramâic. It wis the day afore the Passowre, an the time wis about twal hours, less or mair. Syne he said tae them, 'Luik, here is your king.' But they raired out, 'Tak him awà, take him awà! Tae the cross wi him!'

'Wad ye hae me crucifíe your king?' said Pílate.

'We hae nae king binna Caesar,' the Heid-Príests answert. Pílate than haundit Jesus owre tae be crucified.

---

siccart secured   guid-faither father-in-law   sair serve   ingle fire   beikin warming themselves
forenent in front of   cauldrif cold   in hidlins in secret   speir at ask   lent gave
haffit blow on the side of the head   luif palm of his hand   clour strike   outbye outside
sib related   sneddit cut off   lug ear   fyled defiled   fautor wrongdoer   leisome legally allowed
reiver robber   leash flog   lysses twigs   ploy joke   belyve soon   wyte blame
plainstanes pavement, paved area in centre of town   binna except

JOHN 20:1–29 (NISBET)

Ande in aan day of the wolk Marie Magdalene com airlie to the graue, quhen it was yit mirk. And scho saw the staan mouet away fra the graue. Tharfor scho ran, and com to Symon Petir, and to ane vther discipile, quham Jesus luvit, and sais to thame, Thai haue takin the Lord fra the graue, and we wate nocht quhare thai haue laid him. Tharfore Petir went out, and that ilk vthir discipile, and thai com to the graue. And thai twa ran togiddir, and the ilk vthir discipile ran before Petir, and com first to the graue. And quhen he lowtit, he saw the schetis liand, neuirtheles he entrit nocht. Tharfor Symon Petir com followand him, and he entrit into the graue, and he saw the schetis laid, And the sudarie that was on his hede, nocht laid with the schetis, bot be itself wympilit into aan place. Tharfore than the ilk discipile that com first to the graue, entrit, and saw, and beleuet. For thai knew nocht yit the scripture, that it behuvit him to ryse agane fra deid. Tharfore the discipilis went agane to thame self. Bot Marie stude at the graue without furth wepand. And the quhile scho wepit, scho bowit hir, and beheld furth into the graue; And saw twa angelis sittand, in quhite, aan at the hede and aan at the feet, quhare the body of Jesu was laid. And thai say to hir, Woman, quhat wepis thou? Scho said to thaim, For thai haue takin away my lorde, and I wate nocht quhare thai haue laid him. Quhen scho had said thir thingis, scho turnit bakwart,and saw Jesu standand, and wist nocht that it was Jesus. Jesus sais to hir, Woman, quhat wepis thou? quham sekis thou? Scho gessand that he was a gardinare, sais to him, Sir, gif thou has takin him vp, say to me quhare thou has laid him, and I sal tak him away. Jesus sais to hir, Marie. Scho turnit, and sais to him Rabboni, that is to say, Maistir. Jesus sais to hir, Will thou nocht tuiche me, for I haue nocht yit ascendit to my fader; bot ga to my brether, and say to thame, I ga vp to my fader and to youre fadere, to my God and to youre God. Marie Magdalene com, telland to the discipilis, That I saw the Lord, and thir thingis he said to me. Tharfore quhen it was euen in that day, aan of the sabotis, and the yettis war closit quhare the discipilis war gaderit for drede of the Iewis, Jesus com and stude in the myddis of the discipilis, and he sais to thame, Pece to yow. And quhen he had said this, he schewit to thame handis and side; tharfore the discipilis ioyit, for the Lord was seen. And he sais to thame agane, Pece to you; as the fader send me, I send you. Quhen he had said this, he blew on thame, and said, Tak ye the Haligast; Quhais synnis ye forgefe, tha ar forgeuen to thame; and quhais ye withhald, tha ar withhaldin. Bot Thomas, aan of the xij, that is saide Didymus, was nocht with thame quhen Jesus com, Tharfore the vther discipilis said to him, We haue sene the Lord. And he said to thame, Bot I se in his handis the fixing of the nailis, and put my fingire into the place of the nailis, and put my hand into his side, I sal nocht beleue. And eftir viii dais agane his discipilis war within, ande Thomas with thame. Jesus com, quhile the yettis war closit, and stude in the myddis, and said, Pece to you. Eftirwart he sais to Thomas, Put in here thi fingire, and se myn handis, and put hiddire thi hand, and put into my side, and will thou nocht be vnbeleeffull, bot faithfull. Thomas ansuerd, and said to him, My Lord and my God. Jesus sais to him, Thomas, for thou as sene me, thou beleues; blessit be thai that saw nocht, and has beleuet.

wolk week   *mirk* dark   *wate* know   *lowpit* bent down   *sudarie* sweat-cloth
wympilit folded   *wist* knew   *yettis* gates

ACTS 9:1–28 (SMITH)

Saul, ragin like a wild beas', is laid haud o' by the Lord. Peter dis some o' the great warks o' Christ.

And Saul, yet belchin oot threatenins and blude again the Lord's folk, gaed to the Heigh-priest,

And craved frae him letters to Damascus, to the kirks, sae as, gin they faund ony o' 'The Way,' aither men or weemen, he soud fesh them in thrall to Jerusalem.

But, as he gaed on, he cam narby Damascus; and a' o' a suddaintie, thar lowed aboot him a licht frae the lift,

And, fa'in to the yirth, he heard a voice sayin till him, 'Saul! Saul! why are ye pursuin me?'

And he said, 'Wha, my Lord, are ye?' While he answer't, 'I am Jesus that ye are pursuin'! It is hard for thee to kick against the jaggs!'

And he, trimlin and ferlin, quo', 'Lord, what wud ye hae me dae?' And the Lord said till him, 'Rise ye, and gang ye intil the citie, and it sal be tell't ye what ye are to dae.'

And the men wha war wi' him stude speechless, hearin a voice, but seein nae man.

And Saul gat him up frae the grund, and whan he opened his een, he saw nane; sae, takin him by the haun, they airtit him intil Damascus.

And he was thrie days wantin sicht, and naither did eat nor drink.

Noo there was a disciple at Damascus, by name Ananias; and the Lord, in a vision, said till him, 'Ananias!' And quo' he, 'See! here am I, Lord!'

And the Lord said till him: 'Arise, and gang awa to the street ca'd "Straucht," and speir in Judas' hoose for ane Saul by name—o' Tarsus; for ken! he is prayin;

And he has seen in vision ane Ananias comin in, and pittin his hauns on him, that he soud win back his sicht.'

But said Ananias, 'Lord! by a hantle o' folk hear I o' this man; and hoo muckle skaith he has dune to thy saunts at Jerusalem.

And i' this vera place he has pooer frae the Heid-priests to bind a' thae that seek thy name.'

But the Lord says to him, 'Gang yere ways; for a favored vessel is this ane to me, for the bearin o' my name afore nations, and kings, and the sons o' Isra'l.

For I wull schaw to him what unco things he maun dree for the sake o' my name.'

And Ananias gaed his ways, and cam intil the hoose: and layin hauns on him, says, 'Saul! Brither! The Lord—Jesus, that thou saw on the way heretill—has bid me come, that ye micht hae yere sicht, and be fu' o' the Holie Spirit.'

And at ance fell frae his een as it war scales; and he gat sicht and raise, and was bapteez't.

And whan he had meat, he was revived. Than was Saul a wheen days wi' the believers that war at Damascus.

And at ance, i' the kirks, he proclaimed Jesus, that he was God's Son.

But they ferlied that heard him: and quo' they, 'Isna this the ane that made havoc o' them that socht this name in Jerusalem? And cam here, ettlin the same, that he micht tak them in bonds to the Heid-priests?'

But Saul gather't strenth the mair, and silenced the Jews that dwalt at Damascus, demonstratin that 'This Ane is the Messiah!'

But, whan mair days war come and gane, the Jews colleagued thegither to slay him.

Hoobeit, their colleaguin was made kent to Saul. And they gairdit the ports day and nicht to kill him.

Than the disciples took him at nicht, and loutit him doon ower the wa' in a creel.

And whan he was come the lenth o' Jerusalem, he ettled to join his sel to the disciples; but they war a' fley't o' him, and jaloused that he was a fause ane.

But Barnabas tuik him, and brocht him to the Apostles, and tell't them hoo, gaun his gate, he saw the Lord, and that he spak till him; and hoo Saul had spoken bauldly at Damascus, in Jesus' name.

And he was ane wi' them: gaun in and oot at Jerusalem.

---

lowed blazed *lift* sky *jaggs* pricks *trimmlin* trembling *ferlin* marvelling *airtit* guided
hantle large number *skaith* injury *dree* suffer *ferlied* were astonished *ettlin* intending
colleagued plotted *ports* gates *loutit* lowered *creel* basket *fley't* afraid *jaloused* suspected

ROMANS 12, 13 (SMITH)

Christ's folk maun do as Christ dis; the warld is lookin on!

I entreat ye, than, brethren, by the mercies o' God, that ye render yersels as a leevin, holie, weel-pleasin offeran to God—a proper, rational service.

And no to be conform to this warld, but to be transformed by the renewin o' yere mind, that ye may pit to the prufe what is God's gude, and perfete, and acceptable wull.

For, say I, by the favor gien to me, to ilka ane amang ye, no to be thinkin ower muckle o' his sel, ayont what he soud think o' his sel, but to think o' his sel discreetly; e'en as God gied to ilka ane his portion o' faith.

For, e'en as in ae body we hae mony pairts, but a' o' the pairts hae-na the same duty.

Sae we, the mony, are a' ae body in Christ; but allenarlie are pairts ane o' anither.

Noo, haein gifts by favor, and gifts differan accordin to the favor gien till us—gin it be prophecie, lat it be i' the proportion o' faith;

Or service, i' the service; or he that teaches, i' the teachin;

Or an exhorter, i' the exhortin; he wha gies, lat him gie in aefauldness; he that leads, to lead tentilie; he that schaws mercie, to do it blythely.

Love withoot hypocrisy, scunnerin at a' that is evil; haudin fast to a' that is gude.

In britherly love schaw tender affection ane till anither; in giean honor, surpassin ane anither.

In yere actions no slothfu' in yere spirit fervent; to the Lord fu' o' service;

In hope rejoicin; in trouble lang-tholin; in prayer perseverin;

Wi' the needs o' saunts haein fellowship; in hospitality aye active.

Gie blessins to persecutors—blessins, and no curses.

Rejoice wi' the rejoicin, and greet wi' the tearfu'.

Ilk ane to anither seek the same thing; no seekin heigh things, but for-gatherin wi' lowly things. Be-na wyss i' yere ain conceit.

Return ill for ill to nane; provide things honorable afore a' men.

Gin it be possible, as far as it lies in you, wi' a' men be at peace.

No seekin vengeance, beloved; but gie place to anger; for it is putten-doon, 'To me belangs vengeance; I wull repay, says the Lord.

Gin yere enemy hung'er, feed him; gin he be drouthie; gie him drink; for, sae doin, ye sal heap coals o' fire in his heid.'

Be-na owercome wi' ill; but owercome ye ill wi' gude.

The saunt is a gude citizen; and walks i' the licht.

Lat ilka saul submit itsel to the protection o' the public authoritie. For thar is nae authoritie but by God; thae existin, exist by God.

Sae he that sets his sel again the authoritie sets his sel again the ordinance o' God: and they that oppose sal receive condemnation.

For rulers are-na a fear to gude warks, but to the ill. But wad ye no be fley't o' the authoritie? Div ye that whilk is gude, and ye sal hae praise o' the same.

For he is God's servant t'ye, for that whilk is gude. But gin aiblins ye are doin ill, hae fear; for he disna cairry the sword for nocht. For God's servant is he, punishin wi' wrath him wha practeeses ill.

And sae thar is a need o' submittin yersels, no only on accoont o' the wrath, but eke on accoont o' conscience.

For sae pey ye tribute as weel: for God's ceevil servants are they, takin tent to this vera thing.

Render, than to a' their dues; tribute to wham tribute; tax to wham tax; fear to wham fear; honor to wham honor.

Awe nae man ocht, save love to ane anither; for he wha lo'es the ither fills up the Law.

Thus: 'Ye sanna commit adultery; Ye sanna commit murder; Ye sanna steal; Ye sanna covet'; and gin thar be ony ither commandment, it is summed up i' this word, namely: 'Ye sal lo'e yere neebor as yer sel!'

Love to ane's neebor works nae ill; love tharfor, is the pith o' the Law.

And, kennin the time, that it is an 'oor e'en noo for us to wauken oot o' sleep: for noo is oor salvation narer-haun than whan we first believed:

The nicht is far gane; the dawin comes on. Pit we awa, than, the warks o' darkness, and lat us tak the wapins o' licht!

Lat us work, honorably, as in the licht o' day: no in bruilzies and druckenness, no in lewdness and wantonness, no in castins-oot and envyin.

But pit ye on the Lord Jesus Christ; and hae nae trokin wi' the flesh and its corrupt desires.

---

aefauldness sincerity   *tentilie* carefully   *scunnerin* feeling disgusted   *lang-tholin* patient
drouthie thirsty   *fley't* afraid   *aiblins* perhaps   *takin tent* paying attention   *bruilzies* noisy quarrels
castins-oot quarrels   *trokin* dealings

1 Corinthians 13 (Lorimer)

Gin I speak wi the tungs o men an angels, but hae nae luve i my hairt, I am no nane better nor dunnerin bress or a rínging cymbal. Gin I hae the gift o prophecie, an am acquent wi the saicret mind o God, an ken aathing ither at man may ken, an gin I hae siccan faith as can flit the hills frae their larachs— gin I hae aa that, but hae nae luve i my hairt, I am nocht. Gin I skail aa my guids an graith in awmous, an gin I gíe up my bodie tae be brunt in aiss— gin I een dae that, but hae nae luve i my hairt, I am nane the better o it.

Luve is pâtientfu; luve is couthie an kind; luve is nane jailous; nane sprosie; nane bowdent wi pride; nane mislaired; nane hame-drauchtit; nane toustie. Luve keeps nae nickstick o the wrangs it drees; finnds nae pleisur i the ill wark o ithers; is ey liftit up whan truith dings líes; kens ey tae keep a caum souch; is ey sweired tae misdout; ey howps the best; ey bides the warst.

Luve will ne'er fail. Prophecies, they s' een be by wi; tungs, they s' een devaul; knawledge, it s' een be by wi. Aa our knawledge is hauflin; aa our prophesíein is hauflin: but whan the perfyte is comed, the onperfyte will be by wi. In my bairn days, I hed the speech o a bairn, the mind o a bairn, the thochts o a bairn, but nou at I am grown manmuckle, I am throu wi aathing bairnlie. Nou we ar like luikin in a mirror an seein aathing athraw, but than we s' luik aathing braid i the face. Nou I ken aathing hauflinsweys, but than I will ken aathing as weill as God kens me.

In smaa: there is three things bides for ey: faith, howp, luve. But the grytest o the three is luve.

dunnerin rumbling *flit* move *larachs* sites *skail* disperse *graith* possessions *awmous* alms
bowdent swollen *mislaired* rude *hame-drauchtit* selfish *toustie* easily angered
nickstick tally *drees* suffers *dings* beats down *keep a clam souch* keep calm *sweired* reluctant
misdout distrust *by wi* finished *devaul* cease *hauflin* incomplete *manmuckle* adult
athraw awry

1 Corinthians 15 (Smith)

A' aboot the Risin-again: mair here nor in a' the lave o'the Word. It is ane o' Paul's special messages frae the Lord till us.

Noo, I mak kent t'ye, brethren, the Joyfu'-message whilk I mysel spak till ye, whilk eke ye received, and in whilk eke ye staun.

And throwe whilk ye are saved, gin ye haud siccar the word I tell't ye, in whilk I spak till ye the Joyfu'-message; gin ye hae-na lippened in vain!

For I deliver't till ye, the first thing, hoo that Christ dee't for oor sins, as said i' the Scripturs;

And that he was bury't; and that he has been raised—on the third day, as said the Scripturs;

And that he schawed his sel to Peter; eftir, to the Twal.

Eftir that he schawed his sel to mair nor fyve hunder brethren at ance; the feck o' them remainin till noo, but a wheen are faun asleep.

Eftir that he schawed his sel till James; and eftir, till a' the Apostles;

And last o' a', as to the untimely birth—e'en to me!

For I am but the least o' the Apostles, wha am-na fit to be ca'd an Apostle, for that I persecutit the Kirk o' God.

But by God's favor I am what I am: and his favor to me wasna made vain; but, mair aboundin than they a' was I in toil: hoobeit, it wasna I, but God's favor wi' me.

Sae, gin it be I or they, sae we preach, and sae ye lippen'd.

Noo, gin Christ be proclaimed, as bein risen frae 'mang the deid, hoo say a wheen amang ye that 'Thar is nae Risin-frae-the-deid?'

But, gin 'Risin-frae-the-deid thar be nane,' than no e'en Christ has been raised!

And gin Christ hasna been raised, oor preachin, at last, is vain; and yere believin is a' vain!

And mair: we are schawn to be fause-witnesses o' God; for we bure witness o' God that he raised Christ; wham he raised-na, gin the deid be-na raised!

For gin the deid are-na raised, Christ raise-na!

And gin Christ raise-na, yere faith is a' in vain; ye are yet in yere sins!

And thae, too, wha fell asleep in Christ, perish't!

Gin we hae but hopit in Christ in this life alane, we are o' a' men maist to be pitied!

But noo, Christ has been raised frae 'mang the deid, a first-frute o' them wha are faun asleep!

For sin' throwe a man cam death, throwe a man comes eke the Risin-frae-the-deid.

For as in Adam a' dee, sae in Christ sal a' be made leevin.

But ilk ane followin in his proper place: Christ, a first-frute; than they wha are Christ's, at his comin:

Eftirhaun, than the end—whane'er he delivers up the Kingdom to God the Faither; whan a' rule and authoritie is dune awa' wi'.

For he maun rule till whatna time as he has putten a' his faes aneath his feet.

The last fae that is dune awa' wi', is Death.

'For a' things are to be putten aneath his feet.' But whaur ane says, 'A' things hae been putten-aneath,' it is plain that thar is an exception o' the Ane wha pat a' things aneath him.

But, whan a' things are putten-aneath him, than sal the Son his sel become subject to the Ane wha made a' things subject till him—that the Godheid may be a' in a'!

Or else, what is for them that are bapteez't for the deid? Gin the deid be-na raised ava, why than are they bapteez't for the deid?

And why soud we be rinnin intil danger ilka 'oor?

Ilk day I am deein, brethren—by a' the gloryin whilk I hae ower you in Christ Jesus oor Lord!

Gif, like a man, I battled wi' wild beass in Ephesus, what is the profit to me? Gif the deid are-na to be raised, 'Lat us eat and drink! for the morn we dee!'

Dinna be taein-in: 'Ill company corrupts gude conduct.'

Wauken ye to soberness, richtously; and sin-na; for a hantle ken-na God. To yere shame speak I.

But some may speir, 'Hoo are the deid to be raised? and in whatna body are they to appear?'

Doitit ane! what seed, e'en ye saw, isna made leevin till it dee:

And what ye saw—no the bouk that sal come to be div ye saw—but a bare pickle: be it wheat, or ony o' the lave.

Hoobeit, God gies it a bouk e'en as he has been pleased; and to ilk o' the seeds its richt bouk.

A' flesh isna ae kind o' flesh; but ane is flesh o' men, anither flesh o' beass, anither flesh o' fowls, and anither o' fishes.

And thar are heevenly bodies, and yirthly bodies. But ae kind o' glorie is the heevenly, and anither kind that o' the yirthly.

Thar is ae glorie o' the sun, and anither kind o' glorie o' the mune, and yet anither glorie o' the starns. Nay, thar is a differ, starn frae starn!

And sae i' the Risin-frae-the-deid. It is sawn in corruption; it is raised in incorruption:

It is sawn in abasement: it is raised in glorie: it is sawn in fecklessness; it is raised in pooer.

It is sawn a nateral body; it is raised a spiritual body. Gin thar is nateral body, thar is eke a spiritual body!

And sae it is putten-doon, 'The first man, Adam, becam a leevin bein.' But the last Adam, a life-giean Spirit.

Hoobeit, the spiritual cam-na first, but the nateral: eftir that the spiritual: The first man, o' the yirth, yirthly; the second man o' heeven.

Like as the yirthly ane, siclike are they that are yirthly; and like as the heevenly ane, siclike are they that are heevenly.

And e'en as we bure the likeness o' the yirthly ane, we sal e'en bear the likeness o' the heevenly ane.

But I say this, brethren, that flesh and blude canna inherit God's Kingdom; nor is corruption to inherit holiness.

Tak tent! I unfauld till ye a riddle: We sanna a' fa' asleep; but a' sal be cheenged,

In a moment, in a blink, at the last trumpet; for the trumpet sal soond, and the deid sal be raised, incorruptible; and we'se be cheenged.

For this corruptible-man maun needs cleed itsel wi' incorruption, and this mortal cleed itsel wi' immortality.

Sae whane'er this corruptible has cleedit itsel wi' incorruption, and this mortal has cleeded itsel wi' immortality, than sal come aboot the word putten-doon, 'Death was victoriously swallow'd up!'

'Whaur, O Death! is yere victory? Whaur, O Death, is yere sting?'

Noo, Death's sting is sin; and sin's pooer the Law:

But God hae thanks, wha gies us victory throwe oor Lord Jesus Christ!

Sae than, brethren beloved, be aye abidin, no to be moved; unco aboundin i' the Lord's wark aye; kennin yere toil isna in vain in the Lord.

---

eke also *siccar* secure *lippened* believed *feck* greatest part *wheen* few *hantle* large number *doitit* foolish *bouk* bulk *pickle* grain *fecklnessness* weakness *cleed* clothe

2 CORINTHIANS 11:16–31 (LORIMER)

I say it again: lat nane o ye tak me for a fuil; or, gin ye maun, syne tak the gate ye wad wi onie ither fuil, an lat me hae my bit voust like the lave. Whan I blaw an blowst at sic a rate, I am no sayin ocht at the Lord hes bidden me say, but juist blawin like a fuil. But sin monie ithers is blawin o their warldlie fores, I maun een hae my blaw an aa. Ye ar that wyss, ye haena ill tholin fuils. Deed no, ye thole onie-ane at maks snuils o ye, herries ye out o houss an hauld, taks ye in his girns, lairds it owre ye, an gíes ye a rap i the jaw! I think shame tae say it, but I hae wantit the smeddum tae dae siclike.

Still an on—I am speakin again as a fuil—I hae nae mair need tae be blate nor onie ither man. Ar they Hebrews? Sae am I. Ar they Israelítes? Sae am I. Come they o Abraham? Sae div I. Ar they mínisters o Christ? I am horn-daft tae say it, but I am a mínister o Christ faur mair nor them. I hae trauchelt an tyauved bi faur mair, been jyled bi faur affener, haen a fell hantle mair flaggins—ay, an been ithin a haundbreid o deith, monie's the time an aft! I hae haen the nine-an-thertie straiks frae the Jews five times; three times I hae been beaten wi wands; aince I hae been staned; thrice I hae been shipwrackit; ae time I wis a haill nicht an day i the sea. I hae been constant on the road, an monitime hae I been in danger—danger frae rivers, danger frae rubbers, danger frae Jews, danger frae haithens, danger in touns, danger i the muirs, danger on the sea, danger amang fauss brether. I hae trauchelt sair an been dung wi tire an monitime wantit sleep the haill nicht throu; baith hunger an thrist hae I dree'd an monitime gane ithout mait an been cauld an ill-happit. By an atowre the lave, I hae my hairt's care for aa the kirks tae dwang me ilka day. Wha's waik conscience e'er gíes him fash, an I amna fashed an aa? Wha is led agley, an my hairt gangsna alowe? Sae, gin there is tae be voustin, I s' voust o aathing at shaws hou waik I am. The God an Faither o the Lord Jesus, him at is blissed for iver an ey, is witness at I líena.

---

voust boast   *lave* rest   *blaw* brag   *blowst* boast   *fores* advantages   *snuils* cowards
girns snares   *smeddum* spirit   *blate* modest   *horn-daft* utterly mad   *trauchlet and tyauved*
toiled and moiled   *dung wi tire* worn out with fatigue   *dree'd* suffered   *ill-happit* ill-clothed
by an atowre the lave besides other things   *dwang* worry   *fash* trouble   *agley* astray   *alowe* on fire

GALATIANS 4:8–5:12 (LORIMER)

I the time bygane ye kentna God, an war slaves tae gods at isna nae gods avà: but nou at ye hae gotten on tae ken God, or raither tae be kent bi God, hou is it ye ar seekin back tae the sairie, feckless spírit-pouers, an ar fain tae become their slaves aa owre again? Ye ar keepin halie days an months an saisons an years. I fear o ye: can it be I hae waired aa my trauchle on ye for nocht?

Become ye like me, een as I becam like ye, I prig ye, brether. I am no sayin at ye hae wranged me onie: deed, no! It wis owre the heid o a bodilie ail, as ye ken, at I preached the Gospel tae ye the first time: but for aa my complènt wis ane at micht hae tempit ye tae lichtlie or ugg me, ye did naither the tane nor the tither, but gae me sic a walcome as ye wad hae gíen an angel o God— ay, or Christ Jesus himsel! Sae happie an crouss as ye war i thae days! Troth,

I s' warran ye wad howkit the een out o your heids, gin ye coud, an gíen me them. What, than, hes comed owre ye? Am I become your onfríend for tellin ye the truith?

Thir men is haudin up tae ye, but no out o guid: they want tae steik ye out o the Kirk tae hae ye haudin up tae them. Mind, I'm no sayin at it isna a guid thing tae hae fowk haudin up tae ye, an that at aa times, an no juist whan I am wi ye, my bairnies—weill may I sae caa ye, for I am aince mair in sair grip wi ye, or Christ be formed ithin ye. Oh, gin I wis amang ye eenou, an coud speak anither gate til ye, for I am fair fickelt about ye!

Tell me nou, ye at is sae fond tae be subjeck tae the Law, kenna ye what the Law says? It is written there at Abraham hed twa sons, ane bi a slave-lass, an the tither bi a freewuman. The son o the slave-lass wis begotten as onie ither bairn is begotten, but the son o the freewuman wis begotten as the effeck o a promise. There's a hodden meanin aneth that. The twa weimen is twa covenants. The tane o them wis gíen furth frae Munt Sínai, an beirs childer at is slaves. That is Hâgar, for Munt Sínai is hyne awà in Arâbia, an she answers til the praisent Jerusalem, at is ey in bondage tae the Law wi her childer. But the Jerusalem abuin is free, an she is our mither. For it is written:

> Be mirkie an blythe, thou barren wuman at ne'er fuish hame bairn,
> lilt wi joy, raisin loud thy stevven, thou at ne'er faund birth-stoun;
>   for monie is the bairns o her at hed nae marrow,
>   monie mae nor the bairns o the waddit wife.

Ye, brether, like Isaac, ar childer o the promise. But een as i thae days the son begotten as ither bairns is begotten misgydit the son begotten bi the wurkin o the Spírit, sae is it nou. But what says Scriptur? 'Cast furth the slave-lass an her son, for the son o the slave-lass sanna heir alang wi the son o the freewuman.' Sae, brether, we arna the childer o the slave-lass, but the childer o the free-wuman. Christ set us free at we micht bruik freedom: staund steive, than, an pitna your craigs again anunder the yoke o bondage.

Hairken me, Paul, as I tell ye this: gin ye hae yoursels circumcísed, ye s' get nae guid o Christ. Aince mair I warnish ilkane at hes himsel circumcísed at he is bund tae keep the haill a the Law. Ye ar twined frae Christ, ye at wad be juistifíed bi the Law; ye ar forfautit an deprived o grace. For, for our pairt, it is faith an the wark o the Spírit at we lippen on tae bring us the juistificâtion at we howp for an wait on wi greinin. For whan a man is in Christ Jesus, it maksna an he be circumcísed or no: the ae thing at maitters is faith wurkin warks o luve.

Ye war comin speed; wha marred ye frae obayin the truith? The fair-farran rede at ye hairkent ne'er cam frae him at caa'd ye; an I'm wae tae mind hou 'it needs but a flowe o barm tae tove the haill daud o daich.' But I weill belíeve for aa i the Lord at ye will think the same gate as me. As for him at is pittin ye in a stír, he will een hae tae beir the hivvie juidgement o God, it maks nae odds wha he is. For mysel, brether, gin I am ey preachin circumcísion, what for am I ey persecutit? An what is there, than, i the Cross for oniebodie tae reist at? Sall, but I wiss thae din-breeders amang ye may gang on an libb themsels!

sairie puny   *feckless* impotent   *waired* expended   *trauchle* labour   *prig* beg
lichtlie scorn   *ugg* feel disgust at   *crouss* contented   *howkit* dug   *onfriend* enemy
haudin up paying court   *steik* lock   *grip* wrestle, contention   *or* until   *fickelt* perplexed
hyne-awà far away   *mirkie* merry   *fuish* brought   *faund* felt   *birth-stoun* labour-pains
marrow spouse   *misgydit* ill-treated   *bruik* enjoy   *steive* firm   *craigs* necks   *warnish* warn
twined separated   *lippen* trust   *greinin* yearning   *maksna* does not matter   *comin speed* making
good progress   *fair-farran* attractive-seeming   *rede* counsel   *flowe* small quantity
barm yeast   *tove* cause to rise   *daud* lump   *daich* dough   *reist* balk   *sall* indeed
libb castrate

EPHESIANS 6:10–20 (SMITH)

Be ye strang i' the Lord, and i' the pooer o' his micht!

Pit ye on the hail graith o' God, sae as ye may be fit to staun again the wiles o' Sauton.

For oor struggle isna again flesh and blude, but again the pooers, again the authorities, again the warld-rulers o' this mirkiness; again the spiritual hosts o' ill i' the lift.

Whaur-for tak till ye the haill graith o' God, that ye be strang to withstaun i' the ill day; and, haein dune a' things, to staun.

And sae staun! beltit aboot the mids wi' truth, and haein put on the prufe-coat o' holiness;

And shod yere feet wi' the readiness o' the Gude-word o' Peace;

Aud wi' a', takin up the shield o' faith, in whilk ye hae pooer to kep a' the lowin shafts o' the Ill-ane.

And the heid-piece o' salvation tak ye; and the sword o' the Spirit, whilk is whatsoe'er God has spoken.

Wi' a' prayer and pleadin, prayin aye i' the Spirit and watchin i' the same, wi' a' tholin and pleadin, for a' the saunts;

And for me, that to me soud be gien utterance, that wi' freedom o' speech I may mak kent the Gude-word;

For sake o' whilk I am like an ambassador in a chain; that in sic behauf I may be bauld to speak, as I soud speak.

graith armour   *mirkiness* darkness   *lift* sky   *kep* intercept   *tholin* endurance

Hebrews 11 (Lorimer)

Nou, faith is the warrantie o our howps, the pruif at things at downa be seen
is rael. It wis for their faith at the men o auld is weill spokken o in Scriptur.
Bi faith we ar insensed at the warld wis made bi God's Wurd, sae at aathing
we see cam furth o things at downa be seen.

Bi faith Abel offert up a better saicrifíce tae God nor Cain, an we read at
his gift wis acceppit, whilk is God's testimonie at he wis a richteous man; an
efter he wis felled, he ey spak, throu faith.

Because he hed faith, Enoch wis flittit frae the yird onpree'd deith; *hilt nor
hair o him wis seen*, we ar tauld, *because God hed flittit him*. For witness is borne
him in Scriptur at, afore he wis flittit, *he hed pleised God*, an wantin faith a
man can nane pleise God; for him at comes tae God maun belíeve twa things—
first, at he is; an, saicond, at he rewairds them at seeks him

Bi faith Noah, whan wairned bi God o ills tae come, o whilk there wis ey
nae kythin, tentit weill the warnishment an biggit an airk for the saufin o his
houss-hauld. Throu his faith he duimed the warld an becam heir o the
richteousness at comes o faith.

Bi faith Abraham tentit the caa tae gae furth til the kintra at wis tae be his
heirskip, an tuik the gate onkennin whaur he wis gaein til. Bi faith he sattelt
i the kintra promised him, an there dwalt as an outlan in a fremmit laund,
wi naething tae caa a bidin but the tents at he skaired wi Isaac and Jaucob,
his coheirs i the promise; for his een wis stelled on the cítie wi the siccar
founds, the architeck an biggar o whilk is God.

Bi faith een Sârah gat the pouer tae consave, by her bairntime an aa as
she wis, because she trewed at God wad ne'er gang by his wurd; an sae o ae
man, an him forfairn wi eild, there cam a stock as monie in nummer as *the
stairns i the cairrie* or *the grains o saund ontellin bi the lip o the sea.*

Thir aa díed, as they hed líved, in faith. They díed ithout gettin the things
promised, but they hed seen them an hailsed them frae a lang gate awà, an
awned at here on the yird they war outlans in a fremmit laund. Them at
speaks that gate maks it plain at they ar seekin a kintra o their ain. Gif they
hed been thinkin o the kintra they hed quat, they wadna wantit opportunities
tae gang back til it. But the truith is at they ar greinin for a better—that is, a
heivenlie—kintra. An sae God thinks nae shame tae be caa'd their God; he
hes een a cítie waitin them.

Bi faith Abraham, whan God preived him, offert up Isaac: ay, him at hed
gotten the promises wis ettlin tae offer up his ae son; him at hed been tauld,
'*Bi Isaac thou s' hae the stock will be caa'd for thee.*' God, he thocht til himsel,
maun be able tae raise frae the deid; an get him back frae the deid he een did,
in a mainner o speakin.

Bi faith Isaac gae Jaucob an Esau his blissin, prayin for things at wis ey tae
come. Bi faith Jaucob gae Joseph's twa sons his blissin at his wagang, an
wurshipped God owre the heid o his rung. Bi faith Joseph, whan he wis slippin
awà, spak o the outgaein o the Israelítes frae Egyp, an gae commaunds anent
his banes.

Bi faith, whan Moses wis born, his pârents wis dauntont nane bi the Kíng's edick, but derned him three month, because they saw what a bonnie bairn he wis. Bi faith Moses, whan he wis grown manmuckle, wadna lat himsel be caa'd the son o Phâraoh's dachter. He choiced raither tae dree misgydin wi God's fowk nor bruik the pleisurs tae be gotten o sin for a weeock. I the warld's scorn o Christ he thocht he hed gryter walth nor aa the treisurs o Egyp could gíe him, for his een wis stelled on the rewaird tae come. Bi faith he quat Egyp, an no in fear for the wraith o the Kíng, for aathing there wis tae bide he bade, like ane at saw him at downa be seen. Bi faith he keepit the Passowre, an strinkelt the bluid on the doorcheeks an doorheids, at the Angel o Deith, whan he killed the firstborn, micht hain the bairns o the Hebrews.

Bi faith the Israelítes gaed throu the Reid Sea as gin it war biggit laund, tho the Egyptians wis drouned, whan they socht tae dae the like. Bi faith the Israelítes gart the waas o Jericho faa doun wi mairchin round them seiven days efter ither. Bi faith the hure Râhab escapit the ill end o the onbelíevers, because she hed fríendit an hairbourt the spies.

What needs I say mair? I want the time tae lay doun the stories o Gídeon, Bârak, Samson, an Jephthah, o Dauvit, Samuil, an the Prophets. Throu faith they waured kinricks, ruled wi juistice, obteined the fulfilment o God's hechts, dittit the mous o lions, slockent the bensil o fire, wan awà frae the face o the swuird, frae mauchtless becam strang, kythed feckfu in weir, gart fremmit airmies turn an flee. Mithers o bairns at hed díed gat them back again raised tae life. Ithers loot themsels be swabbelt tae deid raither nor mouband the wurd at wad free them, sae fain war they tae rise til a better life nor this. Ithers pree'd scornin an screingein—ay, een fetters an firmance! They war staned; they war sawn sindrie; ⟦they war tairged⟧; they war felled bi straik o swuird. They gaed hither an yont, happit in pellets an gait-hides, misterfu, dwanged, ill-gydit. They war owre guid for this warld—an thair they gaed, wanderin owre the muirs an amang the hills, wi nae bíeld but weems an clifts i the grund!

Nane o thir, athò they ar weill spokken o in Scriptur for their faith, gat what God hed promised: he wis een providin something better for us, because he wantitna them tae win tae perfyteness themlane

downa cannot insensed made aware flittit removed onpree'd deith without experiencing death hilt nor hair not a vestige kythin appearance tentit paid attention to warnishment warning biggit built duimed condemned heirskip inheritance outlan foreigner fremmit foreign bidin dwelling skaired shared stelled fixed founds foundations forfairn wi eild worn out with old age cairrie sky ontellin innumerable hailsed greeted greinin yearning preived tested ettlin preparing wagang departure rung stick dauntont intimidated derned hid grown manmuckle grown to adulthood dree endure misgydin ill-treatment nor than bruik enjoy weeock little while bide endure strinkelt sprinkled doorcheeks an doorheids the sides and top of a doorcase hain protect biggit inhabited gart made waured conquered kinricks kingdoms hects promises dittit closed mous mouths slockent quenched bensil fury wan awà frae escaped mauchtless powerless kythed showed themselves feckfu powerful swabbelt beaten mouband speak pree'd suffered screingin flogging firmance imprisonment tairged vigorously questioned happit clothed pellets undressed animal skins misterfu destitute dwanged harrassed ill-gydit ill-treated bíeld shelter weems caves clifts crevices

REVELATION 5 (LORIMER)

Syne I saw at him at sat on the Throne huid a buik-row in his richt haund. It hed write on ilka side, an wis sealed wi seiven seals. An I saw an angel, stairk an strang, at wis cryin wi a loud stevven: 'Wha's wurdie til apen the Row an brak its Seals?' But there wis nae-ane in heiven or on the yird or aneth the yird docht apen the Row an luik inside it.

I fell ablirtin an cownin at there wis nae-ane tae be fund wurdie til apen the Row an luik inside it. But ane o the Elders said til me, 'Greitna: the Lion o Clan Judah, the Shuit o Dauvit, hes wan i the fecht; he will apen the Row an its Seals.'

Syne atween the Fowr Baists about the Throne an the Elders I saw a lamb staundin 'at luikit as it hed been felled. He hed seiven horns an seiven een, whilk is the Seiven Spírits o God sent furth outowre the haill yird. He cam forrit an tuik the Buik-row out o the richt haund o him at sat on the Throne, an whan he hed taen it, the Fowr Baists an the Fowr-an-Twintie Elders fell doun afore him. Ilkane o them hed a hairp an a goulden bowl lip-fu o incense, whilk is the prayers o the Saunts, an they war singin a noo sang:

'Thou is wurdie til tak the Buik
   an brak the Seals,
because thou wis felled an wi thy bluid
   coft sowls for God
out o ilka clan an leid, ilka peiple an nation,
an made them a kinrick o príests til sair our God;
   an they sal ring owre the yird.'

Syne in my vísion I hard the voice o an ondeemous thrang o angels at stuid round the Throne, the Baists, an the Elders. There wis ten thousand times ten thousand an thousands upò thousands mair o them, an they war cryin wi a loud stevven: 'Wurdie is the Lamb at wis felled til receive pouer an walth an wisdom an micht an honour an glore an blissin!' An ilka creâtit thing i the lift an on the yird an aneth the yird an upò the sea, an aathing at is in them, I hard them cryin: 'Til him at sits on the Throne, an the Lamb, be blissin an honour an glore an domínion for iver an ey!' An the Fowr Baists said 'Amen'; an the Elders fell doun an wurshipped.

---

buik-row scroll   *stairk* strong   *stevven* voice   *docht* was able   *ablirtin* weeping
cownin lamenting   *greitna* do not weep   *shuit* descendant   *coft* brought   *leid* language
sair serve   *ring* reign   *ondeemous* innumerable

REVELATION 21:1–12 (SMITH)

A New Heeven and a New Yirth. The bonnie Bride o' Christ, wi' a' her pearlins and her jewels.

And I saw a New Heeven and a New Yirth; for the first Heeven and the first Yirth war gane-by; and sea was thar nane.

And the holie city, 'New Jerusalem,' saw I comin doon frae God oot o' Heeven, made ready as a bride buskit for her bridegroom

And I heard a soondin voice oot o' Heeven, sayin, 'Lo! God's dwallin is wi' men, and he sal bide wi' them; and they sal be his folk, and God his ain sel sal be wi' them!

And he sal dicht a' tears frae their een; and Death sal be nae mair; nor dool, nor ootcry, nor pain sal be ony mair: for a' the auld things are gane-by!'

And he that sat on the Thron, said, 'Lo! I mak a' things ower again!' And he says to me, 'Write; for thir words are leal and true!'

And he said to me, 'It has come to be! I am the Alpha and the Omega, the forefront and the endin! I to ilka drouthie ane wull gie o' the waal-ee o' the Watir-o'-Life, freely.

He that prevails has a' things for his heritage; and I sal be to him a God, and he sal be to me a bairn.

But as to the dauntit anes, and the unbelievin, and the abominable, and blude-shedders, and lecherers, and eidol-worshippers, and a' leears, their pairt is in the loch that lowes wi' fire and brunstane, whilk is the second death.'

And thar cam oot ane o' the seeven Angels that had the seeven flagons fu' o' the seeven last plagues and spak wi' me, sayin, 'Come awa'! I wull schaw ye the Bride, the wife o' the Lamb!'

And he bure me awa' i' the Spirit till a mountain great and heigh, and airtit my een to the citie, the holie Jerusalem, loutin doon oot o' Heeven frae God;

Haein the glorie o' God; and her glintin was like till a stane maist precious, as a jasper-stane, clear as crystal;

Haein a wa' great and heigh; and had twal ports, and at the ports twal Angels: and names putten thar-on, whilk are the names o' the twal tribes o' Isra'l.

---

buskit adorned *dicht* wipe *dool* grief *drouthie* thirsty *waal-ee* fountain *lowes* blazes
airtit directed *loutin* being lowered *glintin* shining *ports* gates

BIBLIOGRAPHY

A: TRANSLATIONS FROM THE BIBLE INTO SCOTS

Anon, *The Song of Solomon in Lowland Scotch from the Authorised English Version*, London: printed by Strangeways and Walden for Prince Louis Lucien Bonaparte, 1860

Anon, *The Song of Solomon. Printed in ye olde Scottish Dialect*, Kailyard Series, Glasgow: Macaulay and Mackinlay, n.d.

Borrowman, Alex S, *The Buik o Ruth and Ither Wark in Lallans*, Edinburgh: Gordon Wright, 1979

Cameron, Henry P, *Genesis in Scots*, Paisley: Alexander Gardner, 1921

Henderson, George, *The Gospel of St Matthew, translated into Lowland Scotch*, London: printed by Strangeways and Walden for Prince Louis Lucien Bonaparte, 1862

Henderson, George, *The Song of Solomon in Lowland Scotch from the Authorised English Version*, London: printed by Strangeways and Walden for Prince Louis Lucien Bonaparte, 1862.

Lorimer, W L, *The New Testament in Scots*, Edinburgh: Southside for the W L Lorimer Memorial Trust, 1983 (6th impression, 1987)

Murray, James A H, 'The Book of Ruth', Appendix to *The Dialect of the Southern Counties of Scotland*, London, Asher and Co. for the Philological Society, 1873

Nisbet, Murdoch, *The New Testament in Scots*, T G Law (ed), STS 1st Ser. 46, 49, 52, Edinburgh: William Blackwood and Sons, 1901–5

Paterson, T Whyte, *The Wyse-Sayin's o' Solomon: The Proverbs Rendered in Scots*, Paisley: Alexander Gardner, [1917]

Riddell, Henry Scott, *The Gospel of St Matthew translated into Lowland Scotch*, London: printed by Robson, Levey and Franklin for Prince Louis Lucien Bonaparte, 1856

Riddell, Henry Scott, *The Book of Psalms in Lowland Scotch from the Authorised Version*, London: printed by Robson, Levey and Franklin for Prince Louis Lucien Bonaparte, 1857

Riddell, Henry Scott, *The Song of Solomon in Lowland Scotch from the Authorised English Version*, London: printed by George Barclay for Prince Louis Lucien Bonaparte, 1860

Robson, Joseph Philip, *The Song of Solomon in Lowland Scots*, London: printed by George Barclay for Prince Louis Lucien Bonaparte, 1860

Smith, William Wye, *The Gospel of Matthew in Broad Scotch*, Toronto, Imrie, Graham and Co., 1898

Smith, William Wye, *The New Testament in Braid Scots*, Paisley: Alexander Gardner, 1901 (3rd edn, 1924)

Stuart, Jamie, *A Scots Gospel*, Edinburgh: Saint Andrew Press, 1985

Waddell, P Hately, *The Psalms frae Hebrew intil Scottis*, Edinburgh: John Menzies and Co., 1871

Waddell, P Hately, *Isaiah frae Hebrew intil Scottis*, Edinburgh: John Menzies and Co., 1879

B: OTHER BIBLE TRANSLATIONS

The Geneva Bible: A Facsimile of the 1560 Edition, Madison: University of Wisconsin Press, 1969

Good News Bible: Today's English Version, Canberra: Bible Society in Australia, 1987

The Holy Bible (The Authorised Version), London: Eyre and Spottiswoode, n.d.

The Holy Bible (The Revised Version), London: Oxford University Press, n.d.

Knox, Ronald, (trans), *The Holy Bible*, London: Burns and Oates, Macmillan and Co., 1960

Luther, Martin, (trans), *Die Heilige Schrift*, London: British and Foreign Bible Society, 1954

Moffat, James (trans), *A New Translation of the Bible*, London: Hodder and Stoughton, 1935

The New English Bible, London: Oxford University Press and Cambridge University Press, 1970

Nouum Testamentum Latine Secundum Editionem Sancti Hieronymi, John Wordsworth and Henry Julian White (eds), corrected edition, Oxford: Clarendon Press and London: British and Foreign Bible Society, 1920

Purvey, John (trans), *The Holy Bible* in *The Holy Bible in the Earliest English Versions Made from the Latin Vulgate by John Wycliffe and his Followers*, Josiah Forshall and Sir Frederic Madden (eds), Oxford: Oxford University Press, 1850

Robson, Joseph Philip (trans), *The Song of Solomon in the Newcastle Dialect*, London: printed by George Barclay for Prince Louis Lucien Bonaparte, 1860

Robson, Joseph Philip (trans), *The Song of Solomon in the Northumberland Dialect*, London: printed by George Barclay for Prince Louis Lucien Bonaparte, 1860

Tyndale, William (trans), *The New Testament in the English Hexapla*, London, Samuel Bagster, n.d.

C: OTHER WORKS

Anon, *Ane Compendius Buik of Godly and Spiritual Sangs Collectit out of Sundrye Parts of the Scripture* (1567), reprinted as *A Compendious Book of Godly and Spiritual Songs commonly known as 'The Gude and Godlie Ballatis'*, A F Mitchell (ed), STS 1st Ser. 39, Edinburgh: William Blackwood and Sons, 1897

Cameron, Henry Paterson, *History of the English Bible*, London: Alexander Gardner, 1885

Fristedt, Sven L, *The Wycliffe Bible: Part I*, (Stockholm Studies in English 4), Stockholm: Almqvist and Wiksells Boktryckeri-A.B., 1953

Gau, John, *The Richt Vay to the Kingdome of Heuine* (1553), A F Mitchell(ed), STS 1st Ser. 12, Edinburgh: William Blackwood and Sons, 1888

Grant, William and David D Murison, *The Scottish National Dictionary*, Edinburgh: Scottish National Dictionary Association, 1931–76

Jamieson, John, *An Etymological Dictionary of the Scottish Language*, New Edition, revd by John Longmuir and David Donaldson, Paisley: Alexander Gardner, 1879–82

Legends of the Saints, W M Metcalfe (ed), STS 1st Ser. 13, 18, 23, 25, Edinburgh: William Blackwood and Sons, 1887–91

Murray, James A H, *The Oxford English Dictionary*, Oxford: Oxford University Press, 1884–1928

Murray, James A H, *The Dialect of the Southern Counties of Scotland*, London: Asher and Co. for the Philological Society, 1873

Murray, K M Elisabeth, *Caught in the Web of Words: James Murray and the Oxford English Dictionary*, New Haven: Yale University Press, 1977

Robinson, Mairi, *The Concise Scots Dictionary*, Aberdeen: Aberdeen University Press, 1985

Waddell, P Hately, *Genius and Morality of Burns*, Ayr: Ayrshire Express, 1859

Wedderburn, Robert, *The Complaynt of Scotland*, A M Stewart (ed), STS 4th Ser. 11, Edinburgh: William Blackwood and Sons, 1979.

Winzet, Niniane, *Works*, J King Hewison (ed), STS 1st Ser. 15, 22, Edinburgh: William Blackwood and Sons, 1888–90

INDEX

This index covers material in the Introduction. References to 'his Psalms' and so on are to be interpreted as meaning 'his translation of the Psalms'.